KICKIN' ALS

A YOUNG MOTHER'S JOURNEY THROUGH AMYOTROPHIC LATERAL SCLEROSIS

KICKIN' ALS

A YOUNG MOTHER'S JOURNEY THROUGH AMYOTROPHIC LATERAL SCLEROSIS

CARREY DEWEY

EDITED BY BARBARA VICTORIA
AND JOSEPH ROBINSON

BUTLER BOOKS

Proceeds from the sale of this book will be donated to organizations supporting ALS research and education, as well as ALS patients and their families.

A profound thank-you to Eric Crawford for his pieces, "A Valentine Love Story: One Family's Courage and the Light it Shares" and "At Louisville's ALS Walk: A Memory for Mother's Day." His portrayal of Eric and Carrey Dewey's journey through ALS is thorough, nuanced, and wholly compelling. We would also like to thank WDRB for their permission to include transcriptions of these pieces in this book.

ISBN 978-1-941953-87-7

Printed in the United States of America

Designed by Scott Stortz

Published by:
Butler Books
Phone (502) 897-9393
www.butlerbooks.com

Acknowledgments

At the risk of omitting anyone from the legions of people and organizations who stepped up to support Carrey and the Dewey family through four years of amyotrophic lateral sclerosis (ALS), we extend a profound *thank you* to all!

A special note of appreciation is in order to Karlee Puckett. Karlee lovingly took the necessary time to compile Carrey's original posts into electronic form, allowing the text to be edited into a book. Carrey knew of Karlee's efforts and was deeply appreciative.

We could not possibly have taken the steps we did for as long as we did without each and every one whose heart led them to us.

You know who you are. God knows who you are. And Carrey knows who you are.

Contents

Foreword

My sister, Carrey, was 42 when she was diagnosed with amyotrophic lateral sclerosis (ALS). She knew immediately her life on earth was about to get drastically cut short. She was told to get her affairs in order and start working on her bucket list. At the time of diagnosis, Carrey was a happily married mother of three young children (ages five, seven, and nine). She was heavily involved in her children's school and PTA, church ministries, and local community organizations, and could have easily won the neighborhood "social butterfly" award. The diagnosis was devastating.

Within four years, what started as a little left shoulder weakness turned into full-blown paralysis of every extremity and weakness so severe in her breathing and eating muscles that she needed a ventilator and feeding tube to survive.

After a month or so of what Carrey said was "hiding and crying in her room," Carrey decided that she was going to share her story with the purpose of educating and advocating for others with ALS.

The posts in this book give intimate insight—in Carrey's own words, as it was happening—into what life was like for her during the various stages of ALS. It was important for Carrey to provide a raw look into how this disease can create unparalleled anguish, stress, and heartbreak—and ultimately how it can bring family, friends, and an entire community closer than we ever thought possible. Carrey's story is one of unconditional love and triumph.

I'm often left wondering how something so devastating can also be considered one of the greatest gifts of my life. But that is exactly how to describe the five-year journey I was privileged to be on with my sister during her time with ALS. She was an amazing inspiration to so many, and through her strength, we are profoundly changed. I hope that, after reading this book, others will feel inspired to "Carrey on" their own light to honor Carrey, and the many others who have battled through this unrelenting disease.

—Elizabeth Robinson Sorg

2014

August 19, 2014

Yes, I do have ALS, also known as Lou Gehrig's Disease . . . there ya go, I said it. (Gulp.)

I was diagnosed June 5, 2014, after almost nine months of progressive symptoms and testing—followed by a second (and even a third opinion). I will be blogging my journey and raising awareness of ALS and how it can strike anyone or any age. The ALS Ice Bucket Challenge has hopefully given us a head start in raising awareness of what ALS is and why there is no cure leaving *all* people diagnosed with ALS a prognosis of 100 percent fatal in two to five years average (*and*, I have been diagnosed as having "faster-than-average" progression—double whammy).

God has blessed me with a beyond-words amazing husband, three perfect kiddos, a sister stronger than you could ever imagine, my Robinson/Dewey family who support me every step of the way, and friends, new and old, from all parts of my life who have come to bear this overwhelmingly nasty diagnosis with us, lifting us in every way. For this, I am blessed, and I continue to be prayerful.

For all of you inclined to take the ALS Ice Bucket Challenge to raise awareness and funding, please consider ALS TDI research base (ALS.NET) or TeamGleason.org, two organizations that will use all funds wisely and provide the best chance of getting a medication out of research development to save my life.

So, as we carry on our ALS Ice Bucket Challenges, remember *I am a face of ALS* and so are my five-, seven-, and nine-year-old children, my husband, my family, and my friends.

August 19, 2014

I will be using Facebook in the future to share my stories of living with ALS and raise awareness of *what* ALS is and *why* there is not a cure. Through a community page, which is what Team Dewey will become, I can share my story and the story of so many more in an open audience. Thank you for taking an interest. Feel free to direct those who want to follow and support Team Dewey to this open page. XO

August 20, 2014

So, I am absolutely emotionally overwhelmed by the support that has circled us the past few days. The prayers for strength are working; they are felt, and I feel stronger, much stronger than in days prior. It seems absolutely insane to be in the middle of the ALS Ice Bucket Challenge—I can't really make sense of it . . .

My daughter came home from school today to tell me her school staff was participating in the ALS challenge tomorrow (which we knew) and her teacher asked her to be the water dumper. A classmate or two claimed, "That's not fair!" in true second-grade fashion. Anne

Marie replied, "My mom has ALS; that's not fair!"—she gets it.

I'll be back tomorrow with the details of how I got to the final diagnosis of ALS as many of you have asked. Thanks for caring! XO

August 21, 2014

I don't look like I have ALS . . . yet.

Well, for starters, I can thank my hubby and kids for that. They help me wash and fix my hair, get dressed . . . every single morning.

We are starting this journey from the beginning.

I think because ALS started in my upper extremities, left arm, then right arm, I look like I am functioning. Many didn't even notice I had been struggling. I've made a lot of adaptions to how I operate, and my kids and hubby are super helpful. I have no use of my left arm; he's a goner altogether; deadweight, literally. The kids and I call him the "naughty arm." I have limited strength in my hand. My right arm feels like it holds a 20-pound weight on it when I raise it, but I can't complain because he still works enough to manage by myself, for now.

Basic things I once took for granted are gone: getting dressed on my own, flat ironing my hair, fixing hair for my girls, lifting pots and pans in the kitchen (lifting anything for that matter). Putting a purse on my shoulder, lifting a drink—or a fork—or a spoon to my mouth. At first I was relieved it started in my arms, because that meant a wheelchair would come later. But once the reality set in of what working with the use of no arms means—and not just the thought, but the reality of planning for it in the future, the near future—I look at life and everything differently: what I do have, rather than what I don't have. I do have my ability to walk, eat, and most importantly to me, talk! I appreciated none of that before June 5.

Our family and many other new ALS friends of mine feel strengthened by your support. Thank you for caring.

August 23, 2014

ALS Testing

There is none. No easy diagnosis or test; it takes several months of eliminating everything else, all while symptoms continue to progress. In the end, it was obvious—aside from me being young, my symptoms are a classic case of ALS. I'm going on the assumption everyone has taken the time to learn what ALS is and knows the path we will travel.

I started my diagnosis journey with an orthopedist in January to treat my "shoulder injury" that began September 2013. I assumed I hurt my shoulder from holding my sweet hunk-a-lunk nephew all day or transporting him in the gazillion-pound car seat carrier—only thing we could come up with. I did PT (physical therapy) and continued to worsen. The orthopedist then ordered an EMG and results showed nerve problem in all my extremities. That could mean a wide range of things, though.

I was sent to my first neurologist in mid-March who mentioned Lou Gehrig's disease when he evaluated my EMG results. I'd heard of it but didn't know what it was. Boy, was that a punch in the gut when I Googled Lou Gehrig's disease! He repeated the EMG and diagnosed nerve damage in shoulder (brachial plexus lesion): "not a gnarly disease. Come back in three months." (Relief, I'm gonna live.) But then I questioned how two tests three weeks could apart be on the opposite ends of the spectrum.

Hubby and I thought he was a quack and didn't return. (I could write a book on that experience one day, BTW!) Tons and *tons* of tests and doctor appointments to follow: X-rays of neck, spine, shoulder—all clear. Six MRIs including brain, cervical spine, shoulder, neck, brachial plexus, and another brain scan—all clear. Blood tests, lots and lots of blood tests! It was strange to want to test positive for something in my labs, in my MRI, anything, in order to rule out ALS.

Finally, I was referred to a muscular neurologist who is the best in town at EMGs and also treats—I mean sees—ALS patients. Everything else had been ruled out; he performed a third total body EMG and the results showed nerve relay was affected in not only my extremities, but also my breathing and swallowing nerves. He was able to do a muscle ultrasound and see my fasciculation (muscle twitching). With my progressive symptoms (unexplained muscle weakness in my left shoulder, arm, and hand; muscle twitching in all extremities; vibration in my mouth), the final doctor had the answer after spending five and a half hours with us.

I was diagnosed with ALS on June 5, 2014. (Oh, my God!) Our second opinion at a nationally certified ALS clinic not only confirmed ALS but diagnosed it as faster than average based on how quickly it progressed down my arm to hand. (Oh, my God!) So there ya have it: ALS diagnosis in a nutshell. Of course, I've left out lots of other appointments in between, but included ones that give pieces to the puzzle. Yesterday, I counted 24 doctor consultations and tests in a six-month time span to come to three letters—ALS. All wrapped up in a few paragraphs. Blessed by our faith, we feel stronger from your prayers and support.

August 27, 2014

How Are the Kids?

Honestly, I have the strength to talk openly about my ALS diagnosis with one exception—when it comes to my sweet children. I lose my strength to stay tough at that point; it truly is unimaginable. These incredible children are scared, confused, and spiritually challenged.

Each one is processing what this diagnosis means a little differently. These are great kids, loving kids, kids who need me. My second-grade daughter asks me every single night, "Why does it have to be you?" I tried to give her the "right answer" but in the end, I just have to tell her, "I don't know why." We have enlisted the help of spiritual advisors and professionals to help guide us and our children on this path.

Our kids knew something was wrong with my shoulder/arm from the beginning, long before ALS was even suspected. They were juggled between babysitters while Eric and I traveled the maze to figure out the mystery of my naughty arm. Our kids wanted answers as much as we did. Our oldest asked for an update after every doctor appointment. We prayed like a crazy family to slow it down. When we finally told our oldest we had answers, he was relieved, "Good, then we can work on fixing it!" If only it were that easy . . .

Every decision Eric and I make from this point forward revolves around our kids, including sharing our family diagnosis so openly. They wanted everyone to know, they were confused about who knew and who didn't know. They wanted everyone to know their mom had ALS . . . and so we told.

Our kids know there is currently no cure for ALS. *However*, the ALS Ice Bucket Challenge has put a new twist on that (still hard to wrap my brain around that one). They understand awareness and funds can bring a cure. We pray for a cure in my lifetime; we believe in my lifetime. They also know we are not going down without a fight, and we are going to keep fighting this, at least to slow it down. Last night after the nightly, "Why does it have to be you?" question, my middle child prayed the researchers would work around the clock and not take a break to find a cure—I think they are. Amen.

So, how are the kids? Aside from scared and confused, they are great! We are celebrating the start of the school year (kindergarten, second, and fourth grade), losing a front tooth, learning to tie shoes, riding the school bus for the first time, making new friends, gymnastics, piano, cross country, traveling, enjoying daily life, making memories and having fun—life as it should be led for all of us.

September 3, 2014

Now What?

I've been asked this question several times in the last few weeks. Upon the final diagnosis, when the doctor said, "Yes, I confirm you have ALS," I tried to say, "Now what the hell am I supposed to do with that kind of devastating diagnosis?" But all that came out was a quiet, "Now what?"

His reply was simple. "Get your paperwork in order and deal with your current problem at hand." That's it. Nothing else. No change in diet, new drugs (I was already on Rilutek), drink cherry juice, therapy, smoke weed, something—give me *something* I can do! But that was it. Get my paperwork in order (because you're dying) and deal with your current problem of your arms not working.

When I say, "I'm fighting this," I mean it. I am doing more than working with an occupational therapist to learn how to pull my pants up one handed and getting our paperwork in order.

I've researched; my family and friends have researched; we've made calls; I've asked every single ALS friend I've met in the last several months what they are doing or tried to do to slow down their progression. So, after Eric and I started updating legal paperwork, and I had my friend sew loops onto my stretch pants so I could pull them up by myself, we started on our alternative treatment course. Who knows if it will slow down the progression, but what do I have to lose? My holistic medical doctor made no promises but feels optimistic we can at least slow it down. No promises though.

I am doing some crazy stuff, things I would have called "hokey" to put it politely nine months ago. I am now banking on these hokey treatments to extend my life. I have hope that I can slow this bad boy down in time for there to be a cure. It can't hurt. We sought out a doctor outside of town who we thought could help us. I am transparent with my muscular neurologist (my ALS doctor) about what I am doing—he thinks it's false hope, but I disagree. He has nothing better to offer me with traditional medicine. But you know what? I have hope, which is a lot more than he could offer me. I have hope that I can slow down what he calls faster-than-average progression and that a cure will come in my lifetime.

Now what? Aside from continuing my regular ALS clinical visits, I am also digesting coconut oil as well as having weekly massages with it, using fluoride-free toothpaste, removing my mercury cavity fillings, having IVs of vitamins and minerals and taking oral vitamins, having blood cleansing, using water filters on my shower, practicing clean eating, drinking more red wine (hooray!), getting antioxidant injections, and getting more sleep. In addition, I am applying for clinical trials, making distant travel plans current, banking my voice, writing notes and journals to my kids, maintaining a positive attitude, and studying everything I can about ALS research and advocating for a cure or treatment for ALS. I am hopeful, I am prayerful.

I am doing something besides getting my paperwork in order.

September 6, 2014

Team Dewey: Kickin' ALS

TEAM

DEWEY

KICKIN' ALS

September 12, 2014

ALS, No Longer Just Lou Gehrig's Disease

When my (crazy) doctor suspected ALS in February of this year, he told me my EMG test looked like I had Lou Gehrig's disease and to return the following day for additional testing. I got in my car and Googled "Lou Gehrig's disease"—heard of it, heard of him, the baseball player—but I had no clue what the disease actually was and certainly didn't know anyone who had it, or that people even *still* had it. Boy, did that one Google search knock me to the ground.

When my diagnosis became definitive, I would say, "I have ALS. Do you know what that is?" Usually people had heard of it, but, like me, they didn't know what it was. So, I had to follow it with, "It's also called Lou Gehrig's disease. Do you know what *that* is?" I would usually pick up more people familiar with Gehrig—but most often, I would have to take a deep breath and explain.

"ALS is an incurable, progressive, degenerative neurological disorder. The nerve cells of my brain and spinal cord that control voluntary muscle movement will gradually deteriorate. As a result, muscles—including those that control my limbs, swallowing, and breathing—will be affected, leading to death. No treatment, no cure, 100 percent fatal, usually in two to five years."

Yep, that's what I have . . . followed by a bucket load of tears.

But since the phenomenon of the Ice Bucket Challenge started, I no longer say, "Lou Gherig's disease." It's 75 years after Gehrig's farewell speech, and still no treatment, cure, or understanding of the cause. Seventy-five years later, moving forward with *several* new generations, it's my disease—ALS, also known as the Ice Bucket Challenge disease.

I don't have to explain any more how cruel and inhumane this disease is. How, without a treatment or cure in my lifetime, it will steal my body, speech, swallowing, and breathing slowly, leaving a fully functioning and intelligent [wink] brain. People get it now; they've Googled it in the past month. People are aware of my path, unless of course, they live under a rock. Two months ago, ALS was buried under a rock, but this week it was on the *Ellen DeGeneres Show*, front page of the local paper, viral videos, and prime-time specials.

My name is Carrey Dewey and I have ALS.

September 15, 2014

Thank You

Now that fall is rolling in and the Ice Bucket season is rolling out, I continue to be humbled and strengthened by the support that has surrounded us in the past several months. Not just the support for myself, but the support for my husband and my three precious children, the support for my Robinson family, my Dewey family, my friends, and all those who know my story personally, and the support for all my new PALS (People with ALS). Thank you for supporting us *all*! We need it and we *feel* the love.

Thank you for your prayers, your kind words, your offers to help, your cards, your comments on my page and your prayers. (Yes, I know I said prayers twice.) I am, I mean *we* are, stronger because of you all!

September 18, 2014

My new friend, Sarah, over at speed4sarah.com asked me to write a short article about me and my diagnosis for her blog section, "Young Faces of ALS." Sarah, another young mother asked me in early June, but I told her I couldn't because I was still "in the closet." Wrapping up my words now—it's so freeing to not be hiding a secret.

September 19, 2014

Networking in the ALS community, I quickly found the amazing blog, speed4sarah.com written by another young mother with ALS. Her blog quickly showed me, (1) I was *not* too young to have ALS, and (2) there were other moms with children the same age as my babes. Sarah added me to her Faces of ALS section of her website. I wish I could say it's an honor—but I will say, reading the other profiles gave me comfort in knowing, as a mother, I was not alone . . . unfortunately.

> **Speed4Carrey**
>
> *Carrey Robinson Dewey, Diagnosed in June 2014 at Age 42*
>
> Prior to my ALS diagnosis, I was living the dream: truly. After 10 years of teaching, I was a stay-at-home mom to three amazing young children, ages five,

seven, and nine. I volunteered at our children's school and was an active member at our church, a neighbor, Girl Scout leader, PTA school board member, swim mom, party planner, expert shopper, friend, sister, daughter, mommy, and wife. I was busy. I loved my life, every part of it.

My symptoms started with unexplained muscle loss in my shoulder. I couldn't lift the hair dryer or put plates away, and then the weakness progressed through my arm, and then came the muscle twitching. After six months of testing and ruling everything out, it was confirmed: three letters—ALS—changed it all. I had no idea these three letters would not only change my life but would project to *end* it in two to five years, in the most inhumane way.

I Googled "How to tell your children you have ALS," but that search only returned results about telling grown children. So, I networked with the other ALS mothers at this website about what/how/when to share with young kids.

I explained to my children, "I have ALS," and then answered their questions as they asked.

"No, I can't cut my arm off to stop it."

"Yes, I will be in a wheelchair."

"No, there is no cure or treatment—yet."

"Yes, people die from ALS—[but who really knows how we will die.]"

"No, kids don't get it."

"Yes, I will always feel your touch and hugs."

"No, I don't know why it has to be me."

"Yes, I will always be in your heart."

"No, it's Lou Gehrig's disease, not Luke Eric's disease."

I'm still mothering my young. My kids need me, my husband needs me, my sister needs me. ALS does not pick and choose who needs you; without warning, without cause, without treatment, without cure, it will take you, ready or not.

September 25, 2014

What is Team Dewey?

Team Dewey started as a relatively simple concept, formed 13 years ago when Eric and I married. We were a team; we would celebrate our wins and comfort our losses—pretty basic newlywed mentality. Our team expanded and was complete after our third child. "Team Dewey, party of five!" I loved the sound of it, the look of it, and the feel of it. Just a little cozy in the car, around the dinner table, on the couch, and in a restaurant booth.

In the early days of my diagnosis, I couldn't shake the look of Team Dewey as suggested by my doctors. I spent the first month after my diagnosis crying—bawling—in front of my kids. I cried at the grocery, at church, at swim meets, at restaurants, at the sight of every single family I saw together—even at the sight of my own family. I cried at the thought of what our team would look like. One less person. Literally. Too much room, too much space, someone missing. I had flashes of my family without me. I couldn't accept our team shrinking. I was sad, heartbroken, devastated to the point where I couldn't function without tears. My husband was angry—furious—at what our team would become.

In June, we shared our heartache confidentially with a few of our most prayerful friends to let them know what we were up against. They quickly scooped us up and held a meeting. We were unsure of the agenda but clear on their intentions: to help us develop a plan beyond "getting our paperwork in order." It seemed impossible to tackle all that would come. I had no idea how to figure out the logistics. I am a stay-at-home mom; I run the household; I support my husband's busy career; I volunteer; my kids are young—and the doctors say I am dying. Was "figuring it all out" even worth it?

That night, in our friends the Anserts's living room, Team Dewey began to shape into something unimaginable. Our friends made it clear Team Dewey was not shrinking but growing.

The next meeting was a group of family and connected friends who came together to figure out the logistics for our family for living with ALS. Eric and I walked in to find motivating ALS posters with inspiring quotes, Team Dewey T-shirts, banners, Team Dewey candles, and a fighting, cheering spirit. Seriously, a pep rally for Team Dewey?

Unbelievable. These friends knew what we were up against. They were not naïve about my condition, they were well aware of what ALS would look like as I progressed. They had come together as representation to cheer us on in our fight for a cure and for our little party of five. At the close of the meeting, I visualized my family running through the football tunnel, and a huge crowd of people in uniform, cheering us on . . . a metaphor certainly morphed from the meeting. The weight, the weight of not being alone in this fight, was lifted off our shoulders and the shoulders of my entire family. We were not alone.

We've come a long way from my dark, tearful, fetal position, which seems forever ago. Team Dewey is something I could never, *ever* have imagined. It is well beyond my little party of five, more than my family and friends. It is our community, friends of friends, neighbors, classmates, family friends, strangers, and my new PALS (People with ALS) helping in the fight for living with ALS.

Today, Team Dewey is much too big for that cozy booth I visualized. It makes me stronger, makes me smile, humbles me, and takes some of the fear away. Thanks to all of Team Dewey, much greater than our party of five.

September 28, 2014

Some of the younger members of Team Dewey: Thanks for your support, Stopher Cross Country Team, runners, coaches, and parents.

October 12, 2014

Home after an awesomely *amazing* family trip! As first-time Disney doers and cruise goers, we had a lot to get done on our bucket list. Magic Kingdom at gates open, both parades, Space Mountain twice, Elsa and Anna, Dole whips and fireworks; Disney Cruise with all our favorite character friends, dolphin swimming at Atlantis, snorkeling, cruise food and more food, and Colleen's favorite, flying above the clouds. My perspective was different on this trip . . . it really was amazing! I definitely want my family to go back, hopefully with me too.

A very special thanks to Team Gleason for wanting to be a part of our family trip. You guys are *way* beyond awesome—on all fronts. No white flags here!

October 14, 2014

Phasing Out

Our morning routines have been nuts-o here at the Dewey household the past few years. In the morning, I wake up first, craft my edible art we call lunches; get the basic breakfast supplies out; cut fruit; empty dishwasher; greet hubby; fix his collar; hand him breakfast; kiss him good-bye; finish getting lunches, backpacks, folders ready; find shoes; fix bedhead; stick a hair bow in; say a final "don't forget to brush your teeth"; kiss them and put them on the bus.

That was all before ALS.

Now, I can't make lunches—something I loved doing. I can't cut fresh melon. Can't get a carton of milk out, fix a collar, brush hair, or lift a dish. I really just sit at the counter and direct traffic, but I seem to get in the way. It stinks to say, "I can't," but literally I can't move my naughty arm up and can't bear weight in my good arm. I guess that is what faster-than-average progression looks like.

Eric has been doing the morning routine pretty much since school started, and my ability to help has diminished over the past month as my good arm has weakened substantially. Leaving the house at 8:45 just isn't sustainable for the rest of his career. He can do it for the short term, but this need in the morning isn't going away for our family—ever.

We decided we needed to hire help in the morning. A need that, as long as the babes are young, we will always have. Consistent help. Every-morning help. We found the perfect person, Brittani Dodge, willing to come for just a few hours and be my extra set of hands or my assistant during our morning chaos. I reviewed the morning routine: what I do, how I cut, where the lunchbox supplies are, who gets what shape of sandwich cutters, hair brushes, pony tails, and where all the necessary and critical equipment is to make our morning run smooth. I was excited we found someone fast who would still allow me to control the morning and direct traffic. This would alleviate all the stress we have in the morning, as well as enable Eric to get to the office at a realistic time. Yeah, perfect! Problem solved.

As excited as I was to interview this young lady and review our needs, my emotions changed mid-interview. As I gave her a play-by-play of what I did, that now *she* would do, I realized I was passing the first two hours of my "mommy life" to someone else and I would never *ever* get them back. Those basic tasks of mine were no longer mine. Jobs, that while simple and routine, I did with pride and love. Tasks that someone else will always do for my family—always. Losing one arm was tough, but now, the second arm can't bear much weight either. I felt as though I was training someone to take over my mommy jobs so I can phase out.

When Eric got home from work, he was eager to hear about the interview. I wasn't going to share my feelings about our newest team member since we agreed to "outsource" my tasks. I wanted it only to be positive, but he could tell my excitement wasn't what it was earlier in the day. I cried and explained my unexpected emotion of how I felt I was phasing out. After a long, head-down pause, he tearfully replied, "I guess you are . . ."

Because, really, I guess I am.

I absolutely appreciate this sweet girl taking on this critical role in Team Dewey. I just didn't expect this side of the emotions to overshadow the "Yeah, perfect!" excitement I had felt days, even minutes earlier. Moving forward and not looking back—blessed to have her.

October 16, 2014

It's Only Physical

Phasing out is only physical. It's a fact. ALS is taking over my body physically; my nerves are slowly dying as are my muscles. It's my reality. However, this disease will *never* take my mind, heart, spirit, love, or faith. These are all solid and, thankfully, not controlled by nerve cells.

Don't get me wrong; I am slowly phasing out of what I do only physically. It's the cruelty of this disease—and sometimes the reality can be emotional. Not only am I phasing out of the insanity of our school morning routines, but I've already phased out of my abilities to dress myself, cook in the kitchen, do cartwheels (well, I never could do a cartwheel, but you know what I mean). I do, however, participate in all of those tasks. I plan meals most nights, pick out my clothing, write love notes for their lunchboxes, read bedtime stories, and make the grocery list—heck, I even chaperoned a field trip with my kindergartner today. I am not going anywhere soon. I still run the ship and will remain at the helm.

My amazing friend Sarah, a fellow MALS (mom with ALS) even used my post from yesterday on her blog today—speed4sarah.com. Why? Because she understood the reality of every word I said, because not only is it *my* reality, it's *her* reality too and the reality of every person with ALS . . . just phasing out physically.

Your replies to my last post were awesome and inspiring. I cried and laughed and felt so loved. I wanted to reply to each of them. Team Dewey has some amazing cheerleaders onboard. I loved what you all said and wanted to assure you—it's only physical. Love you all!

October 19, 2014

Team Dewey Comedy Night

In the early days when I was going public and many asked what they could do to help, I was beyond overwhelmed. I couldn't think of anything at all other than prayers for strength, lots and lots of prayers for strength. No one could make my ALS go away or make it better. I had more fears than God could lift and felt I had no control over my new diagnosis that I had just had politely handed to me. No way to stop it, no treatment, no cure, no chance of survival from this fatal disease. It was absolutely overwhelming: physically, emotionally, financially, and spiritually.

At our second planning meeting, the one where they had a pep rally for our team, this comedy night fund-raising thing was mentioned by Mike and Dawn Anserts. "Are you free November 14? " they asked. From the get-go, the Team Dewey Comic Relief planning group has set out to help with the financial burden from the unrealistic medial cost we will incur down the road (non-insurance items such medical home modifications, mobility equipment, in-home medical equipment, in-home personal medical care, and speech-generating equipment). I had no idea what these team members really had up their sleeves—I mean, how could anyone imagine this? The shape this event is taking is incredible. These Team

Dewey players are a bunch of movers and shakers, simply amazing.

Is the event overwhelming? Heck no! It is the most inspiring thing one could ever feel—the generous auction items, the elaborate planning in such a short amount of time, the people who have bought or donated via tickets—all coming from my friends, both old and new, friends of friends, and community members. Fills my heart and takes away a part of the burden so we can keep on keepin' on!

Many have asked how connected we are with the planning and details of this event. For those who know me well, my answer may surprise you—not at all. It is difficult to sit on the sideline as this event is right up my alley—planning, decorating, organizing, networking, socializing, and giving. Eric and I go to these events, but to be the recipient of this—still hard to wrap my brain around. It's a strange place to be. We are accepting this night as a gift from you all. They said all we need to do is not be late. Thanks, Team Dewey, for all your hard work and planning and can't wait to see you all there because, of course, laughter really is the best medicine!

October 29, 2014

I'm Good . . . No, Really, I Am Good

"How are you?" I hear it all the time. When I answer, "I'm good," it's usually followed by, "No, how are you *really*?" Well, *really*, I'm good! My dad reminds me though, when he asks how I am, he wants to know specifics: how are my arms, legs, breathing, swallowing, emotions. Fair enough, Dad.

I have so many new ALS friends who are further down the road in their journey. They have to make tough decisions on care, equipment, and surgeries that come with this lovely disease. You may read my story and feel sympathy for me; I feel equally the same when I read stories of my fellow PALS (People with ALS). Seeing these new friends of mine who are further along on their journey, some just 12 months ahead of me: feeding tube, BiPap machine, tracheostomy, Eyegaze, power wheelchair, accessible vehicle, 24-hour care, and many more surgeries and equipment I don't even understand yet. Making tough next-step decisions—several of these friends have young children like I do. It's all part of my journey. I may not have my arm strength, but I can adapt for now. It's as good as it's going to get. But really, when you know what I know is coming—how could today *not* be good? I guess it's all relative, so when I say, "I'm good," I really do mean it.

I am seen at an ALS clinic and my dad is especially interested in these updates. The "I'm good" doesn't fly when he wants a hard-core "how are you?" report. An ALS clinic is like speed dating—only in medical terms. I have my own room and the medical professionals rotate to me. I have a date with the muscular neurologist and nurse, occupational therapist, physical therapist, pulmonary therapist, speech therapist, and mental therapist. They all rotate through my room and when they are done, they convene to talk about little ole me. They can't cure me or make me better. The clinic just treats the symptoms as they progress and plans for the next big problem. After my visit last Friday they noted that I continue to progress.

My naughty left arm is shot, and my right arm is substantially weakened over the past two months. I'm making logistical adaptions daily from how I help my children, how I brush my teeth, what cup I drink from, what foods I eat. I'm still driving, thanks to an adaption on my steering wheel. I'm not sure how long this will last, but I'm trying not to look down the road.

My breathing is still strong—which ultimately is the key—lung capacity. I practice breath exercising to increase my lung capacity. ALS patients usually die of respiratory failure, so lung capacity is measured in real terms. When you diet, you measure in pounds; when you have ALS, you measure in lung capacity. I'm at 71 percent.

My leg muscles are strong, but I have noticeable changes in nerve reflex . . . you can connect the dots there.

I tire easily and am always fatigued, both of which are typical symptoms of ALS. I have to decide how to spend my X amount of energy. In the old days, I could burn the candle at both ends and recoup later. Doesn't work anymore. If I overdo it, I physically can't move the next day.

My muscles twitch and spasm at night when I lie down. I am trying some alternative treatments to help with that, and it seems to be working. It doesn't hurt (yet), but it is a constant reminder when I lay my head down to rest that I have ALS.

My voice is still strong, but I have started banking my voice (recording it for future use on a communication device) before it starts to weaken. My swallowing is still good. I had a swallow study done a few months ago and hopefully that will hold out awhile.

Not too much pain. Mostly from my naughty arm, which is deadweight caused by my arm separating from my shoulder. I can manage that pain at this point, but the biggest issue is to prevent frozen shoulder from lack of movement, so I need to constantly move the arm that has dead muscles. I "sling" my arm via a jacket or vest pocket and I wear my new letter carrier purse. Functional accessory!

Mentally, I'm taking each day at a time and that seems to be working most of the time. There are times I look too far down the road or imagine life for my children and husband down the road—I just can't do that and stay in the game. I am inspired by the community support, Team Dewey, and the power of prayer. Honestly, I think that is the key to being good—being open to all three of those things.

Tonight we carved pumpkins with my three little babes and tonight, in the here and now, I'm good.

November 11, 2014

Stopher Elementary School challenged the WHAS-11 *Good Morning Kentuckiana* show during the Ice Bucket Challenge in August—including Andy Treinen, morning anchor. A few weeks ago, Eric and I sat down with Andy, also a fellow Stopher parent, to talk about our life in the middle of the Ice Bucket Challenge, so I guess this is an "after-the-ice-has melted" kind of interview. Our interview airs tomorrow at 6:45 a.m. and again at 4 p.m.

November 14, 2014

Looking forward to Team Dewey Comedy Night tonight. Can't wait to see old and new friends and laugh my ALS off. I mentioned I wasn't overwhelmed but inspired by the generosity—today I am feeling very emotional, overwhelmed as I prepare to receive the love. Love my team!

November 16, 2014

I keep starting and deleting and restarting my blog. I'm not sure how to thank my friend-family for what just happened. How do I put that in writing? How do I thank my community for such an amazing, inspiring, over-the-top evening? There are no words for my deep appreciation for every single person who gave their time and energy to planning this spectacular night—in three months' time, mind you; to every person who made a contribution to the fund; to every person who donated to the auction, to every person who filled the room to support our family as we travel this path called ALS. For now, it feels like A Love Story, because at this moment in time, that's what it is—A Love Story of my life.

I have been wrapped in so much love this weekend. It's an experience that is indescribable . . . truly. The deep support far exceeded the funds that our friend-family raised Friday night. I know the goal of the evening was to build a medical fund nest egg for us. A fund to have for equipment, care, and needs not covered by insurance so I can live with ALS in our home as long as possible; for our family to focus on living our dreams and members of Team Dewey would focus on the financial/medical end. But Friday was so much more than a medical nest egg. It was about being lifted by our community that has embraced our family living with ALS.

ALS may take my body, but Friday night at the Olmsted, it filled my heart with love from this amazing community that ALS can't ever take away.

November 26, 2014

Thanksgiving and Thank-You Notes

If you've been to my home in the last two weeks, you found me knee-deep in addresses, stationery, stamps, and an array of my favorite pens. Let it be understood, if you stop by my home, you will be handed a stack to stuff, lick, and stamp. My dining room is now thank-you note central. It was suggested I do a mail merge and print out generic thank-you notes, but I wanted to take a few minutes and think about the gift each person has given me. I needed the process time; it's a great problem to have!

So I am taking a break from giving thanks in notes to giving thanks to all. Somehow, this Thanksgiving is different—it goes beyond my usual thanks for family, food, and . . . well, not so much health. This year, my thanks for health is replaced with an abundance of new thanksgivings.

- I may not be thankful for having ALS, but I am thankful for the many blessings this diagnosis has brought my way.
- I am thankful for every person who has educated themselves about ALS because of my diagnosis.
- I am thankful for my massage friend who comes every week to make my aching body feel better.
- I am thankful for my PT and OT friends who come to tape my arm back to my shoulder, so it doesn't fall off.
- I am thankful to my friends who have adapted my wardrobe, either through retail therapy or alterations.
- I am thankful for everyone who has shared a meal with my family so we can sit at the table together.
- I am thankful for my prayer warriors and every single person who has held me and my family in their prayers and mass dedications.
- I am thankful for my photographer friend who captured our silly family on film.
- I am thankful for my friend in Colorado.
- I am thankful for my ALS friends who are holding my hand tightly on this journey, showing me how living with this diagnosis is done.
- I am thankful for a wonderful therapist for my children, allowing them (and me) a place to share their anxiety.
- I am thankful for my girlfriends who lovingly put my collection of kids' keepsakes into scrapbooks for my kiddos.
- I am thankful for all contributors to the over-the-top comedy night—taking future financial stresses away.

- I am thankful for every card and letter of support I've received in my mailbox.
- I am thankful for my community, which has embraced my diagnosis beyond the Ice Bucket Challenges.
- I am thankful to my friends who come to help with my mom jobs—oftentimes, I'm sleeping and don't even know they are there.
- I am thankful for every person who has signed up to help down the road, reminding me of the support I'll have when the time comes.
- I am thankful to every friend who has taken me to the doctor.
- I am thankful to my morning gal who faithfully allows me to work through her arms.
- I am thankful for my crazy friend who said she wanted to buy my kids' love with gifts, so she sent both girls an obnoxious amount of One Direction stuff.
- I am thankful for every person who cares enough to follow my page, traveling this ALS path with me.
- I am thankful for my children's school, which has shown they will do more than just teach my kiddos.
- I am thankful for the ALS research being increased because of the Ice Bucket Challenges.

Who knew having ALS would cause me to be so thankful? This year, in the midst of my diagnosis, I am so grateful and thankful for all that has come.

November 29, 2014

Boston Bound and Ice Bucket Dollars

Shortly after my diagnosis, I applied to be part of ALS research at ALS Therapy Development Institute (ALS TDI), a biotech company in Cambridge, Massachusetts, that works on screening ALS drugs. This disease didn't give me the luxury of waiting until I was ready to accept my diagnosis. I had to get started right away applying for and networking within the ALS community, especially since my doctor says my progression is faster than average.

The first question of the screening for this research gave four simple options—one of which was:

Is your ALS diagnosis (1) suspected, (2) possible, (3) probable, (4) definitive? Answering those questions took me through a warp speed of my recent ALS diagnosis journey, handing me the words to express each stage. I remember tearfully selecting "definitive" for my diagnosis, wishing I could go back in time to when it was just suspected or even probable—and not quite real. But for the sake of this program though, "definitive" was the qualifying answer, so that's good news, I guess. Next, was a phone interview. They said I would be contacted in approximately two weeks. The program was funded to take 25 ALS patients to build their genome. Since every ALS patient is different and often, ALS is used as a broad diagnosis, no two cases are alike. The hope is that they will uncover subgroups and potential treatments of subgroups.

Then, this thing called the ALS Ice Bucket Challenge got in the way of my two-week wait. It took another two months for them to follow up with my phone interview because they were so busy processing incoming research money—great problem to have! It was worth the wait because they now had funding to expand their current research to 400 ALS patients—and guess who is one . . . *me*! So if you contributed to the ALS Therapy Development Institute (ALS.net), as I know many of you did, here are your real dollars at work—right now. Thank you!

Eric and I leave tomorrow for Boston to participate in the ALS TDI Precision Medicine Program Research. It's a rather quick collection of samples—skin sample for them to grow my own stem cells, blood samples, and some tricked-out fancy wrist and ankle bracelets to track my nerve conductions. I am anxious to know more about my ALS, including the genetic gene testing component. They will then run the results through a bank of more than 50,000 different medications to see if there is a possible medication for my potential ALS subgroup.

I have watched several other of my new ALS friends struggle with just getting to Boston to participate in this program because they are further progressed than I am; airplanes and power wheelchairs usually don't mix, dehydration to avoid airplane potty issues, breathing with cabin pressure, torsos not strong enough to sit upright on a plane . . . so I'm not taking my ability to fly with ALS for granted—not at all!

Can't wait to share more details of my trip with you. Until then, Boston bound and Ice Bucket dollars, here I come!

No white flags here.

December 4, 2014

What is the Precision Medicine Program at ALS TDI?

Our quick trip to Boston this week was to participate in an amazing new research program at ALS Therapy Development Institute (ALS.net). As I've shared earlier, ALS TDI is a nonprofit biotech lab that works exclusively on screening ALS drugs. It is also the largest ALS lab in the world, was founded by an ALS patient and family, and many team members still have ALS connections. This is the real deal; their motive is to find a treatment or cure for ALS—nothing else. Thirty scientists are working around the clock, 24/7. Anne Marie was so relieved to hear this update since she has been praying for the researchers.

There are several components to the Precision Medicine Program, and it is all very exciting for all ALS patients. I have two goals in participating: (1) To screen my ALS motor neurons for a potential drug for a possible treatment based on the results, and (2) the researchers and my family will have evidence of my ALS disease and my entire DNA genome for future testing after I'm gone (hopefully a long, long, long time from now). My ALS and DNA will be banked.

Here's what is needed and why.

I gave a blood sample and skin biopsy—a quick, painless 10-minute process at Mass General. The skin biopsy, the size of a pencil top, will be used to grow my very own ALS motor neurons from my very own stem cells. It will take about five months to grow the motor neurons and get started, but as of now, it is two days old in TDI's lab. ALS TDI will then test more than 50,000 drugs against my motor neurons to see if one reacts positively to a specific drug. Additionally, the stem cells will be banked for further testing or potential treatments.

My blood sample will be used to map my entire DNA genome. This will allow them to look for patterns among ALS patients and possible reactions to a tested drug. This mapping will take about two months. They will be looking for patterns and sub-patterns among ALS patients. This will be an amazing piece of information to have personally.

Next, we went to the ALS TDI lab in Cambridge to get my homework and fancy trackers. I was instructed on how to use the trackers and do the exercises—more like weight-free leg lifts and arm lifts. Sounds easy . . . unless you have ALS. These trackers are worn for seven days a month and sent back to TDI for the data to be uploaded and tracked in my patient portal. Big, bulky house-arrest looking monitors—at least they are black and red.

Next, I will receive a phone call once a month to record the saying, "You owe me a yoyo today" five times. Go ahead, try it . . . Eric can't say it with a straight face once!

But, I'll record that saying five times each month, with a straight voice, to measure my speech progression.

The other fancy thing is all of my data will be uploaded to a patient portal for me to see. Open data. If my motor neurons react positively, and the drug is not on the market, there is a push with evidence to fast-track the drug for approval.

While at TDI, we got to meet some great people that I knew from email and Facebook, bringing the lab to life, and we had an unexpected sit-down with ALS TDI's CEO and chief scientific officer, Dr. Steve Perrin, to get answers to some of our questions and hear his promise to answer any other questions I have in the future. These people are so flipping smart and dedicated! He is not there to treat my symptoms; he's there to find a cure—that's who I need on Team Dewey. That's who *all* ALS patients need on their team.

December 12, 2014

My second grader has been asking me to read to her classmates a very special picture book about a teacher who had ALS (*What Did You Learn Today?*). I read this book to my kiddos as a springboard into dropping the bombshell that I had ALS so there is some deep emotion with this book, but I followed her wishes and read it with a smile on my face and a lump in my throat. Thanks, Jodi Ames of Hope Loves Company, for sharing the book with me and being there when I needed you.

December 14, 2014

Bucket list weekend for this Nashville-born gal and family—Christmas at Opryland Gaylord and Rockettes . . . amazing, should be on everyone's list! By chance encounter, we were upgraded to the Porter Wagoner Presidential Suite for a once-in-a-lifetime experience and that it was.

December 21, 2014

Just by Chance

Last weekend, we spent a few days in good ole Nashville, Tennessee, for a country Christmas at the Opryland Gaylord. It's been on my bucket list for a while, but it's pricey to do it all, so I've waited. When my frugal friend said how amazing it was and worth every penny, I knew this was the year—

Upon arrival, Eric asked a hotel lobby employee if there was a wheelchair for use. Long distances wear me out and I had underestimated the size of the 2,900-room hotel. I have a chair for long walking distances but left it at home because it's big, bulky, and draws attention. The hotel employee, about my age I guess, asked if the guest who needed a chair was at the hotel yet. Our little family stood together as I said frankly to her, "I know it's deceiving, but I have ALS and long distances are tough." I felt like I needed to justify the need for a chair because I appear normal.

The employee gave me "the look"—the stunned look that means they have seen ALS firsthand; they know exactly what it is—not from a newfound Google search this summer from the ice buckets, but an up-close knowledge. She was so fast; she lined up alternative transportation to take me around the hotel rather than through it and met up with my family at our entrance of the show that was beginning shortly. We had a very brief exchange while waiting. She intently asked when I was diagnosed (I could see her calculating in her head: three to five years minus seven months . . .) and what brought us to the Gaylord Hotel. I simply explained that Christmas at the Gaylord was on our family bucket list, and we were there to make memories. I figured that's why most people were at the Gaylord that weekend, but I guess it means something different coming from a mother with a terminal diagnosis with her young kids by her side.

This chance encounter with, as it turns out, the bigwig of the hotel, made our trip not only more memorable, but a trip we could never duplicate—unless we want to shell out a smooth $5,000 a night (yes, I am totally serious). She upgraded our room to something that reminded me of the Plaza Hotel Penthouse gone country—2,500 square feet of color and country in the Porter Wagoner Suite. Ask my kids their favorite part of the trip. "The room!" all three will say. Anne Marie counted how many cartwheels she could do across the suite; Colleen played the jukebox nonstop; Ian used the elliptical machine in the workout room while Eric played with the remote control for the curtains and TV that came up from the dresser. Of course, I loved the lavish bed and the "hers" bathroom suite—perfect for an ALS patient after a long day of country Christmas singing.

She also took us under her wing while we were there and gave us Shrek breakfast tickets, arranged private transportation when we needed off-property access, stocked our room with champagne, chocolate-covered strawberries, milk and cookies, and the sweetest, dearest note from her.

We ran into her later in the hotel, and she told us her dear friend's father had *had* ALS ("had"—you know what that means). She told me she called her friend to tell her about our encounter last night and how much I had touched her heart. Her kindness to our family touched me just as much as I had touched her.

It was an amazing trip that I suggest everyone take, even without the extras. It was memorable for sure, due to a just-by-chance encounter with an employee standing in the lobby who knew how to help our family make lasting memories.

December 25, 2014

Merry Christmas, Team Dewey!

May the light continue to shine.

December 26, 2014

Holding on to all I have this Christmas season and not wanting a day to pass. If only I could freeze time. Merry Christmas from our little party of five to yours.

December 31, 2014

My First Christmas

After a death, events seem to happen in firsts—or so I've heard. First birthday, first Christmas, first anniversary of . . . It works the same for a patient with a terminal diagnosis as well; at least for me it does. While my family may not have felt this was the first Christmas since Mommy's diagnosis, I secretly and quietly did. My mind going back and forth between last year—when we effortlessly picked out our tree, decorating it while I reorganized ornaments behind their back, touched and reviewed every gift before I purchased, wrapped like artwork, baked our family favorites, and filled our home with the Christmas spirit while assuming we had many more years of building traditions as the generations would grow.

This Christmas was different. This year was *my* first, my first Christmas truly facing my own mortality, the reality of what ALS does to every person who lives with it. My first Christmas was about deliberate and intentional teaching and passing down traditions that root our family. Taking in the sights, sounds, and smells of the season. Documenting and planning ahead. No more hustle and bustle, shop-till-you-drop, get-it-all-done, I-have-so-much-I-still-need-to-do, I'm-exhausted kind of Christmas like it was in years past. I used every ounce of energy teaching my kids, so they understand the meaning, the origin, and how to continue family traditions in case next Christmas looks different from this Christmas. I wanted to brand their sweet memories the way I did this year but didn't quite know how to manage that without burdening their hearts of what we are really facing. My first Christmas came with enormous waves of unexpected emotion—trying to stay present with the people I am blessed to have, followed by dark and fearful flashes of my future—their future.

I love our home fully decorated for Christmas and we had sweet friends come in and do that for us. We took pictures so the kids could remember where things went for next year . . . just in case. After the kids unwrapped their gifts and threw their gift tags in the trash, I panicked, and Eric pulled them out of the trash to save for future gifts. Would I have the ability to write next year? Then I wrote extra gift tags the next day for my whole family . . . just in case. Last night I ordered 10 new nutcracker ornaments for our family nutcracker tree . . . just in case. I also fell to the Elf on the Shelf ridiculousness this year—late to the ballgame, I know. My babes always wanted one, but I knew that with keeping up with the Advent calendar, I couldn't also do this elf thing . . . *but*, I didn't want my kids' memory to be "Mommy was a scrooge and wouldn't let us have an Elf on the Shelf," so "Nash, the good elf" hopped in our luggage from the posh room we stayed in at Nashville.

2015

January 1, 2015

Happy New Year, Team Dewey! Thanks for bringing me hope, inspiration, and the ability to be open to miracles in many forms in 2015. I am strong because of what this team has become.

After celebrating with a host of awesome friends last night, we are continuing our New Year's Day tradition at Great Wolf Lodge with the rest of the world. Cheers!

January 14, 2015

ALS and My Sweet Momma

My sweet beautiful momma had a series of strokes two and a half years ago; she was 64 at the time. She has a feeding tube, weak voice, cannot walk on her own, and requires 24-hour care—which comes along with many other daily functions we all take for granted. Mom has less of a filter now (she really never had much of one before though), but her mind is sharp, and her heart is still huge. Mom was better than Martha Stewart in her prime because not only was she clever and crafty, she was thoughtful, meticulous, and incredibly gracious. It was who she was. She was a well-known gardener, baker, and the ultimate hostess. She taught me everything I know about gift wrapping and entertaining—not so much gardening and baking.

I've witnessed firsthand having all the things stripped away. Her losses happened instantly and overnight; mine are happening over time. We share many of these loves. I went through my first holiday season struggling to open Christmas cards as they arrived, decorating the tree as an instructor, and not being able to open gifts, let alone wrap gifts from my custom wrapping station inspired by her craft room. I've watched my mom struggle with these simple tasks for more than two years. Now it was my turn.

Mom and I shared a good cry together the other night on the phone. What she wanted more than anything was to help me, physically help me, and physically, she couldn't. I assured her the little things she was doing for me were of big support because they are. I felt so bad for her—for my mom—as a mother. I could not imagine being in her shoes; having some understanding of what I am going to face and not being able to help physically but just have to be a bystander and witness to this um . . . "messed up" disease. When I try to imagine my little Anne Marie or Colleen facing what I am facing and not being able to help—my mind and heart just can't go there—yet that is what my mom's reality is. I cried for her.

I reminded my sweet momma, as though I was reminding myself as a mother, it's how she loves me that matters. And that she does.

January 22, 2015

Don't Judge a Photo by the Pose

I posted this photograph of Eric and me on my personal Facebook page this summer when all appeared quiet in my world. The photo was taken this past June on Sanibel Island during our annual family trip, a tradition that dates back to my early childhood. I stood in the water with the man of my dreams; I mean that literally, not figuratively. It's one of my favorite pictures taken of us and it was snapped just 19 days after we received the news of my ALS diagnosis. We had both cried so much the weeks prior, our eyes are visibly puffy. At this moment in time, Eric and I laughed as the waves crashed against us and our youngest screamed in concern as the ocean drenched my dress, but the smiles on our faces are authentic. I think that's what I love most about this captured moment—our smiles. Knowing what lay ahead and looking out at my children playing on the beach, when their hearts were not yet heavy with the news of why Mommy's arm didn't work. This snapshot in time is frozen in my memory even without my favorite photo.

My naughty arm was beginning to show signs of atrophy as I had noticeable muscle loss. Eric had to physically lift my hand and place it on my hip for my "skinny arm pose" since my arm didn't have enough strength. "Skinny arm" for me was due to atrophy, ALS, not the hand-on-hip pose. If you look closely you can see it—where the shoulder and arm have a dip—that's muscle atrophy—today, it's significantly more noticeable.

Once I posted my beach photo to my Facebook page, the compliments rolled in. They were sweet, flattering, and complimentary of our family. Comments like "You are so lucky to find each other," "I'm so happy for you and Eric," "You both look amazing," "Your family is so blessed," "You all are perfect for each other," "Life doesn't get any better than this." But I had a secret behind the photo, and I felt deceptive as all the compliments continued. I was anxious as my friends commented. I wanted to pull down the photo I had shared with my Facebook world and remain quiet. Eric assured me the photo itself was authentic; I presented nothing deceptive in my post. Ours were genuine smiles, in an authentic setting, of two people honestly in love. At that moment, that snapshot in time, we were genuinely happy. We were determined that ALS was not going to rob us of our happiness on this trip.

January 31, 2015

Well, I Have Some Bad News . . .

Although when I say I have "bad news," it's not worse than being told I have ALS, so that helps with the perspective of *this* bad news.

I have been participating in the exciting Precision Medicine Program at ALS TDI in Cambridge, Massachusetts, since the first of December. You may recall my posts; I had several of them. I was one of 400 ALS patients selected for this hopeful research program. Disappointingly, I have been eliminated from the study due to some antibodies that came back in my blood work. This is not a cause for alarm for my doctor or me, but it does enough to disqualify me from further participation in the PMP study.

So . . . no tracker movement, no DNA mapping, no genetic testing, no stem cell growing, and no testing of my ALS against the 50,000 potential medications for ALS.

I've known for a few weeks now. I just needed some time to adjust my attitude. I still believe in the program and a positive outcome from ALS TDI. My kids still pray for the researchers and I still direct research dollars to ALS.net. I am just disappointed (to put it politely) that I can't be a part of their research for a cure and that my family won't receive my personal data from my participation in the program. It's a tough blow. I feel like I've been cut from the squad, but that just means I need to educate and advocate more since I can't contribute to this promising program. I'm not stopping; another door will open.

February 5, 2015

Eric comes home from work and finds me showered and hair flat ironed, house cleaned, beds changed, laundry done, dishes done, fridge cleaned out, groceries stocked, dinner on the table and dessert in the fridge, Ian at basketball practice, birthday gift purchased, and V-day projects picked out from Pinterest. My friends help me make ALS look easy. Couldn't do it without them! XO

February 6, 2015

So This Just Happened

My little sister, Elizabeth, and her husband, Mickey, moved in two houses from us! Well, it didn't happen just like *that*, but it did *just* happen.

It's been in the works for several months . . . maybe since August. Seemed impossible. She and my awesome brother-in-law own a beautiful home about 15 minutes away. They purchased it less than two years ago, and they called it their forever home. They have a 20-month old hunk-a-love and expecting baby #2 soon. Moving for me, for my family, just seemed ridiculous. But they both reminded me, my family is *their* family, and that's why they are moving. To live with ALS firsthand—ugh, who the heck signs up for that? My awesome sister and brother-in-law do!

If you live on my street, you probably got a knock on the door or a call from my dad asking to let him know you were if interested in selling. Two doors down just so happened to be interested in selling their home in the coming months—and that is the very short version of how it happened.

It's a beyond-crazy act of love from my sister and her husband. They both knew that to really help me, to help Eric, to help my children, they needed to be right by our side. Although if you know either of them personally, it doesn't surprise you.

I am beyond blessed.

February 21, 2015

Cabin Fever

Louisville, Kentucky, just had five straight snow days. I'm scared to mention how many inches for fear my Boston friends will sling a snowball my way, but it's a lot considering our area and it's colder here than Alaska—literally. This unusual weather left my kids with unexpected snow days stacked Monday through Friday.

Am I going stir crazy? How am I holding up? Do I need anything? Do I need to get out? All valid questions from my concerned friends and neighbors. Honestly though, it's been an amazing week. I have loved every minute of it, and I consider this unexpected week with my family my little gift—truly. One full week stuck inside with my favorite people. Just my family in our home. We've had occasional trips to the neighborhood sledding hill, but other than that, my snow plans have not been any different than most with young children.

I'm confident my change of perspective is my internal clock ticking as I live my life. I just feel blessed I have been able to escape cabin fever this year and enjoy every day, every minute, every second.

February 23, 2015

Here we go again. Eric and I are headed to Johns Hopkins Hospital in Baltimore to see the only rheumatologist-neurologist in the country.

These trips stink—my kids cry, I cry, I think Eric wants to cry—but we are still strong enough to travel, so off we go! Lots of uncomfortable testing, but we're hopeful for some answers and maybe a few ideas to slow down this nasty ALS. I continue to progress at the same anticipated rate despite my efforts to slow it down. I'll keep you posted.

February 25, 2015

After 26 vials of blood, my fifth EMG (a test equivalent to electrocution), a nerve conduction study (like total body shock therapy), lip biopsy (including stitches), MRI of my glands, and a spinal tap, I am done . . . for now.

Many times I was on the verge of tears from the painful testing and emotional nature of my diagnosis; I took my mind to the prayers and supportive comments shared with us. Thank you all for reminding me I have Team Dewey behind me.

Exhausted, sore, bruised, and beat up, I'm ready to reunite with my talented and silly family tomorrow!

March 1, 2015

Dear Friends,

My fellow ALS momma, Trickett, is at the end of her ALS road. I have struggled this week on what to do, how to help, what to say, how to feel. How can this really be the reality of parenting until the end with ALS? She has an amazing team behind her, much like you all!

A mother of three, with one son and two daughters just like me . . . kids only a few years older than my babes. Same age as me. Diagnosed exactly one year ahead of me.

Trickett reached out to me weeks after my diagnosis as I was looking for another mom with younger children to connect with. She friended me, invited me into a moms' group, shared advice and showed me how to live with ALS. She offered advice on how to tell my young children I had ALS and what that meant to our family in an age-appropriate way. I admired her beauty, strength, grace, and honesty as she lived with ALS and I felt if Trickett could do this, I could too. I was inspired to create my team page because of her. I fed off her strength and was fueled in admiration of her ability to be so honest and public, educating and advocating along the way. Friends, things have changed quickly, and I *cannot* do what Trickett is doing now. Her respiratory system is failing, and she is saying her final good-byes, planning her ending with hospice. The reality of what Trickett is facing, what I am facing, what *every* patient with ALS is facing is overwhelmingly frightening. Love you, Team Trickett Wendler: Farewell to Fight ALS.

March 6, 2015

No More Snow Days!

I'm on the bandwagon now because we've had a shift in plans. Out of our Johns Hopkins visit last week came a potential treatment to blast and reset my immune system to potentially slow down my ALS progression. I've had issues with my immune system in the past, so it's possible a preexisting condition is an accelerant to this nasty disease . . . maybe. . . . hopefully. . . . prayerfully. Great news! This is exactly what we were looking for on our visit to JHH, something to try next.

Bad news is, it's administered in the hospital as inpatient. My doctors wanted to start immediately because of my progression rate. In addition to both my arms, my core muscles and lung capacity are also affected.

So, with very little notice, I was admitted to the hospital on Snowpalooza snow day. Darn it! This separation would be easier on us if my babes were in school. I would love to be snowed in with my favorite peeps and a winter wonderland rather than be stuck in a hospital, but these are the choices we must make. Being separated is painful for all of us and the snow days just are not helping.

But, if my doctors think there is a chance to potentially, possibly, maybe slow my progression even the slightest, we all agreed to gamble the heartache and two weeks (gulp) for this immune system blast.

Day #3, but who's counting?

March 17, 2015

After my seven-hour treatment today, we were able to pull off our annual St. Patrick's Day dinner celebration. Family traditions and celebrations are instilled in our family; it's part of who we are and hopefully always will be. I am so proud that even though my arms don't work, Eric, kids, our morning gal, and sweet friends helped pulled it off. Notice the wee lil' lad in the middle making his party debut.

March 19, 2015

Trickett Died Last Night

Her three young kids are without a mom, her husband without his wife because a treatment or cure for ALS has not been found. I swing from heartbroken to shocked, devastated, mad as hell! This is my reality if we do not find a treatment or cure; my new friends will continue to die, all of them . . . until it is my turn.

March 21, 2015

Here is another amazing mom friend of mine, Jodi Oliver, diagnosed May 2013. We are in a small Moms with ALS support group. I affectionately call her "Hollywood" because she lives in California and was a guest of Hillary Swank at the You're Not You premier last year. Jodi directed me on the books to teach my kids about ALS; put me in contact with a company that made a journal video for my family; encouraged me to start voice banking before my voice changed; passed on information, resources, and connections; and checked in with me often. Jodi and I talked about bucket list items and wanting to take our girls to see Taylor Swift in concert this year. She said she is afraid she won't make it to her August date when TS comes to her hometown. Love me some Jodi "Hollywood" Oliver!

March 24, 2015

What Else Can You Do?

Email the FDA today! It literally took me three minutes to write a short intro, then copy and paste the info below.

While our supporters are fighting for us in DC, you can show your support beyond signing the petition by emailing the FDA at: druginfo@fda.hhs.gov.

And cc these people:
margaret.hamburg@fda.hhs.gov
william.dunn@fda.hhs.gov
stephen.ostroff@fda.hhs.gov
jim_jeffries@alexander.senate.gov
margaret_atkinson@help.senate.gov
kristin_chapman@help.senate.gov
Elizabeth_Schwartz@help.senate.gov

Here's what to say:
Share your personal story, how you know me or any other ALS patient, or simply explain

why you support the ALS Community in our self-advocacy efforts in getting a viable treatment to market. Then include the following—you can even copy and paste:

> On 23 February 2013, the FDA held its first public hearing to address the urgency and disparities faced by the ALS Community. The meeting was standing-room only and was also attended by the ALS Association (ALSA) and the Muscular Dystrophy Association (MDA). Following the meeting, these two advocacy organizations sent a joint statement detailing action items that were expected to change the design of future clinical trials and make treatments more readily available to people with ALS (PALS).
>
> It has been over two years since that joint statement was offered to the FDA and still the ALS Community finds there has been absolutely no change with regards to preclinical development or clinical trial design. Neither has the consideration of benefit-risk assessment been implemented in getting new treatments to patients suffering a horrible death.
>
> Additionally, it is hard to ignore that the 2012 Food and Drug Administration Safety and Innovation Act (FDASIA) is quite clear in its intent and that the FDA is strongly encouraged by Congress to grant Accelerated Approval (AA) to treatments that benefit all serious and life-threatening diseases. We see that the FDA has done very little to move itself further in this regard. As Congress is crafting the 21st Century Cures Act, you now have an opportunity to show them that you are on board. GM604 is a perfect fit for the AA Program.
>
> Please approve Genervon's GM604 so all PALS can have access to this promising new treatment and hope for a future.

April 2, 2015

My friend Jodi Oliver, "Hollywood," died today.

Diagnosed 13 months before me, there are three children without a mother and a husband without his wife—sound familiar? Seventy-five years after Gehrig, we still are without a treatment or cure for ALS! How is this okay? Jodi has been a friend to me since the beginning of my journey, advising me on conversations I needed to have, offering me advice on how much to tell my kiddos, ways to accept help, and she shared resources available to me. My advisors, friends, and mentors keep dying. It's not going to stop until we find a cure. *This is not okay!*

April 4, 2015

While you all enjoy the warmer weather, we are packing our coats and boots for our next big trip—skiing in Colorado. It's been on the bucket list since we had kids. Unfortunately, we no longer have the luxury of waiting till the kids are more self-sufficient to plan this trip. It's now or never, so I'm dragging my weak ALS body to Colorado to attempt the slopes one last run. Not sure exactly how it will look, but I will show my kids the place I spent many spring breaks and introduce them to a sport Eric and I share a love for. Nervous but excited.

I dug up an old photo from when Eric said, "Will you . . ." and I said, "Heck, yeah!" Poor digital quality 15 years ago.

April 15, 2015

Family tubing, *not* ALS friendly for me. Won't say I'll do that again, but not disappointed to retire the sport. I couldn't hold on to the tube or hold my trunk and neck up or get my weak self off; it took two people. Kids had a ball and I got another family picture out of the deal, so it was worth it.

April 16, 2015

Say Yes to the Dress

Anne Marie's First Communion is coming up soon. I've attended First Communion classes by her side to help prepare her for this holy sacrament and be present in the moment with her. I didn't do this with Ian who prepared two years prior. Honestly, it's something I'm doing because I have a terminal illness. I want Anne Marie to remember us preparing together; that I was present, by her side, in her heart, as I will be always.

A rite of passage for female First Communicants is "the dress." It's what I remember about my First Communion . . . my white lacy dress, new shiny patent leather shoes, and a fresh daisy halo hairband. It's a big deal. Even a bigger deal because I have ALS and . . .well, this will likely be the last sacrament dress we shop for together. I knew shopping for the dress needed to be special, our time, and our memories, magical in the eyes of an eight-year-old . . . just in case, you know.

I scoped out a few places we could shop for the dress, inspecting their selection, fitting rooms, sales associates. I was looking for the perfect setting as it really wasn't about what she would wear, but the memory we would make together. The reality of why I *had* to make this dress shopping special brought me to tears at each inspection stop—I wanted to share my story with other moms browsing the dress selection as my eyes filled. I tried not to blink because I'm prone to the waterfall effect.

I considered calling the local bridal boutique where I tried on and bought my own wedding dress 14 years ago. I would explain my situation and politely ask to borrow their beautiful fitting room for a few dresses I would bring in with me. But I knew, emotionally, I would create a memory I didn't want Anne Marie to have—eyes welling up and snot dripping over her and these beautiful dresses in a bridal shop. Anne Marie would have no idea why her First Communion dress would make me emotional, and honestly, I'm okay with that. I don't want her to know . . . not yet.

With four weeks left to create the perfect memory and contemplating my dilemma with a friend, she asked, "What did you do with *your* wedding dress?" My dress? My dress was literally slung on a hook, not even in a covered bag, let alone sealed or preserved. It just hung with my scarves and purses from when my girls played dress up in it last. And that was it. With the generous gift of a talented friend, I turned over my wedding dress—shopping was done. The perfect dress had been hanging in my closet all along.

I challenged my amazing and talented friend to make two dresses: one for Anne Marie and one for Colleen later. I didn't want my girls to share—I wanted them each to have a piece of my wedding dress. I knew it was an over-the-top request; I understood. Blessed by her gift, talent, and prayer on both ends, my friend made this last-minute dream a beautiful reality and memory with the dress—a dress for Anne Marie, designed to save enough fabric to make one for Colleen in a few years or sooner if needed. We will have more memories with these perfect dresses than any shopping experience ever would.

April 23, 2015

Thank you all who supported the Steve Gleason Act allowing ALS patients without a voice to have access to speech-generated devices connected to Internet and environmental controls. PALS everywhere say thanks—passed the Senate, now on to the House.

April 24, 2015

Moms with ALS

Early in my diagnosis, I prayed for a very specific support group. Support from mothers with ALS—if such a group even existed. I was fearful I was the only mom with small children and a diagnosis of ALS—literally. It was such a dark and lonely feeling thinking I was the *only* mom on this journey. Selfishly, my prayers were answered when I connected with another mom who started just that, a group called Moms with ALS. It's a small support group (not because there are only a few moms with ALS; unfortunately, there are way too many). However, the group was intended to be intimate so bonds would be formed; I was mom number six. I felt fearfully alone in my diagnosis until I found my way into this unique support group and met the most amazing young mothers living with and parenting around ALS.

My new friends answered my questions that no one else in the world could guide me on: not my husband, therapist, parents, sister, friends, clergy, the ALS Association, or even my ALS friends whose children were older. We are moms still parenting young minds and hearts; our children range in age from four to 15. Only these women could guide me and answer my questions about what to share, how to share, when to share. Only these women could give me a safe place to put my fears: what's next, how to explain, how to leave memories, marriage, hardships, resources, gifts to buy, finances, advocating, and much more. These moms inspired me with their courage, openness, beauty, and strength. I consider this group and these amazing women one of my many miracles on my ALS journey. I am blessed to know them . . . or to have known them.

That's where the reality of ALS comes in. You see, half my amazing support group is dead. Just like that. I joined the group in July and by the beginning of April, three of the six beautiful mothers, mothers I took my fears and anxiety to, who I sought advice from, looked at and said, "I can do this!" are now dead. Seriously. Somehow I thought we'd be together forever—however long that is. I have witnessed their journeys to the end, and this *is* the reality of ALS until a treatment is found. I promised I would stay present and not look down the road of my own path, at times an impossible promise to keep to myself, as my friends share their time is near, they know. It turns quickly—the breathing. And then it's over.

My emotions are mixed. I feel blessed to have these inspiring and strong women in my life, women who wrapped their arms around me in the early days when most of the world didn't know my fate. Women I have not met physically but love them all. I feel the pain of their loss, the fear of who is next. This is the reality of knowing Moms with ALS.

April 26, 2015

First Communions . . . one down, one to go! Having Anne Marie in the dress on sacrament day was amazing!

April 29, 2015

Ian: Mom, if we find the cure for ALS, can we change the team name to Team Dewey Kicked ALS?

Me: Hell, yeah!

April 30, 2015

What Does ALS Feel Like?

Have you ever had a muscle spasm or a charley horse? Imagine that in your legs, arms, back, stomach, and throat—yes, my throat!

May 3, 2015

I Love May

May is full of celebrations for our family with Kentucky Derby festivities, Mother's Day, Memorial Day Weekend, and end-of-school shenanigans. What I didn't know until my diagnosis was that May is also amyotrophic lateral sclerosis or ALS Awareness Month. I had never heard of this three-letter disease until it was suspected I had it. In addition to ALS changing the course of my life, it has also changed the course of my May. Combined with our fun-filled family celebrations, May also includes the Kentucky ALS Walk, Advocacy Days in Washington, and opportunities to educate people on the fatal disease that has no treatment or cure. I will be participating in all three.

I will use the Team Dewey FB page in May to answer questions that have been commonly asked of me about ALS. Thank you in advance for allowing me to educate and happy May!

May 8, 2015

Shoot It to Me Straight

I've wanted to share a physical update for a while to educate and let you know how I am progressing—to show you how ALS runs its nasty course physically. It's important that you see, that you understand, how ALS breaks down. This is the kind of update I give when my dad says, "Shoot it to me straight and don't sugarcoat . . ." It's long overdue because honestly, I owed my children an update first. Since my progression wasn't noticeable to my babes, I didn't feel the need to share with them for their obvious concern.

I look the same, my arms are weakened, and I adapt. My kids are waiting for progression to move to my legs and be in a wheelchair fulltime. That's how I thought my ALS would look too—left arm, right arm, left leg, right leg, core, diaphragm, but since every case of ALS looks different, that's not how *my* ALS looks. Good news first: I'm still walking. Getting in a car, up steps, and even down a mountain is not a problem physically. Bad news: The disease is still progressing. Specifically, it's progressed substantially in my diaphragm, the main muscle used in breathing. I was expecting this muscle to weaken later on, after my leg muscles, not now. I've explained before, when you lose weight, you measure in pounds; when you have ALS, you measure in lung capacity. Mine is now 49 percent. A substantial drop since my last clinic visit 12 weeks ago (gulp).

With the drop in my diaphragm strength, my progression of the disease will become more noticeable to my kids because I started using breathing equipment to allow my diaphragm muscles to rest. This made my progression obvious to them. I like to focus on what I can do, rather than what I can't; however, for the sake of educating, I'll simply explain through my lost abilities.

My left arm is done, and the hand is substantially weakened.

My right arm is weak. I struggle to get a fork to my mouth, lift a cup, turn a key, pull a blanket over me, or give a gripping hug. The simple things. I need complete assistance dressing.

My core is weak. I can't lift myself out of bed or get out of a low chair without assistance.

My neck muscles struggle to keep my head up. I rest often to take the weight of my head off my neck. (Did you know an adult head weighs 10 to 11 pounds?)

My body continues to have total body muscle fasciculation (twitching); these are not painful but a constant reminder I have ALS.

I have total body muscle cramping; hurts like hell *but* at least I have muscles left.

With my weakened diaphragm, I am short of breath when I walk short distances, including room to room.

I'm progressing, but that is no surprise since ALS is a progressive disease. It's usually about what *rate* you progress. I am still progressing at a faster than the two-to-five-year average rate despite my intense efforts to slow it down; that doesn't mean I am done trying though!

Mentally, I still feel like Kickin' ALS! Thanks for your continued prayers, comments and gestures.

May 9, 2015

Our family participated in the Walk to Defeat ALS today. I feel I advocate through my Facebook page and didn't know if I could mentally or physically do the walk, but my kids wanted to rally their friends and participate . . . and so we did! Today was their day to advocate, their pep rally for raising awareness as it becomes more their disease. In the end, it is my kids who are left with the reality of my prognosis of ALS and the responsibility to advocate for a treatment or cure for ALS. I'm so glad we participated today; my kids loved seeing their classmates and families show support and I met some amazing members of the ALS community—plus our team won a few awards.

May 10, 2015

Never in a zillion years would I have imagined leaving all my loves on Mother's Day to travel to Washington DC for ALS advocacy. It's a tough one, but I felt called to go. My family understood, but when it came time to say good-bye, I could see the excitement on their faces.

May 12, 2015

I felt the need to go this year to Capitol Hill to share my story, my children's story, and the story of so many others. ALS doesn't give me the luxury of waiting until next year to do anything, and this trip was no exception.

Today I shared my story in meetings with Senator Rand Paul and Senator Mitch McConnell.

May 14, 2015

Super excited to introduce you to my rock star friend, Deb Quinn . . . or as I call her "Deb from New York." Deb was one of the bodies I needed to squeeze as soon as I got to DC. By fate, she was the very first person I ran into when the elevator door opened at the conference; God brought her right to me! Deb really is an amazing friend; we've known each other almost a year, keeping in touch via email, text, and phone. She is the very first person I met with ALS and she reached out to me immediately. Ironically, my friend did a Google search for "mom with ALS" to help me connect and Deb came up first. Deb is a fierce advocate for ALS patients' needs and immediate research, and she has known the disease upfront for many years. She has "familial ALS," which means it's hereditary, and this type of ALS accounts for 5 to 10 percent of reported cases. The other 90 percent are called "sporadic"—no known reason or cause.

Deb's great aunt died of ALS; Deb's grandma died of ALS; Deb's dad died of ALS; Deb's adoring little sister Rhonda died of ALS; and Deb is living with ALS . . . along with her 28-year-old son, Dustin. That's exhausting just to type! Actually, she was able to trace 26 members of her family who had ALS. I'd say she knows this monster all too well.

I love Deb from New York to pieces and meeting her was beyond awesome—her love, her friendship, her advocacy, her generous handmade gifts. I'm blessed to know her. As I wrapped up my post today, I saw that my sweet mom friend Sarah at Speed4Sarah.com featured Deb as her newest face of ALS today! I'll link so you can read this rock star's story firsthand, plus you should follow Sarah's blog. She is awesome! http://www.speed4sarah.com/speed4deb/

May 16, 2015

Every single person in this picture has ALS. We are living with but dying from this disease without a treatment or cure soon. Time is not on our side.

I had an absolute anxiety moment when this picture was taken. The PALS are really amazing and inspiring people, but I just wanted out. I wanted out of the photo, out of the group, out of ALS altogether. Unfortunately, that's not how it works . . .

ALS
ASSOCIATION

May 22, 2015

I am one of 30,000 living Americans who have received the diagnosis, "You have ALS—no treatment, no cure, fatal, average prognosis two to five years." ALS is *not* okay!

May 26, 2015

My sweet Anne Marie prays nightly for a cure and prays directly for the ALS researchers. She was happy to add these new faces to her prayer list.

A direct impact from Ice Bucket Challenge funding: the addition of *four* new members to our science team! As our CEO Dr. Steve Perrin says, "Adding new talent in the lab allows us to do more and go faster, which is what a commitment to developing treatments for ALS requires." Learn more at http://www.als.net/Media/5488/News/. *Thank you* for your support in our mission to end ALS!

May 28, 2015

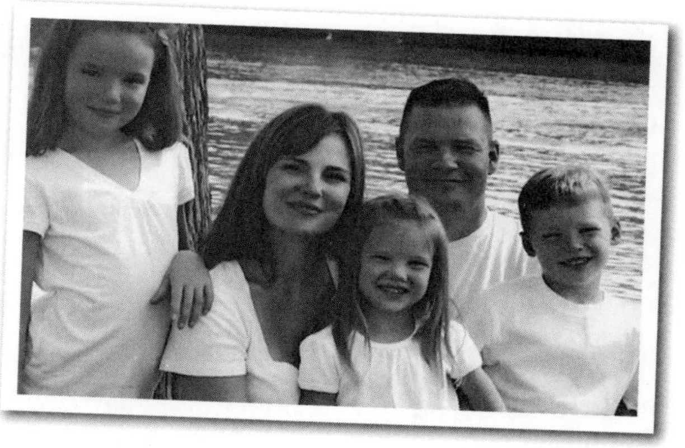

Thank you to all who watched and shared Trickett's educational video. She gave so much of herself to educate and advocate for a treatment or cure for ALS.

If you didn't get a chance to watch her educational video, I've reposted the link.

After less than a year from my diagnosis, I'm on the same breathing machine at night that Trickett was on. It's what you don't see that is so hard. Thank you for watching her video—there's no better educational material for ALS than what this brave momma left us.

May 30, 2015

I'm glad I was open to connecting to Dads with ALS or I would have missed becoming friends with Jay!

He's fierce and speaks the truth, plus he's an amazing advocate and writer, and his 90 Minutes Foundation raises big bucks for ALS research. Jay was the inspiration behind my ski trip as well. Rock on Jay (and Melissa too)!

Is a picture really worth a thousand words? It's been over 70 years since ALS was named Lou Gehrig's disease and we still have no treatment for it. But what we do have now is social media and patients speaking out like never before. You see, ALS is an ugly disease for a number of reasons. First, it can happen to anyone and usually targets fit and very active people. No one wants to be reminded of that. Second, it takes away your muscles and you atrophy into a paralyzed body that's completely useless. Third, if you're lucky enough to be able to afford it, you can be kept alive on a ventilator with a tube in your neck to breathe for you; people don't want to look at that either. Finally there are no survivors or feel-good stories. No one goes into remission, no one gets better, and everyone dies a slow crippling death.

June 5, 2015

One Year Ago Today

One year ago today, June 5, 2014, the doctor said, "You have ALS. I am so sorry . . . you're so young." My kids' summer break would start the very next day, and Eric and I had just learned my diagnosis was a rare terminal disease, 100 percent fatal—no cure, no treatment, two to five years if I'm lucky. Take *that* on your summer break! Oh, my God.

I'm really not sure how I feel today on the day that marks one year. It's been on my mind with anxiety and anticipation of what today would look like, what today would feel like. Is today an anniversary date? Is today a birthday of sorts? Is today a black Friday? Eric even asked me last night if he was supposed to buy me a gift—he wasn't really sure the protocol or etiquette of a diagnosis date or what support I would need today—do we celebrate, or do we mourn?

Now that June 5 is finally here—as we reached the one-year mark of living with ALS and the start of our summer break with our three young kids, I'll just say simply—I'm thankful. I'd miss the enormous blessings of my life if I wasn't thankful for what we have received in the months following my devastating diagnosis. Never in a bazillion years did I think this time a year ago, as the doctor delivered a shattering blow to our family's dreams and changed our lives in one sentence, that the next year would play out with:

Beautiful family photos on our Sanibel trip; American Girl and Legos in Chicago; Magic Kingdom, Disney cruise, and swimming with the dolphins as a generous and unexpected gift from Team Gleason; an unimaginable display of love and support from our friends and community at the comedy night/benefit auction; supersized Gaylord suite at Christmas; Copper Mountain skiing; Anne Marie's First Communion and keepsake dress; first concert with my precious girls; my sister and her sweet, growing family becoming our neighbors; deepened relationships and brand new friendships; Team Dewey morphing into something greater than our party of five; friends and strangers dumping buckets of ice on their heads in my name in support of a cure for ALS; and the strength to live this monster out loud to help educate and advocate for a cure for a disease I had not heard of the year before. I didn't think I'd have a Facebook community willing to travel my journey with me. There have been heartfelt displays of love and support through gifts toward my family, from concert tickets and airline flights to dinners, massages, and financial contributions to my medical fund. I have received only the good, the love, the gifts from friends and strangers alike. It's still mind blowing.

This past year has been a honeymoon year of sorts with ALS. My doctor told us to work on our bucket list and make memories, and that we did—and we aren't done yet! Year two will bring getting down to business, as my breathing continues to decline, and we begin home renovations to make our house accessible for me as I continue to progress. I understand we will have new challenges, but there is so much left! My two-year post (because there will be one) will be filled with more bucket list memories, but progression is certain. So, as I close out one year, we celebrate our babes completing kindergarten, second, and fourth grade. We celebrate a Facebook feed full of school accomplishments and graduations, and certainly, we celebrate the gift of life we all have today. Cheers!

June 12, 2015

Eric and I held on to my diagnosis secret pretty tightly until we were able to get a confirming second opinion. We confided in only a few, telling them the direction my diagnosis was taking. Eric told only one person when I was diagnosed. The one person he trusted and would seek advice from, his role model, no doubt. We spent the next seven days shocked and devastated over our outcome, crying on the shoulders of only a few.

Seven days after my diagnosis, we got a call. Eric's role model, his close friend, lost his perfect daughter—and I mean that literally. Tragically and instantly. She was 24, just getting life started. She had an impressive life resume, even at 24—a sign of living life to the fullest. It wasn't fair. We had seen her a few days before walking the dog with her dad, smiling and laughing, of course. And then it was over. Just like that. No good-byes, no last letters, no last bucket list trips, no special gifts, no warning, no getting paperwork in order, no last hugs, no last beach trips. Our heart broke for our friends, as it still does today.

Our devastation and shock focused on their family and the instant loss of this amazing young women we knew, that our children knew. We witnessed the heartache and devastation of losing such a precious life too soon, without warning. We naturally put our diagnosis aside to bear witness to a raw heartache that is unrepairable. We cried and hurt for the entire family.

Seven days after my diagnosis, I changed. I had time, I had a heads-up. I have today and I appreciate being able to get paperwork in order, to work on my bucket list, to write letters, to leave gifts, to be alive even as my body is failing.

Her dad shared with us how special her social media footprint was to him: her Pinterest page of quotes, her Twitter comments, her Facebook pictures. I became more diligent on my own Pinterest page, on my Facebook page, and diligent in living today as tomorrow is not guaranteed to any of us.

June 13, 2015

Just home from another medical trip to accommodate the symptoms of ALS progression. After taking the advice of some of my dear PALS friends, Eric and I traveled to Cleveland to have extensive pulmonary testing to see if I qualify for the diaphragm pacer.

The FDA approved the pacer in 2011 for spinal cord injury patients and ALS patients. The device has the potential to buy me more time with my babes and that's the motivation.

Bad news is, my diaphragm is weakening. Good news is, its weakened just enough to qualify me as a candidate for the pacer—I'm within a good window of time. Now I have to decide if I should have the feeding tube placed at the same time even though my swallow is intact at the moment. With ALS and a constant decline of function, you *always* want to be ahead of the next big problem as my doctor explained to us, especially with the weakened respiratory system. This is just the beginning of big medical decisions we'll have to make as we live with ALS.

June 14, 2015

The nurse in Cleveland said to me, "You're doing good since you still do your hair and make-up."

Eric laughed and quickly told her *he* did my hair and makeup! I'm still good though.

June 18, 2015

Damn! I took my first fall today. With my arms not working, my balance is a little off and I couldn't catch myself to break my fall. My mind told my arms to grab the ledge, but they didn't respond. I have a big ole knot on my noggin, but it could have been worse, so I'm lucky, I guess. I just hate when ALS progression sneaks up on me. Adjust, move forward, and keep Kickin' ALS.

June 29, 2015

We take an annual trip to Sanibel Island with my family. I've gone almost yearly to the same condo since I was eight. I know all the tips and trips to maximize this family beach vacation. It's a family tradition that continues with my own children, and I love sharing the memories and experiences with them. This year was obviously different. Showing up with a full year of ALS progression under my belt caught me off guard; my progression was so altering and obvious. While I deliberately live in the moment and appreciate the abilities and support I do have, I was emotionally overwhelmed on the first day with how different this trip was with my uninvited guest, and how different my life is from a year ago while living with ALS. They were emotions I didn't expect and certainly wasn't prepared for when I arrived for a week of sun and sand.

I've adapted over time with our family trip as a small child, teen, college student, bringing Eric, new family members as we've married, then each new baby. We've had lots of special "firsts" on this trip, and I've always adapted to the change—but this year, the adaption was different. This year was instantly and noticeably different. It wasn't about a growing or maturing family; the adaption is obviously for my ALS. While my progression is daily at home, I had a benchmark on this vacation—how was I on my trip last year with ALS? I've had a full year to compare my progression. We had lots of firsts on this year's trip thanks to ALS. First time I had to be fed, first time I felt paralyzed (stuck on a beach chair unable to lift my head or arms), first fall as I prepared for the trip, first time I couldn't unzip my purse, first time I couldn't open a car door, first time I needed help in the bathroom beyond what my children can provide. But, I'm putting Sanibel 2016 on the bucket list! Not just that I'll be alive, but that I will have the strength and motivation to adapt, adjust, and return to the island I love with my sweet family.

July 3, 2015

Date Night with My Hubby

He bathed me, dressed me, then took me to dinner . . . where he helped feed me once my fork became too heavy to lift. Boy, have times changed! Adapt, adjust, move forward.

July 4, 2015

Today marks the 76th anniversary of Lou Gehrig's farewell speech. He was one of the first people to put a face to ALS.

Unflippin' believable that 76 years later, there is still not a treatment or cure for this 100 percent fatal disease.

Happy Fourth of July from our little family to yours!

July 7, 2015

AM: Mom, is your diagram a muscle?

Me: Yes.

AM: Will you still be here when it quits working?

Me: (Long painful pause) . . . I'm trying to keep my diaphragm muscle working so I'll be here when a cure comes.

Absolutely ridiculous and heartbreaking bedtime conversation to have with an eight-year-old.

July 10, 2015

My cluttered garage is such a strange reminder of my life—past, present, and future. I see abilities I've lost: my minivan, my golf clubs, my tennis racket, my bike, corn-hole (okay, I never really had that ability). My new abilities: wheelchairs and electric scooter. And what's to come: wider doors and materials for making our home handicapped-accessible. Who knew a garage could tell so much about your life in one quick glimpse?

July 10, 2015

Thanks for all the donations and shares, Team Dewey.

We are almost halfway to our financial goal of donations to ALS research and less than two weeks away from our Awareness Week kick-off, August 1 to 8—can you give up the use of one of the following for one day or even just an hour: your arm, hand, legs, voice, or ability to swallow?

July 17, 2015

I am joining my awesome friend and fellow ALS mother warrior, Sarah, at speed4sarah.com, to raise awareness and research dollars for direct ALS treatments.

What will I give? I am giving my life, slowly but surely. I am giving every ability I have—my ability to hug, hold, write, drive, my hobbies, my ability to walk distances, shower, eat, speak, and ultimately breathe. But as long as I can, I will give of my heart and mind to raise awareness and knowledge of this disease that is 100 percent fatal.

What will my children give? My children are giving up their mother tucking them in at night, helping with their hair, helping with their homework, the security of knowing their mommy will always be there, holding them when they are hurt, driving them where they need to be, fixing family meals, crafting, joining them on field trips, giving them hugs, rubbing their backs at night, joining them in family sports, being with them physically, and eventually, my children will give their mommy—not by choice.

What will *you* give? Will you give up one physical ability for one day during the week of August 1–8 and document on Facebook to raise awareness? Will you donate funding for direct ALS research through this campaign to ALS TDI (no amount is too small)? Will you share this campaign and give awareness?

August 4, 2015

Celebrating 14 years of marriage with my hubby and littles. ALS certainly changes a marriage in ways you could never imagine, but I'm more in love with these people than ever! We are blessed!

August 12, 2015

First day of school for my babes. It's incredibly hard not to think about what should've been or what their school year will look like as I continue to progress in my second year. I didn't want to let them go today, and I think the feeling was mutual. They are amazing little caregivers. The good news is, they had a great first day and are in the hands of some amazing teachers! Now I'll work on not thinking about what should've been.

August 16, 2015

Adapt, Adjust, Move Forward

I've been whispering these words internally since the onset of my progression; long before my ALS was confirmed. It's critical for me to keep these words embedded mentally in order to avoid the abyss of depression that ALS can cause. I've had to adapt and adjust how I function and think in order to move forward. My progression is constant despite our numerous attempts to slow down my nerve loss—I absolutely wish I could report a success story, and honestly, I felt I was going to be able to share a miracle with all of you. I'm not giving up, but as of today, I have to report that nothing has slowed down my ALS, despite some pretty crazy and aggressive attempts—blood cleansing, replacing all my plasma (a process called plasmapheresis), mistletoe injections, heavy antibiotics, an arsenal of vitamins and supplements, IV treatments, chemo drugs, mercury screening, changing what I eat and drink, massive amounts of prayer, and the lists goes on and on . . .

I'm now at the point where I'm not only continuing to try new regimens to slow down my ALS, I must also accept reality and manage the symptoms of ALS to prolong my projected lifespan. My decreased respiratory symptoms are managed by a breathing machine 10 to 12 hours a day. My inability to cough and keep my lungs clear is managed by a machine that forces me to cough (or gag rather). And if you see me with my arm in a sling or taped with medical tape, it's because the deadweight of my arm is separating from my shoulder. If you see me in a neck brace, it's because my neck muscles are weak and having a hard time keeping my head up.

Sometimes adapting and adjusting is more difficult. I retired my car keys four months ago. It's not as easy to function without both my arms—typing and handwriting are skills of the past. Processing thoughts on paper with pencil and keyboard are no longer options. Blogging my journey and educating about ALS have been immensely therapeutic for me and adapting all my writing to voice-to-text is taking a bit longer to move forward. I miss my handwriting, my ability to write my children lunchbox love notes, my personal thank-you notes, my mental therapy of the keyboard.

Sometimes moving forward takes a little longer with the loss of some abilities than others. I'm still learning my new life, but not getting too comfortable because it changes on a regular basis.

Adapting, adjusting, moving forward . . .

August 20, 2015

The Rest of the Story

Thank you all for your kind concern about my fall yesterday.

My photo was intended to educate about the realities of ALS. For patients fortunate to be somewhat mobile like myself, falling is no stranger. This wasn't my first fall, nor will it be my last. But my sister pointed out after my post, my face and fall only told half the story. She said the "real ALS story" is what happened *after* my fall.

So, the rest of the story is—not only could I not break my fall, but when I fell, I couldn't get up. I couldn't move my arms; I couldn't lift my hands; I couldn't lift my head; I couldn't turn my torso. I was stuck face down on the floor because my upper body is either too weak or paralyzed to move, making it impossible to get up on my own. Luckily, I wasn't alone, and my sweet assistant was here and we problem-solved getting me up off the floor.

We have already started the process of making sure I have someone with me 24/7; this was just a bold reminder it's not too early to implement.

So, today I'm good—sore and swollen, but good. As always, adapting, adjusting, and moving forward.

August 22, 2015

2015 ALS Ice Bucket Challenge, Round 2

It's much more than a fad and a thing of the past. The Ice Bucket Challenge has changed the course of my journey through awareness, education, and advocacy. *You* do know someone with ALS and all of Team Dewey is challenged for round two! Please tag or post your videos. Send donations to #whatwouldyougive campaign, als.net, teamgleason.org, or alsaky.org.

Thank you!

August 23, 2015

Big Decisions

After much research, consultation, and prayer, Eric and I decided the diaphragm pacer would be a good option for me since my progression is picking up speed. There is no guarantee the device will work for me. The doctor will know more once he puts the electrodes on my diaphragm muscle during surgery. It will not repair my breathing, but we hope it will slow the progression of my failing respiratory system and buy me a little more time. I'm having a hard time completing a full sentence without a breath of air this week. I'm not sure if it's progression or anxiety, but either way, it's scary as hell.

We also decided (I think), to get the feeding tube at the same time. Surgery for ALS patients is very risky because our bodies are weak and breathing is compromised, so we're encouraged to undergo surgery only once.

I'm beyond anxious as Eric and I make the six-hour drive to Cleveland for my scheduled surgery early tomorrow morning. Continued prayers to ease my anxiety, the anxiety of my littles, and for a successful surgery. My sweet Ian buckling me in as my kiddos say good-bye . . . again. Thank you for your continued support.

August 24, 2014

A Quick Update on Today's Surgery

Carrey's diaphragm pacer and feeding tube surgery were both successful. Stomach muscle spasms from ALS and two new devices implanted in her stomach are tricky, so we are trying to manage the pain. If all goes as planned, we will head home Wednesday. I read all the comments to Carrey, and we deeply appreciate all of the prayers and love shown by Team Dewey.

—Eric

August 25, 2014

Date night for the Deweys! My honey plugged my wires into the pacer, flushed the feeding tube, helped me with my hygiene, fed me dinner in bed. Watched me pop pills all night and was still willing to cuddle with me.

September 9, 2015

My Teeny-weeny was sick, like stomach-bug sick, like need-your-mommy kind of sick. My sweet child crawled in my lap and said she would be so sad if I wasn't here to take care of her . . .

Little does my innocent six-year-old know, we are facing a head-on collision with ALS that will likely make this unimaginable situation her reality.

After two very difficult weeks—physically and mentally—I felt a true surge of anger and adrenaline in my fight to kick ALS!

September 11, 2015

How's the Diaphragm Pacer?

Now that I've survived two weeks post-op recovery, I can speak to the pacer. The last two weeks have been a bear—it took me two full weeks to get my breathing back to baseline. Recovery was ridiculously scary. I wasn't expecting gasping to breathe as part of my recovery—only discomfort and pain. I seriously thought my progression had accelerated and the worst was happening . . . add anxiety to a hard time breathing and you have one hot mess. *But* we made it, and I'm all better and back to my 44 percent lung capacity and the discovery of a little white anxiety pill.

The pacer is not an instant fix by any means. My pacer is set with different "voltages" and I will gradually increase to the maximum setting. The device is external, and I sleep with it at night along with my BiPAP breathing machine. I have not noticed any changes yet, but I'm still building up to the highest voltage. It's not expected to improve my breathing, but rather help sustain or slow down my diminished lung capacity.

During surgery, the doctor had the pacer at the highest setting, and I was breathing better with the pacer than without, so I'm realistically hopeful it will work!

We went with the feeding tube. I'm not using it for nutrition yet and hope I won't have to anytime soon. We just have to flush it every couple of days. Since my recovery was so difficult, I'm definitely glad I had it "installed"—that's Eric's word; he's such a guy. No regrets so far.

September 14, 2015

Another quick medical trip for Eric and me. I wanted to cancel this appointment because I'm tired, really tired . . . and I ache at leaving my littles. But my surge of adrenaline carries me on—plus, I'm able. There will be a point in my fight when I'm unable to get on a plane or stay in a hotel. Not exactly sure what I'm looking for, but hopeful for something . . . anything.

September 23, 2015

I'm applying for a state grant to help offset the cost of my caregiver/assistant. Based on my answers, you'd think I'd be eligible immediately. Unfortunately, there is a two-year wait . . . certainly not what a patient with ALS wants to hear.

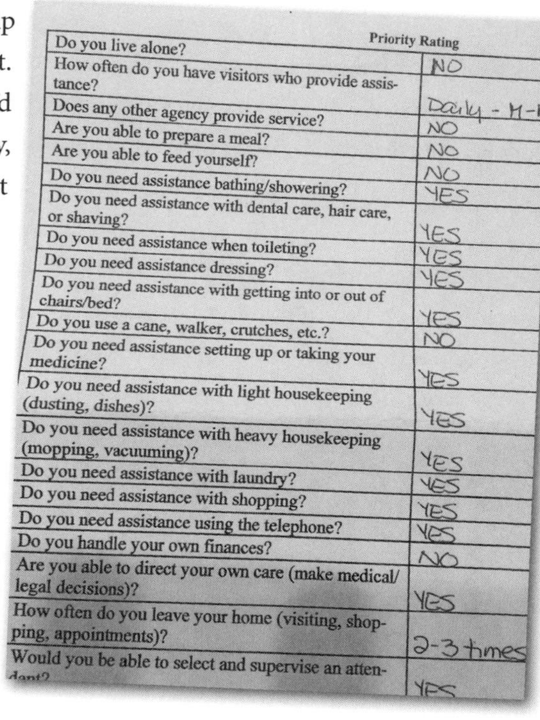

	Priority Rating
Do you live alone?	NO
How often do you have visitors who provide assistance?	Daily - M-F
Does any other agency provide service?	NO
Are you able to prepare a meal?	NO
Are you able to feed yourself?	NO
Do you need assistance bathing/showering?	YES
Do you need assistance with dental care, hair care, or shaving?	YES
Do you need assistance when toileting?	YES
Do you need assistance dressing?	YES
Do you need assistance with getting into or out of chairs/bed?	YES
Do you use a cane, walker, crutches, etc.?	NO
Do you need assistance setting up or taking your medicine?	YES
Do you need assistance with light housekeeping (dusting, dishes)?	YES
Do you need assistance with heavy housekeeping (mopping, vacuuming)?	YES
Do you need assistance with laundry?	YES
Do you need assistance with shopping?	YES
Do you need assistance using the telephone?	YES
Do you handle your own finances?	NO
Are you able to direct your own care (make medical/legal decisions)?	YES
How often do you leave your home (visiting, shopping, appointments)?	2-3 times
Would you be able to select and supervise an attendant?	YES

September 30, 2015

I spent my cold and rainy day at my kiddos' walkathon!

Last year, I was a few months post-diagnosis and serving popsicles. This year, I sat in my chair the whole time since my arms don't work, doing what I love most—just being with my kiddos. I've let go of not being able to be in the thick of things, and just appreciate being there, being here.

October 10, 2015

Hello, Dolly

This time last year, I was riding Space Mountain at Disney with ALS. So this year, a trip to Dollywood, Dolly Parton's amusement park, didn't seem too ridiculous. Surely I could still sit in a roller coaster!

We made sure I rode the ride where my upper body and neck were fully supported since those areas continue to weaken. A fully supported roller-coaster ride didn't seem, at least at the time, to push my physical limitations.

Since I was using a handicap pass for assistance, I was required to sit on the outside of the coaster, which threw a kink in our how-to-ride-a-roller-coaster-with-ALS logistics plan we had carefully crafted. Eric held one hand and I sat firmly on my right naughty hand to secure it . . . but I didn't account for g-force or upside-down loops. Every loop, my paralyzed arm unleashed to dangle and jerk outside the ride. When everybody else was clenching their arm support, I was the one with my arm up in the air like an unruly guest—I hoped they would stop the ride because I wasn't following the rules of keeping arms inside, but no luck. I was pretty confident my arm was ripping off like a cooked chicken leg. The good news is, when the ride finally stopped my arm was still attached . . . in pain but attached.

In hindsight, it may not have been the best idea for my body, or a *really* bad idea in my sister's opinion. My roller-coaster days are officially over, but I made a great memory with my family.

October 16, 2015

I was slightly hesitant when Norton Neuroscience Institute asked me to be the face of ALS for an upcoming event. It's a difficult commitment when I can't get dressed on my own, put on make-up, or even brush my teeth or hair. But in a continued effort to educate and advocate for a cure or treatment for this devastating disease I've been handed, featuring a face of an early 40s female was a great opportunity to show that ALS is affecting patients younger every year; it's not only a grandparents' disease, it's a young parents' disease, as well. And so I agreed to be a face for living with ALS.

October 21, 2015

I never thought I'd say it, but I can't wait for my power wheelchair to come in. I got emotionally overwhelmed during my chair fitting, but now I'm ready. My youngest wanted me to go on her field trip today and I had to say no. It's one of my favorite trips that I've done with my other two, but the farm wasn't quite manual-wheelchair friendly.

Chair ordered a month ago, just waiting for insurance clearance and, of course, the ridiculously expensive van to transport it in and then I'll be field trip-ready again.

October 30, 2015

My morning started with my quarterly ALS clinic. It's a three-hour appointment where I meet with all of my doctors and therapists and they rate my progression. The team tells me how much worse I've gotten and how to adapt to the changes that are coming. These appointments beyond suck—and today was no exception—but I guess they are necessary to keep up with the crazy adaptions needed to live with this disease.

The good news is I had a lunch date with my hubby at my favorite café. We ordered carry-out to eat in the car, but Eric encouraged me to sit at a table. He's really awesome about not letting ALS get in our way. We avoided our progression discussion and mapped out a game plan for the next four hours of our crazy day.

After a quick lunch, we joined the class parties with our children at school, wrapped up another successful Dare to Care food drive (our school is amazingly generous), rushed home for three rounds of piano lessons and getting ready to head out for a Halloween party—I'll process that ALS progression later. For now, I'm too busy living.

October 31, 2015

After reprimanding my two girls for screaming and being ridiculously unkind to each other this morning, I sent them both to their beds for timeout. "How long?" they yelled.

"Until I get out of bed!" Crap, I forgot, I need them to help me get out of bed. Oh, and while you're at it, can you take me to the bathroom and help me get dressed? So much for that time out!

November 10, 2015

Just to be clear, when somebody asks me how I'm doing, I *always* answer from a mental standpoint—unless of course, you ask me about my physical condition. Living with ALS is just as much mental as it is physical, at least from my perspective at this point. Usually, I'm doing good, appreciating what I have and living in the moment.

So when I give a positive reply and a smile, please don't assume my body is well or my progression has stopped.

I had a well-intentioned acquaintance ask me if I was getting stronger.

Here's how ALS works—it's progressive, my body gets worse by the day. It is 100 percent fatal. I'm putting up my best fight to kick the crap out of ALS and slow down my progression (no luck yet), but I'm not getting better and I'm not getting stronger. My left and right arms don't work; I can't write; I can't go to the bathroom by myself; I can't feed myself. Heck, I can't do *anything* that requires hands—think about that for a minute. I have a hard time holding my neck up; I can't get up out of a low chair; I can't get myself out of bed. I can't walk to my children's classrooms, walk a flight of steps, or have lengthy conversations without being out of breath.

So, how am I? I am strong in my faith; I am well loved; I am well supported; I am in a faithful marriage; and I'm mothering three beautiful children who need me . . . so today I am good!

November 13, 2015

She's Here! Introducing the Newest Addition to My ALS World

Female Permobil

Born: November 11, 2015

Weight: 400 pounds of steel, foam, and wires

Height: 4 feet, 2 inches

I'm not really sure what to call her yet; she's going to be my sidekick for the duration of my journey. I feel she needs a proper name with the amount of time we will be spending together—to call her a wheelchair, a power wheelchair, or call her by her model name seems unfriendly. I already feminized her when, upon a family vote, I selected pink as the accent color. Cardinal red was a close second! It is a chair to not only move my body, but fully support my body. She will adapt with me as I continue to progress. Some parts of me have already quit working—I've progressed past the initial joystick they ordered because I don't have the strength anymore to move the standard joystick.

My core stomach muscles have weakened to the point where I need help being lifted out of a low chair. My new wheels will lift me up to an almost standing position so I can walk out of my . . . whatever I'm gonna call her.

In addition to my core muscles, my neck has substantially weakened, as well. She has a headrest and will allow a recline for my neck muscles to rest. This should help with the constant head-, neck-, and backaches, and I won't be faced with the droopy neck that most ALS patients get while I'm in the chair.

My unnamed chair will obviously take me farther distances than I can walk due to my breathing issues and allow me to navigate my own body on grass and uneven terrain. I'm looking forward to getting back to the parks.

My right hand is extremely weak, and the controller is set to be used with minimal muscle use. When my hand is completely paralyzed, the navigation is outfitted to be controlled by my chin (no, I couldn't say that without crying) or the attendant controllers on the back, so my caregiver can move my chair. Eric said he'll finally be able to control me (hardy, har, har).

She will recline into a flat position, and I can use it as a bed if Eric is not here to help me transfer or as therapy to stretch my legs.

She will hold my Trilogy (my breathing machine). My lung capacity dropped another 10 percent the last three months. If you're new to this journey, that's how ALS progression is measured. I'm not there yet, but in time when I need my breathing machine throughout the day, I'll have it with me wherever I go.

When I was fitted for the wheelchair almost two months ago, I was unexpectedly teary at the overwhelming number of needs I would grow into with this big, scary, black chair. Now that she is here, I'm ready to embrace her abilities because I'm ready be more mobile.

I've spent the last couple of days navigating around my home and neighborhood. The destruction I've done to our molding and cabinets in the last 48 hours is painfully pathetic. We widened doors this summer, but clearly no doorway can be wide enough. I'm really wishing we went with that open floorplan I was completely opposed to five years ago.

How much does this piece of equipment cost? It's a custom-built chair, custom to my unique growing needs. MSRP is $44,000; my insurance covers a large portion of it. I'm still waiting for my out-of-pocket total.

I'm still getting to know her and deciding on a name. Consider me a driver in training until then.

November 26, 2015

We are thankful for everyone who has prayed, cooked, shared a talent, transported, supported, donated, listened, cheered, commented, shared a gift, carried a burden, loved, and been a part of our enormous blessings. From our little party of five, Happy Thanksgiving.

—Team Dewey

November 28, 2015

I always knew I was going to host a party for Eric's 50th birthday.

He *loves* a party and I love to party plan.

Eric is five years away from the big 50 I've been planning; unfortunately, ALS has taken the luxury of waiting away. If there is something I want to do, I need to do it now. So, a surprise 45th for my awesome husband it was! Such a fun night—really, really fun! So much fun, I cried when it was over. I didn't want it to end. I don't want anything to end.

December 3, 2015

My birthday was yesterday. I turned 44. Birthdays become major milestones, especially at the rate of my consistent decline in breathing. I was just happy to have another birthday, *really*! Happy to be 44, happy to be here, happy to be alive and loved. I've watched many not make it this long. Heck, my dearest high school friend didn't make it past 16. Years are to be appreciated and celebrated. We have many friends celebrating turn-of-the-decade birthdays and cringe at the thought of being "that old." It's highly unlikely I will turn a new decade without an expedited treatment or cure, while remaining faithfully optimistic that will happen. I wish friends wouldn't cringe at getting older but appreciate the year and decades they have.

I watched my mom celebrate her last birthday this summer. We knew her life was coming to an end—to serenade someone with one last "Happy Birthday," the song never sounded so beautiful!

I had a great birthday. My mom and dad came for a visit, my friend came in town to help my kids make dinner, my morning friend made a beautiful cake and helped my kids plan an early morning birthday party before school. The only sign of ALS present was the three breaths it took to blow out my 10 candles; oh, and my kids feeding me my birthday cake.

December 5, 2015

My sweet momma died on Thursday evening at age 69. My dad asked that I share with those who knew her. To know my mom was to love her.

Robinson, Ellen McGuire, 69, died peacefully at her home surrounded by family, Thursday, December 3, 2015. She was born to James and Adelaide Klosterman McGuire in Chattanooga, Tennessee. She was a retired flight attendant with United Airlines and a member of Epiphany Catholic Church. She is survived by her husband of 48 years, Joe Robinson; her children Christopher (Eva) Robinson, Carrey (Eric) Dewey, Ryan (Michelle) Robinson, and Elizabeth (Mickey) Sorg. She is also survived by her seven grandchildren, Drew and Layne Robinson; Ian, Anne Marie, and Colleen Dewey; and Jameson and

Joseph Sorg; and her sister Terri (Tommy) Farmer. Ellen graduated from Sienna College in Memphis, Tennessee. She met her future husband while cheerleading for his basketball at Christian Brothers University, and they were married four years later. They had four children and after living in Bethlehem, Pennsylvania; Cincinnati, Ohio; and Nashville, Tennessee, they made their home in Oldham County, where they have lived for 38 years. Ellen was admired for her beautiful gardens, the wreaths on the front door, and her famous chocolate chip cookies. She was also known for her plentiful scarf collection; her love for crafting, pottery, and art fairs; and incorporating her Southern roots in just about everything she did. Ellen was a second mother to many and made an impact on any who knew her. Funeral Mass will be on Monday, December 7, 2015, at 11 a.m. at Church of the Epiphany, 914 Old Harrods Creek Road. Visitation will be on Sunday, December 6, 2015, at Ratterman Brothers Funeral Home, 12900 Shelbyville Road, East Louisville, from 11 a.m. to 6 p.m. Expressions of sympathy can be made to the ALS Therapy Development Institute, 300 Technology Square, Suite 400, Cambridge, MA 02139.

December 14, 2015

The Loss of My Sweet Mom

While the death of my mom wasn't a shock, it's still been a painful loss. I'm trying to adjust to the physical loss and feel the presence of her in my life every day—I'm 10 days in. I think about my own mortality and faith challenges often with the lessons my mom taught me, especially the very unique lessons since my own life-changing diagnosis.

My mom fought through numerous life-threatening medical conditions. She was a woman of amazing strength, and if my mom had even the slimmest chance to overcome, she would take the odds and beat them. Her medical complications were much deeper than her cancer diagnosis delivered in June. When the doctors said there was no treatment for her, and the cancer would eventually end her life, she knew what that meant. We, mother and daughter, then had something uniquely in common—we both had a 0 percent survival from our diagnoses. She entered hospice care while I began to watch the process.

My sweet mom lost many things I will eventually lose, such as my ability to eat, walk on my own, and a strong voice. We shared our losses, too: our ability to drive, our ability to stand up on our own, the control of our kitchens, our ability to bathe on our own, our ability to breath comfortably, and even our independence as we both needed 24-hour assistance. We both lost abilities that were important to us—hands-on decorating, entertaining, and even traveling without an arsenal of medical equipment. My mom was disappointed with her fatal diagnosis; she understood what it meant and got even busier living! She always focused on what she could do, and while things were difficult, she continued to bake, write her beautiful letters to others, buy thoughtful gifts, visit craft fairs, and continue to add to her scarf and pottery collection. My mom was always put together; she never let herself look sick. People would always tell me how good my mom looked, and I was quick to clarify, she looked better than she felt. But that was my mom, always doing her best to represent herself well.

Honestly, it has been a painfully surreal experience shared with my mom. Before her diagnosis in June, I really believed she was invincible, and that I might die before her. It's unnatural to die before your parents. I certainly didn't want my mom to die, but I didn't want to die before her either.

My mom told me she loved me; she told me I was a good mother; she was proud of my advocacy efforts; and she loved reading my blog and all the comments. The only gift she wanted for her birthday was a copy of my printed Facebook page with all the comments. While my mom was obviously devastated by my ALS diagnosis, she took comfort in the community we are surrounded by and would often say "if anybody could live with ALS, you can." She called the many people who help our family live with ALS "angels sent from God."

Mom was loved by many, a true example of what a shepherd is—all who knew her will attest to that. She appreciated the gift of time, and while every task was difficult, she was too busy living to prepare for dying. And so her passing was quick.

Mom helped celebrate my 44th birthday on Wednesday at my house and she died the next day in her home meticulously decorated for Christmas, with all of her ingredients on the counter for her scheduled baking day Thursday that never happened. My mom was definitely living.

I learned many lessons about the end-of-life process and the difficult decisions I will have to make on my journey. At times, I felt like God was stretching the process out so I could be aware of every scenario. I pretty much watched from the sideline, as my dad and sister modeled what amazing and dedicated care looks like. It was an emotionally awkward and draining experience that I'm still trying to process. Even on her last day of life, she continued to teach me much-needed lessons for this, at times, painful journey I'm on. Witnessing my mom, in the presence of our family and priest, take her final breath immediately after receiving her last rites sacrament was something I needed to witness to help remove some of my own fears and bear witness to my faith.

My mom designated ALS TDI, the only dedicated ALS research lab, for her memorial contributions. Even in death, she's still advocating for a cure for me and everyone else living with ALS. My sweet mom is my newest angel.

December 20, 2015

Merry Mobility to Me!

Eric just bought me the most expensive car I will ever own. It's not the fancy car I wanted after I outgrew my minivan-mom chapter of my life. Never did I dream it would be *me* keeping our family in a minivan for the duration of my life. Honestly, every part of ALS is absolutely ridiculous and van shopping proved to be no different.

My new van looks very much like my old van, except the accessibility conversion puts my new van into the price range of my dream car that I'll never have. Take the cost of a van and add $25,000 to convert it to be accessible for a wheelchair. No, that's not a typo and, no, insurance does not help with the accessibility conversions. You're on your own: happy handicapping!

Shopping for an accessible van was difficult. A stark visual and financial reminder of our reality. I also had feelings of guilt as I watch many ALS families set up GoFundMe accounts or undergo extreme burdens to cover the cost of their accessible vans. Through my medical fund, I have the ability to cover the cost of the conversion without a great financial hardship. I fell somewhere in between feeling extremely grateful and seriously pissed off.

Test driving for the van literally meant how I maneuver or drive my power chair in while my three kids sit on the back bench bickering—but then again, they argued in my old van, too. This test driving takes minivan-mom status to a whole new level. I hated every one we looked at. The back ends are jacked up because of the lowered floor, and I lost the ability to carry two to three people in the middle to make room for my chair. I literally cried on one test drive because of our reality and finally told Eric to just buy a van. We settled on a used Honda Odyssey—we are the third owners of this accessible van, so it's far from new. Somehow, the Odyssey made me feel most "normal," whatever that means. I guess because I've driven an Odyssey the last 10 years it wouldn't be a huge change.

I'll appreciate my accessible van, ramp, lift, and racing stripes. Okay, Eric says it's the footplate, not racing stripes, but that's what they look like to me. In keeping with the spirit of this complete ridiculousness, the antlers and red nose are included.

December 31, 2015

2015 in Review

We rang in 2015 with our annual New Year's Day Great Wolf Lodge trip.

My sweet sister and brother-in-law moved in two houses down from our family.

We enjoyed an excessive number of snow days.

We taught the kids to snow ski in Colorado for spring break.

Anne Marie received her First Communion and got her ears pierced.

I made an ALS Advocacy trip to Washington DC.

All three children progressed in their piano lessons.

We enjoyed another annual family trip to Sanibel Island.

Anne Marie made the school cheerleading squad and is working hard to master a back handspring.

Colleen joined the chess club . . . and hated it.

We spent fall break in the Smoky Mountains.

I continue to serve on the school PTA board as an advisor.

I joined my high school girlfriends on a trip to DC.

Ian was selected as a *Louisville Magazine* Super Kid.

Eric and I both continue as scout co-leaders for our children.

The girls went to their first concert, Taylor Swift.

My sweet baby nephew was born just in time for our annual St. Patrick's Day celebration.

I continue to navigate in the kitchen from helping prep dinner to baking my favorite, banana bread.

All three kids have created a YouTube Channel and filmed hair tutorials and toy reviews.

Eric and I celebrated 14 years of marriage.

Ian is in his last year of Webelos, getting ready for Boy Scouts.

Spent time in Costa Rica with the notorious "church ladies."

The kids are halfway through first, third, and fifth grade, meaning a middle school decision is on the horizon.

I continued to stay busy advocating for ALS research, spreading the word of what ALS is, and fighting for a treatment and cure.

We appreciated every ride in the Jeep with the top down.

I hosted a surprise birthday party for Eric.

We caught Santa in our home on Christmas Eve.

I turned 44.

I spent Christmas Eve at my parent's home for the 44th time.

My mom died.

I lost my ability to drive.

I had a feeding tube and diaphragm pacemaker implanted.

I began using the BiPAP machine to help me breathe at night and the cough assist machine to strengthen my diaphragm.

I left my children four times for out-of-town medical trips.

I spent a week in the hospital receiving an alternative treatment.

My breathing went from 77 percent to 44 percent (as of three months ago).

I lost my ability to get out of bed on my own and feed myself.

We installed two bidets—out of necessity, not luxury.

We put in place 24-hour assistance for me as a safety measure.

We widened the doors on the first floor for accessibility.

I lost my ability to sit upright on my own.

I lost my handwriting.

I got a power wheelchair and an accessible van.

Two of my ALS mom friends died, along with many other people I've connected with.

We canceled our annual Great Wolf Lodge trip.

I'd really like to say, "Bring on 2016," but that's not really the truth. Each day gets harder. I'd like to freeze time, but I know I can't. So, I will take the good with the bad and continue to feel the love, the outpouring of support, and the physical actions of faith from both friends and followers, that lighten our burdens as we continue to adapt, adjust, and move forward through 2016.

2016

January 9, 2016

Physical Update

I had my quarterly ALS clinic appointment yesterday. I go every three months to have my progression assessed. It's usually a three-hour appointment that I never look forward to because I always find out how much worse I've gotten and what's coming my way next, forcing me out of living in the moment. These appointments are physically and emotionally draining. Since my progression is consistent and my breathing has been affected since onset, I never get good news and this appointment was no different—except they brought in a palliative care doctor to this appointment. That word is as scary as ALS.

While my area of weakness continues to grow throughout my limbs, significantly my neck and core muscles have suffered the most dramatic muscle loss as measured at this appointment. These are the muscles that help me sit upright in a chair, cough, have a bowel movement, balance, keep my stomach tucked, and blow my nose. While my legs definitely continue to weaken, I can still walk very short distances with caution. I've stumbled more times than I care to share.

I've really struggled with my breathing the last six weeks. I just thought it was the amount of high energy and emotion of things going on, and I would rebound. But with ALS, rebounding isn't typical. My lung capacity is currently 39 percent. I'm out of breath with minimal activity, such as talking and walking even 15 yards. I can't yell anymore—my kids are really disappointed about that! I use the breathing machine at night to give my diaphragm a rest, but sometimes during the day I use it as a necessity when I am gasping and can't catch my breath; usually after I've attempted the stairs on my own or a shower. It is definitely something I will need to incorporate more during the day now that my respiratory numbers are under 40. I'm starting to feel more comfortable at home where I have all of my equipment such as my lift chair, and stairlift that will take me up the steps, plus all of my breathing equipment.

I really hate sharing these updates, but I know it's important for my continued advocacy efforts. I'd love to share I've made progress, or I'm gonna start a treatment, or the FDA approved a new drug, but at this time, I can't. I'm still hopeful and prayerful that will occur in my lifetime though.

I'm connected with ALS patients in all stages all the way to the end. I know what this beast looks like as it continues, so I still really appreciate all that I do have. I can speak clearly; I can eat any food I crave; I still live in my home; I can shed my wheelchair if places are not accessible; I'm still healthy outside of ALS. I still say I'm good. It's not my attitude, it's what I know is coming.

January 10, 2016

My littlest helper giving me a lift on the stairlift. I don't have enough strength in my hands to hold the chair control, so she does that for me. All the little things make a big difference.

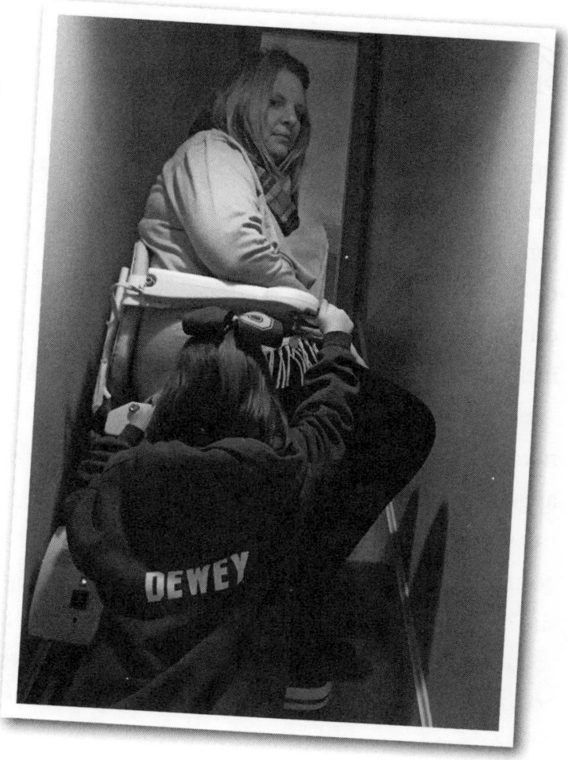

January 15, 2016

Inheritance of Hope

I've always felt a real need to connect with other young parents who have a diagnosis similar to mine. If patients didn't have children, young children, children who are still under our wings, I couldn't really relate—even if we shared a diagnosis. My torment and sadness lies with leaving my children and husband too early and not necessarily the inhumane process my body is going through.

In early December, Inheritance of Hope organization called and invited us on a Legacy Family Retreat in Orlando starting this weekend.

Inheritance of Hope is a volunteer-based Christian nonprofit that brings young families together whose parents have a life-threatening diagnosis to create memories, provide counseling, and build unique friendships. IoH is equipped with therapists and volunteers who will be there for my family as we face the harsh realities of what ALS will do to us. The description of this family retreat is a beautiful blessing to our family, so of course, we accepted their generous invitation.

January 25, 2016

Our family was a recipient of the Inheritance of Hope Legacy Retreat.

I've been anxious to put our experience into words, but our experience was something greater than words could explain—so full, so moving, so emotional, so comforting, so inspiring, and truly so full of hope. Hope far beyond my diagnosis: hope for Eric, hope for my three children, and hope for my sister.

Our family planned on attending a Christian retreat for parents with a fatal illness. I had no idea how serving and loving and hands-on IoH was. Twenty-three families carrying a heavy burden, 34 volunteers (11 of whom came as family recipients and returned to serve), five coordinators, seven counselors, and five staff members—all physically and spiritually there for us. I feel so incredibly blessed to be one of the 300 families Inheritance of Hope has served on the Legacy Retreat since the beginning in 2007.

Going into the Legacy Retreat, I desperately needed guidance as our family continued to travel down our inevitable path. We needed human connections from other parents and children who face similar circumstances as well as connections with families that have experienced the worst but come back on the other side to share their love with us. I needed tools to continue on as I leave behind my three children and spouse and my sweet sister.

Inheritance of Hope was this beautiful hand-delivered blessing. IoH said not only are we going to provide the retreat, we're going to provide it free; we're going to be the hands to help cover all the logistics as difficult as it may be; we're going to help you with all the details while you're here; we'll provide you with tools to utilize on the retreat and when you return home; we're going to help you make a legacy video for your family; we're going to counsel your children; we're going to give caregivers an opportunity to connect; we're going to shower you with priceless gifts; we are going to pray with you; and we're going to hug you and love you forever. They didn't know us at all. They only knew—I mean understood—our circumstances. Seriously, that just happened to our family, provided by people who started as complete strangers and ended as family.

I am equally inspired by the circumstances and beginning of this amazing organization, which in itself is a beautiful story of a faithfully devoted and courageous husband-and-wife team. Kristen Milligan died of cancer in 2011, five years after she and her husband, Deric, established this organization. But boy, did she leave our family a much-needed and priceless gift—because they knew what we needed, what all the families on the retreat needed. Additionally, her husband and three children, as well as a few of their other family members were volunteers on the retreat with us.

I actually came home a little more paralyzed and struggling a bit more to breathe, but it was totally worth it! I am forever grateful to Inheritance of Hope for the gift that will continue on in our family long after I'm gone.

To learn more about this organization or to see lots of pictures and videos from our trip as well as ways to gift other families in our exact situation, see https://inheritanceofhope.org. Because every parent with a fatal diagnosis deserves a Legacy Retreat.

January 29, 2016

This was a quick sketch by Colleen.

January 31, 2016

All the muscles in my body have been twitching since diagnosis; those twitches are called fasciculations. It's new to my vocabulary since ALS. Sometimes they are visible; sometimes they are not. Fasciculations are a common symptom with ALS patients. They are caused by the muscles backfiring when the nerves don't work.

Please note: Just because your muscles are twitching *does not* mean you have ALS!

The past few months, my tongue has been twitching slightly. Fasciculations don't hurt; it's more of a reminder my tongue will be affected, weakened, or even paralyzed. Recently, I've been biting the sides of my tongue because the muscle is in fact, getting weaker. It's not going into place between my bottom teeth, it's resting on top of my teeth, which is, I guess, how I bite it. I'm pointing out the obvious—this muscle loss will affect my speech and eating. I think it's fair to say I will be eating at all my favorite restaurants and finishing my voice recordings ASAP!

February 13, 2016

Both girls had Valentine's Day parties yesterday, and they wanted me to come. It made sense. I've never missed a party—heck, I used to be the room parent planning the party. I should be thankful I have a valid reason for not having to put in the work to party plan and just showing up, but it doesn't work like that.

I made it through most of Colleen's party but needed to leave toward the end. I was starting to get anxious, which in turn affects my breathing. I'm not quite ready to go out in public with my breathing machine, but we're getting to that point. I went home, took an hour nap and a little white pill, and went back for Anne Marie's party. Just trying to make the day matter for the people that matter most.

February 19, 2016

I had my first real ALS scare on Sunday. I hate to even retell it, but it's important in terms of understanding ALS . . . and my reality.

On Sunday, Eric took Ian to swim practice while I rested at home with the girls. I was lying in bed so I couldn't fall or choke and had recently been to the bathroom. I was completely comfortable in a resting position with only the girls home. As time passed, my breathing started to become slightly labored. I'm sure it was a combination of anxiety and my body sliding down in bed leaving my chest unelevated. I ran through my breathing strategies, but it didn't work—what I really needed was my breathing machine. Anne Marie has assisted putting my mask on many times, but never solo.

She tried to put the mask on me but was having a hard time getting it latched. As minutes passed, my breathing became more labored. Anne Marie called Eric, but he was 30 minutes away. She called my sister Elizabeth: no answer. She proceeded to call two more nearby neighbors: no answer. I guess it's fair to say, I was panicked. I definitely should've thought earlier to have her run to my sister's house two doors down first. That is the entire reason her family picked up and moved next to us—to physically be there when I needed them immediately.

I can only imagine the message Anne Marie relayed to my sister, but Liz was here super-fast. She readjusted me, gave me anti-anxiety medication, and put my breathing mask on, and all was back to normal in my ALS world.

Honestly, it scared the hell out of me. We are using this as a learning experience and making a list of people to call in case of emergency and at what point to call 911, as well as teaching Anne Marie or anyone else at home with me how to put the mask on.

My biggest takeaway, though, was not my breathing struggles, but how my nine-year-old handled the situation. She was calm and quick thinking as my breathing declined. Even when my sister came to help, my sweet girl lay in my bed and rubbed my hand, trying to provide comfort. ALS is scary and my children are the real faces of this disease, but I'm watching my children develop in ways I never imagined. I'm beyond proud of my sweet girl and super thankful for my nearby sister.

March 9, 2016

This morning Colleen was attempting to have a debate with me. I was in bed with my breathing mask on, and she was insisting on being homeschooled for the day. This is her way of saying she wants to stay home. It's hard to have a discussion with anyone when air is being forced down my throat in two-second intervals with my mask muffling my weak voice. She always tries though. The best I could do was, "We'll . . . talk . . . about it . . . tonight." With that, she turned and looked at me, and sassed, "You're homeschooling me tomorrow! End of discussion. Period" and walked out the door.

I lay in bed paralyzed and completely inaudible to reprimand her for her ridiculous disrespect. Where in the world would she have heard that? Oh Lordy, we must find a cure for ALS quick because this girl needs me!

On a separate note, Colleen lost her first tooth at school today. Good thing she went, because if she was homeschooled her teacher-momma wouldn't have been able to pull it for her. It's a simple milestone, but when ALS was mentioned several months before I was actually diagnosed, I cried to Eric about the possibility of missing her losing her first tooth. The Tooth Fairy throws a special party in the Dewey household, and of course, I am her assistant. It's crazy to think that was actually one of my first fears; it's really hard to grasp reality when you're diagnosed with ALS, but that's where my confused mind took me—missing out on Colleen losing her first tooth. So tonight we celebrate a once-in-a-lifetime losing her first tooth and making every memory count, sassy or not.

March 17, 2016

Our family never misses an opportunity to celebrate and share in traditions, and tonight was no exception.

Hard to believe this time last year we had a five-day-old nephew, my mom was here, and I was in the middle of my aggressive plasmapheresis treatments, hoping to slow my progression. What a difference a year makes.

Happy St. Patrick's Day from our wee little Irish family to yours!

March 19, 2016

My Next Biggest Problem

With ALS, you have to look ahead and start preparing for your next biggest problem. In my case, my next biggest problem snuck up on us. After feeling confident with my maneuverability skills and navigating in and out of the car (which is no easy task, by the way), I'm transitioning again. I'm struggling to control my wheelchair because of the weakness in my "good" right hand. I already have a sensitive joystick since I have weakness in my hand, but even with that, I basically control my wheelchair with the tip of my thumb. I'm not able to put my hand on the joystick by myself and sometimes my wrist gets so tired it falls off the controls completely and then I'm stuck.

When we were at our retreat in January, Eric was leading the family and I was in the back, mothering my ones ahead of me. But my wrist gave out and fell off the chair, my voice was too weak to yell at them and I was stuck. Literally. I was just getting ready to ask a stranger to put my hand back on my wheelchair when Eric eventually realized I wasn't behind them and came running back toward me. Another lesson learned.

When I lose an ability, I always hope it's just because I'm tired, and I'll be stronger in the next few days, but rarely does that ever happen. It's just progression, another loss. So this week I've needed help controlling my wheelchair. The next big step is to set up the controls to work through my chin, but I really don't want to be there yet—or ever. But with ALS, you never get your way, and you better adapt just to move forward or you're going to be stuck. I'm holding onto any strength I have in my thumb. I never appreciated my thumb as much as I do now. He's really my only working finger and is critical to my ability to be independent and move. I'll never take my thumb for granted again. Ever.

April 1, 2016

The Only Thing Worse Than ALS

The only thing worse than ALS, from my experience, is severe chronic mental illness. Our family had to painfully watch my brother's life disintegrate into complete darkness and debilitation because of his mental torture. He could not experience the beauty of God's wonderful world, the deep love and support his family felt for him, or the joys of everyday living.

My brother kept up with my ALS progression and was proud of the way I was open and honest. Chris shared with me that he had a hard time being around me because he was such a "downer" and I really needed "uplifting spirits"—his words. He was hesitant to tell me how he was feeling because he said I was fighting a real fight. I assured my brother our diagnoses were equally devastating, and my heart hurt that he could not experience the love and support that has carried me through my own devastating diagnosis. I shared with my friends who have been aware of my brother's health, that I wouldn't want to trade him illnesses. I'd much rather have two to five years feeling the love, support, and God's strength instead of the darkness my brother endured, even while under the care of medical professionals and family. My brother did everything asked of him by the doctors. Unfortunately, they were still not able to get any light into the deep dark hole of depression in which he lived.

It is with deep sadness, I share my older brother Chris died last week at the age of 46 from severe chronic depression.

Christopher Kerry Robinson
July 24, 1969—March 21, 2016

April 19, 2016

Colleen asked me if I thought I'd be alive when she was married and had children.

Eric and I have chosen to explain my diagnosis to them by answering their questions honestly, and so each child understands ALS differently.

I reminded my seven-year-old that we are praying for a cure or treatment in my lifetime.

"I know what we're praying for, Mommy, but what do you *think*?" She stumped me on how to answer honestly. After a long pause, I told her there's a possibility I won't be, but I was going to do my best to live as long as I can.

Answering these kinds of question sucks!

April 28, 2016

Does ALS Hurt?

Specifically ALS, the dying of the nerves, does not hurt. It's the damage and destruction of ALS that hurts.

My specific pain is in my arms where the destruction started. Since they weakened first, I was still able to walk and carry the unsupported deadweight of my arms. In the beginning, I tried putting my arm in a sling so the weight wouldn't pull down, but that disrupted my balance, and I believe caused my first fall. Consequently, carrying the deadweight on my arm caused subluxation, which means my arm bone is separated from the shoulder socket, pulling all of the muscles and ligaments in my arm. It's about a one-and-a-half-inch separation.

To manage the subluxation, my physical therapist friend, Michelle, comes over weekly to gift me with her amazing ninja taping skills. She's a badass when it comes to Kinesio tape, which temporarily lifts my arm back into the shoulder socket. It's not pretty and leaves quite the tan line, but it eases the pain, so I am thankful for her gift.

I also have some pretty intense muscle spasms and cramping. The ones that hurt the worst are in my throat and hands, which is why I take a hefty dose of muscle relaxers.

Fortunately, we are able to manage my pain with therapy, taping, and medication, so no big complaints yet.

May 1, 2016

Thank you to my awesome friends who ran in my name when I couldn't run. Running the mini-marathon has always been on my bucket list, but I waited for no good reason, and now it's impossible. One of my few life regrets. My friends rallied the troops and ran for Team Dewey helping me run the mini by proxy. Well done, Team Dewey!

May 2, 2016

My amazing seamstress friend Sarah did it again! She was able to make a second dress for Colleen out of my wedding gown, like she did for Anne Marie, to wear for their First Communions. What a beautiful gift to give my girls and me. There isn't much fabric left, but she's making small hearts I can share with them to sew into their wedding gowns and a small handkerchief for Ian; I can leave these for them to use on their wedding days. Little did I know my wedding gown would get this much mileage.

May 4, 2016

Colleen's First Communion

Colleen received the Sacrament of First Communion one year ahead of schedule. Typically, kids prepare for the sacrament as second graders in the Catholic Church. My church made a special exception and allowed Colleen to prepare during her first-grade year. It isn't because I don't think I will live that long; it's because I wanted to help her prepare spiritually by attending all of her preparation classes with her, by her side, and not just be here to bear witness.

Last summer, my good friend and First Communion teacher, Becky Brown, first mentioned the idea of Colleen preparing a year early. I thought the idea was ludicrous and honestly, I was half offended my friend didn't think I would live that long. But the more I thought, the more I understood her intentions of me being an active participant with her class. I knew I could give Colleen more this year than next year. And without question, our church granted a special exception for her.

Colleen and I definitely made the most out of our preparation together. It gave me an opportunity to answer lots of questions and revisit my own understanding of this holy sacrament. Now, she's holding me to the promise of getting her ears pierced for her First Communion, something that I promised them years ago.

May 8, 2016

It's a bittersweet Mother's Day, the first without my sweet momma and the clock ticking on my own mortality. If I must be diagnosed with ALS, this is how I would like to spend my Mother's Day, with my family serving as amazing advocates.

I left my family last Mother's Day to attend this conference. I promised them if I came back this year, they could join me. I feel very fortunate to be here this year with them by my side.

May 10, 2016

Making memories and making a difference. Insanely busy but productive day in Washington, DC. We started our morning at the White House for unofficial business, followed by back-to-back meetings with our senators and representatives. My kids did an amazing job being the faces of ALS and I know their sweet young voices made an impact.

May 11, 2016

I was on the fence about making this trip to DC for ALS advocacy. I was tired and still recovering from my last trip. But I knew how much I wanted my kids to be with me last year and honestly, I felt blessed to be here and be able to go, so I put my heart all in and rallied. Couldn't have brought the kids without my loving husband and supportive father.

The kids may not have understood all the technical talk during some of the ALS conference sessions in Washington, DC, but they definitely took away the different stages of ALS, the inspiration that they are not alone in their fight for a cure, the inspiration of seeing other people living with ALS, as well as ways to pimp out my wheelchair—more to come on that later. They also enjoyed meeting many PALS they have heard me speak of.

So glad we made the trip, my babes were amazing advocates, and a stark reminder that my little people are the faces of ALS.

May 13, 2016

Physical Update

I usually try to do a physical update right after my quarterly ALS clinic visit. I'm about a month behind on this one because honestly, I hate sharing the updates, but I know how important they are in my continued efforts to educate people about ALS and advocate for research and support for ALS patients.

So here goes . . . my body continues to weaken, which is what ALS does. The biggest difference noted during my clinic visit was my inability to support my neck and my left leg is much weaker than my right. The real blow to the gut is the continued decrease in my breathing. My lung capacity went from 39 percent to 31 percent—which continues a consistent decline of 3 percent a month. So, what 31 percent looks like is I'm out of breath when I walk from my bed to my bathroom; I can't cough up secretions in my chest without a cough assist machine; and I'm on my breathing machine 12 to 14 hours a day and counting.

My speech is still good, which is great because I love to talk! My voice is softer, and my pitch is lower, but my speech is still clear. I do have to talk less because I get out of breath, and that's a real bummer for somebody who always had poor conduct grades for too much talking in class.

One of my new changes is my swallowing. I am not able to get my pills down with water anymore, and I'm starting to move to softer food. I choke often drinking water—I have to be very conscious that fluids go down the right way, so I don't choke, since I can't cough.

I've had too many "crumbles"—or falls as my physical therapist defines them—to count. No wounds, thank goodness, but my body will crumble when I'm being transferred off the toilet or out of the chair. This is because my legs and core muscles have weakened. I can't give myself a lift anymore because my core muscles are so weak. And core muscles have a direct impact on your bowel movements . . . you can fill in the rest.

It's a little tricky because ALS can be so deceiving. You see me out and about with an authentic smile, and other than using my power wheelchair, I look fine. But my body is failing me. My thumb is holding in there enough to control my wheelchair, but he's so weak he can't even push the round iPhone button, which is a priority around here.

The good news is, aside from ALS, I'm perfectly healthy. I need to make sure that I remain healthy and free of congestion and lung infections, as these are potentially fatal for ALS patients.

I hope that after my next ALS clinic update, I can report a plateau because I would be perfectly happy to live out the rest of my life if we could just freeze my ALS in the state I'm in now. Until then, thank you for all your love and support.

May 20, 2016

Shortly after I was diagnosed with ALS, I received a letter from my dad's neighbor—someone I had never met before. In the letter, this man and his wife generously offered to build my wheelchair ramp when the time came. I set the offer aside because I was quite sure the time would never come. But unfortunately, the need came months ago.

Like all the other equipment added to our home, it was to be another visual reminder of all my disability and physical deterioration. I've been resentful every time I've had to add equipment. I cried when we bought our accessible van; I cried when I got my power wheelchair; and I even cried when we had to put a stairlift into our staircase. I knew the ramp would be no different. When my dad called his neighbor to accept his offer, he said he wanted to build the ramp in memory of my mom, Ellen. Somehow that changed my perception of the new ramp that was to come.

When my dad's neighbor, a complete stranger to me, showed up at my home to begin construction I watched him from my kitchen window. This white-haired, gentle older man, who I now know as Dennis, dressed in what most would consider church clothes, arrived to begin the ramp. I kept waiting for that tearful feeling, but my emotion surprised me as I watched this generous man construct my ramp.

My dad offered to help, but his neighbor wanted to work alone. After watching him for several days, I could see why. He was meticulous; he was thorough; he built it in several stages; and I believe his plans were sketched on a napkin.

Sometimes I would come into the kitchen and watch Dennis outside working. I could share by tapping on the window and waving with my foot as he constructed what was becoming a beautiful family-friendly ramp with the kids' quick exit steps, all in my mom's memory.

Dennis finished the ramp a while ago. We just had the opportunity to get our families together with his wife, Jane Anne. I'm so happy his grandsons were in town to join us, so they could witness the impact of their grandfather's generosity and compassion and participate in the dedication of "Ellen's ramp." And like everything else in our family, we take advantage of opportunities to celebrate—prayer and cake included!

May 22, 2016

My kiddos, along with the help of my friend Emily, captained Team Dewey for the ALS Association of Kentucky walk last week. My babes were incredible organizers and advocates, rallying support from their friends, families, and teachers. They were proud to bring home the Team Spirit Award for the second year in a row.

Sweet Colleen asked, "Will we walk next year if they find a cure?" I told her we would throw a party like she's never seen before when that happens.

May 23, 2016

After my last clinic appointment, Eric and I met the kids at the bus stop after school. We expected big smiles, but what we got was Colleen running off the bus.

"Mommy, how was your doctor's appointment today?" she asked with hope in her voice.

My entire body immediately filled with fear, anger, and sadness because I couldn't tell her my appointment went well. I couldn't tell her they had a treatment or cure. I couldn't tell her my breathing level had plateaued. I couldn't tell her I was going to get better.

It hurt my heart to know Colleen carried this throughout her day and eagerly wanted to know the outcome. Honestly, it broke me I couldn't tell her my appointment was fine. I promised I would be as honest as possible for their questions.

I didn't have a lot of time to prepare an answer, but I knew I needed to be truthful. I told Colleenie I still wasn't getting better—but she already knew that. I told her the doctor said I really need to be careful about being around germs and staying healthy aside from ALS. As a family, we need to make sure everybody who comes in our home washes their hands, the kids can't drink after my straw even when I'm not looking, and I have to limit my exposure to school germs, so I won't get sick.

I explained if I got sick, I would most likely need to go to the hospital, and that is one of Colleen's biggest fears. Breaking it to her slowly.

May 25, 2016

Big shout-out to Stopher's National Elementary Honor Society and the fifth-grade class for sponsoring the Rainbow Run, raising over $600 for the ALS Association, Kentucky Chapter.

This project is much deeper than the disease that is affecting our family, as at least two other students in this class have lost grandparents to ALS, a disease that some people call rare.

June 1, 2016

ALS is a complete nuisance, with my arms and legs not working. But now struggling to breathe at times and panicky to get on my breathing machine, ALS is becoming scary, very scary.

June 4, 2016

My high school friends, affectionately known as '89ers (the year we graduated), wanted to take me out on the town. Reluctantly, I went, but I knew I could be a burden.

I enjoyed a great evening with my friends. When I needed to go to the bathroom, I took my trusted friends who have lifted me off the toilet before, but I did warn them I had weakened in the last six weeks. When we opened the stall door, we saw that the toilet was exceptionally low for a handicap-accessible bathroom. I knew it was going to be difficult for me to get up, but I could have never even imagined what was to follow.

After the second attempt, we FaceTimed my sister who has always gotten me out of complicated positions. We had her coach us on how to put the gait belt around me. She instructed my two friends in the stall while my third friend held the phone so my sister could continue to coach. On the third attempt, with my sister watching and coaching, I was almost up, but my legs gave out. At that point, with my underwear and pants around my ankles and my entire body on the floor, I knew we needed outside help.

One of my friends quickly came back with two strong staff members. It took several attempts to get me up safely—by that I mean my neck didn't get whiplash, my shoulders were not further separated, my feeding tube and diaphragm pacer ports weren't ripped out, and no gashes or broken bones, only sore muscles. Eventually I was lifted and placed into my chair, but by that time, I was having a difficult time breathing. When I finally got into my chair, I tried to catch my breath and take a drink of water, but that only resulted in choking and me having to spit everything out. I caught a glimpse of my friends' eyes, all of them tearful about what they had not only just witnessed, but participated in, and in my sister's eyes and her helplessness from being a spectator to a simple transfer that spiraled out of control.

Honestly, I don't remember the entire bathroom break. What I do know was anybody who was in the ladies' bathroom with us got a real crash course on what ALS really looks like. I asked my friend how long she thought we were the bathroom. I estimated 20 minutes and she estimated 45; either way, when we eventually returned to our table, they told me how proud they were of me and how good with my words I was in coaching. I reminded them that many ALS patients lose their voice and the ability to do that coaching. What they saw was only a glimpse of ALS. My sister was a great cheerleader, reminding me this was just a bump, and we would take our lessons learned and keep on going.

June 5, 2016

Happy anniversary. Well, not really "happy," but today marks the two-year anniversary ALS joined our family. June 5, 2014, I was diagnosed with ALS. Actually, the doctor said I had "motor neuron disease." I think he didn't have the heart to look me in the eye and tell me I had ALS. I knew enough to ask, "Isn't that ALS?" He said, "Yes . . . I'm so sorry. You're so young." Followed by what most patients hear:

There's no treatment or cure.

Life expectancy is two to five years.

Go home and get your affairs in order.

We did just that, but we also sought the opinions of several expert doctors, hoping it was something else. I received treatment for Lyme disease "just in case." We tried various alternative treatments and traveled all over the United States to meet with experts to find a possible treatment that would work for me. Unfortunately, my ALS has continued to progress at the same consistent rate. I'm still praying for a miracle though.

The tremendous acts of kindness and generosity shared with my family have been a blessing most people won't ever receive. As I enter year three, I'll continue educating and advocating for those with ALS, living in the moment and taking it day by day. I plan on going until the wheels fall off, while continuing to prepare a safety net for my family. This next chapter of ALS is going to be scary . . . but I'm definitely not done.

June 8, 2016

People ask what I've done to my hands because I've been sporting a new set of fancy blue boxing gloves. They're not really boxing gloves, they just look like it. *I* didn't do anything to my hands, ALS did. The muscles between my thumb and index finger are so atrophied they separate into almost a "splits" position, which is painful. My hand muscles also spasm, causing my hands to clench into a tight fist position. When the spasm is over, I don't have enough strength in my hand to open my fingers back up, and they're stuck in a closed fist, which is not painful, but uncomfortable. I frequently ask my caregiver to open my hands. These new fancy splints help keep my hands straight and provide a little relief. So if you see me sporting them, you'll know what ALS did to my hands.

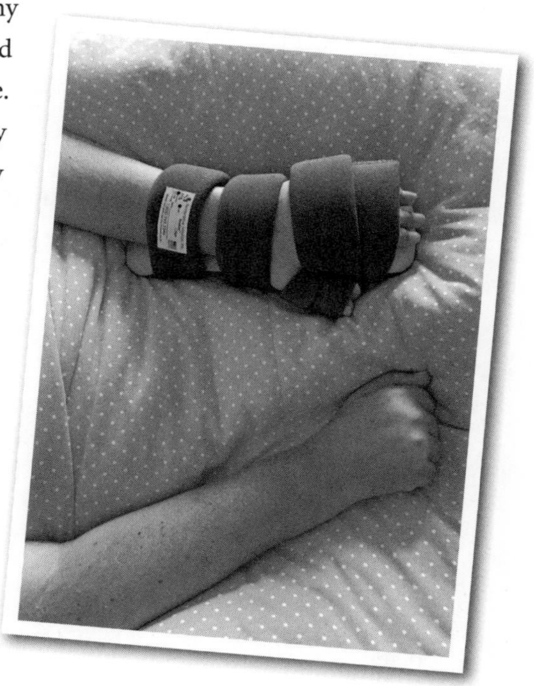

June 9, 2016

She *Had* ALS

In the beginning, when Anne Marie heard someone "had" ALS, she always asked how they got rid of it.

After a year, she learned if someone "has" ALS, they are alive; if they "had" ALS, they died. Death was the only way to get rid of ALS.

Now when she hears someone had ALS, she asks, "How long did they live?"

Last night she met a sweet husband and daughter who lost their wife and mother in March. As expected, Anne Marie asked, "How long did your mom have ALS?" What followed was a question I've never heard her ask before: "Was your mom's progression faster or slower than my mom's?"

People often ask how my children are. They have been in therapy since the beginning to help them process the multitude of changes ALS would force them to experience. Anne Marie doesn't like to ask questions because she is scared to hear the answers, but I know she is quietly calculating. Damn you, ALS!

June 16, 2016

We're leaving today for our annual family Sanibel Island trip. I've vacationed there my entire childhood and adult life—this is my third visit since ALS invaded my body. This annual adventure will likely be my last, not because I think I'm gonna die anytime soon, but because traveling is getting more difficult, especially with my breathing. Plus the growing amount of equipment I need is ridiculous! It was bittersweet reading my Sanibel post from last year.

Honestly, I've had enormous anxiety about traveling this time.

My family and caregiver have gone to great lengths to make sure I have everything I need to be comfortable and safe:

Trilogy breathing machine, backup chargers, and masks

Cough assist machine

Wedge pillow, horseshoe pillow, small pillow, neck pillow—heck, two suitcases full of pillows

Heating pad

Baby monitor

Arm splints

Transfer mat

Gait belt

Portable threshold ramp

Portable bidet
Medication
Astronaut pants
Feeding tube supplies
Power strip
Kinesio tape
Diaphragm pacer and batteries
Power wheelchair and charger
Manual wheelchair neck support
Handicap-accessible van rented
MAC daddy beach wheelchair rented
Elevated toilet seat rented
Manual wheelchair to hoist me up the steps rented
Shower chair rented
My caregiver Suzy hired
Plus my normal beach vacation packing list.

ALS is trying to crash our party, but we're not gonna let it happen! Sanibel 2016, I'm happy to meet you!

June 18, 2016

We made it! We had to do a few modifications to get into our condo, which is up a flight of steps. Carrying my 380-pound wheelchair up the steps was not an option. Thank goodness for strong beach friends and a confident husband. Raising lots of ALS awareness today on Sanibel Island.

June 19, 2016

I knew Eric would be an amazing father long before I married him. I was looking for not just a husband to fall in love with, but also one who had all the characteristics of a great father and role model. Eric is loving, faithful, devoted, energetic, patient (usually), calm, adventurous, resourceful, intelligent, outgoing, loyal, and committed.

Our hope and dream was definitely raising our three children together. But ALS is wedging itself in between our parenting roles, leaving Eric and I at polar opposites—my role being eliminated and Eric carrying the burden of going it alone.

There is great comfort in knowing my children will have an amazing father to continue to take care of them. Eric has demonstrated true tender loving care so I have confidence that my children will be in good hands under his wings.

Happy Father's Day, Eric. We love you. From our little party of five.

June 26, 2016

A huge shout-out to my Robinson family for raising a ruckus and awareness representing Team Dewey in the St. Louis Chapter Walk to Defeat ALS. Thanks for your continued love and support from afar. You guys are awesome!

June 28, 2016

Last year we rented a manual beach wheelchair with big balloon tires for our Sanibel trip. This year my power chair supports my whole body but will not move on sand. Eric surprised me with a better solution, making me the bad ass of the beach. In a chair with treads—just like a tank!

The back of the chair had a big "Rent Me" sign. We decided if I'm going to be a rolling billboard on the beach it's going to be what I would advertise: "Cure ALS."

June 30, 2016

From my chair to the pool was another big transfer. The pool had an accessible pool lift, but I was a dumb ass and didn't want to use it. I insisted on having my family walk me into the pool. It was a pretty dangerous spectacle. We did it once and I was a dumb ass for trying. From that point forward, we used the pool lift, and I was thankful it was there.

I'm on my breathing machine most of the time now, so I was usually attached but took small breaks where I didn't feel leashed.

I definitely lose some of my ALS disability when I'm in the water. We put a noodle under my arms and under my wrists. I have enough leg strength where I can walk in the pool and feel weightless.

I've seen these awkward pool-lift chairs covered at the hotels we stayed at, but I've never seen one in action. It's pretty easy to use and definitely a must to get me into and out of the pool from this point forward.

July 2, 2016

Sand Dollar Ceremony

Sanibel Island is more than a vacation spot to me. It's where we've gathered as a family in the summer and created memories since I was eight years old. This year was different with the loss of my mom and brother and them not being with us. The landscape of our family is changing, and it was certainly felt on this trip. My mother was an avid sheller and my brother enjoyed conversation at the beach and inspecting changes to the property. I knew this would be my last trip, not because I'm projecting when I'm going to die, but because this type of travel has become too difficult. I needed closure for my family and myself. This island, this beach, this ocean, this sunset, these shells, and the breeze will always be a part of my mother, brother, and me. I wanted my family to feel our presence and everything we felt when they came back without me.

Right after we checked out, I asked my whole family to join me on the beach for prayer. Eric tearfully purchased 15 sand dollars—one for every member of my family. Sand dollars have always been a treasured find on Sanibel Island and a symbol to my entire family of our love of this beach. I reminded them I would always be a part of this annual trip, whether in body or in spirit. Everybody said a prayer and quietly "Frisbeed" their sand dollar into the ocean.

There are many legends of the sand dollar, but this year, I adapted them to fit my own symbolism for my husband, children, and myself. The sand dollar has five keyholes. I named each keyhole, with me at the top and Eric and the kids below, lifting me up. Then I showed them something they didn't know. If you shake your sand dollar, you can hear the tiny treasures inside. I broke open a sand dollar and showed them inside—five tiny, dove-shaped shells. I gave them each a dove from my sand dollar to represent our little party of five.

I sweet-talked my brother, sister, and husband into walking me into the ocean one last time. I said my prayer and Eric tossed my shell into the salted water for me.

The sand dollar ceremony was full of tears and hugs. I feel blessed to have been given the time to have closure and create this symbolism with my family. I do feel comfort knowing my family will continue to gather together at this place I have grown to love so much, but it was very difficult to give it my final good-bye.

July 7, 2016

There was only one charity Colleen wanted to contribute to . . . it really was a no-brainer. Inheritance of Hope *continues* to inspire me. Thank you for your continued support!

July 9, 2016

Meet Suzy

Suzy is my angelic caregiver and friend and wears many hats in both roles. My sweet caregiver could feel my anxiety about being away from my help (outside my family) as we prepared for our annual beach trip. The week of our trip, my anxiety level increased. Suzy felt called to join me on our trip to relieve some of the burden from my family. When I mentioned bringing her to my family, everyone was super excited at the possibility. They all know how much help she gives me, plus the kids *love* Ms. Suzy! With minimal details to work out, and her own supportive family behind her decision, the week before we left we booked a last-minute plane ticket, and she joined us on vacation. I immediately felt at ease.

When Suzy arrived on Saturday, I called her "a genie in a bottle at the beach." We kicked off her arrival with a round of piña coladas. It was so comforting to have Suzy with me, and my entire family appreciated her dedication to my well-being. I was definitely expecting to share a week of poolside and beachside tropical drinks with her in our downtime, but my intentions were not reality.

On the first full day of vacation, my brother-in-law was advised to come home because his father's health was failing rapidly. He left Sanibel and arrived in time to be by his father's side with his family. (RIP, Jack Sorg.) Having lost our mother recently, our hearts could understand and mourn for Mickey and my sister and the entire Sorg family. With Mickey gone, I was hesitant to ask my sister for help because she needed to tend to her itty-bitty ones—but that was okay, because Suzy was there.

Early Monday morning, Eric fell ill with sharp abdominal pains. After our home remedies failed, my dad took him to the ER. We were pretty confident he had gallstones, because of his extreme pain, which could make a grown man cry—literally! Without going into too much detail, Eric was down Monday and Tuesday, barely up Wednesday, started to come around Thursday, and felt well on Friday as we were leaving—but that was okay, because Suzy was there.

Instead of Suzy being added help and sharing poolside drinks with us, her role replaced Eric as commander of my care, with the help of my family and beach family. Not just my care, but Eric's care and the care of my children. My heart was divided between mourning for the Sorg family, aching for my husband, and making lasting memories for my family. In short, I had to introduce you to Suzy because she literally saved my vacation.

July 14, 2016

Three-Month Physical Update

I had my quarterly ALS clinic check last week—an appointment I never look forward to. The first thing my sweet Colleen said to me when I woke up was, "I hope you have a good appointment, Mommy." This is the same child that after my last appointment, when we picked her up from the school bus, immediately asked what the doctor said. My sweet children are holding out hope that one day I'll get good news, but again this is not the case. Sometimes I wonder if it's even worth my time to go sit through a four-hour appointment to find out how much worse I've gotten, but I always want to know my progression rate—so I go.

As expected, after we got home, the kids wanted details, especially since this was a really long appointment. Just like last time, we stressed the importance of not cross-contaminating germs and helping me stay free from any infections. The biggest stress of the appointment was not to get sick; with my lung capacity now at 21 percent, it would be really hard for me to recover from an infection. I've lost all ability to cough, so the secretions would settle in my lungs and do me in. We came up with a game plan if I get sick—who to call, what hospital to go to, and other decisions to make at that time.

I shared with my doctor that a few days prior to that appointment, at the end of the night, I was struggling to breathe even with my breathing machine on. I looked fearfully at Eric and thought this was it. I thought I was going to suffocate in my sleep. I can't tell you how happy I was to see the clock say 6:30 a.m. and my breathing back to "normal." My doctor assured me that situation is not likely to happen without warning, but rather he said to watch for me sleeping more, having lower oxygen levels, and being more lethargic as my CO_2 levels rise. Sounds crazy to say, but I found comfort in this.

My disappointment was really no different than after all the other visits. My lung capacity decreased from 31 percent to 21 percent (and not because of lack of effort). I looked at my sister and I could see her eyes well up. That's no surprise considering I wear my mask 23 hours a day now, and I know I couldn't survive without it.

My total body continues to weaken. My right leg can still bear weight so that's the good news. Not done yet at all! Eric and I are planning to renew our wedding vows; we're planning a birthday slumber party; and we're in the middle of a 10-year-old's surprise bedroom remodel. I've got lots more to do and am busy doing it.

July 16, 2016

What's Going on with Carrey's Breathing?

Submitted by Eric Dewey

(I tried to get him to dumb it down; bear with him.)

The diaphragm is a big sheet of muscle under your lungs; it moves down when you breathe air in and up when you breathe carbon dioxide out. The lungs absorb oxygen from the air. The two, moving and absorbing, work together to provide oxygen to the blood. In ALS, the diaphragm weakens as the nerves that allow the muscle to move are dying. The muscles fail to pull air in and push CO2 out. Now Carrey is leashed all the time to a noninvasive ventilator called a Trilogy. The Trilogy is helping her pull air in and push CO2 out. This machine does not provide oxygen. Oxygen may need to be added at some point if enough air is not moving in and out for her lungs to absorb adequate oxygen. But at this time, her oxygen levels are at 99 percent. Good job, Carrey Dewey. Bad news, the amount of air her diaphragm can pull in and out without ventilation, in her case the Trilogy, is 21 percent of a healthy person of Carrey's height.

July 18, 2016

My sweet Anne Marie turned double digits today. It's a strange feeling to want my children to age quickly. I wanted to make sure that she would remember this milestone birthday. Anne Marie was so excited when she woke up to 10 balloons, each dangling a five-dollar bill. I hope she remembers this as much as I did when my mom did it for me.

Anne Marie is a natural caregiver. I proudly watched her tend to my mother in the years following her stroke and never imagined she soon would become one of my primary caregivers. She is a different child since my ALS diagnosis. She has enormous compassion toward me and others. She doesn't want to disappoint me, and she has learned to say she is sorry. She always asks what she can do to help and never disappears during the many tasks it takes to get me prepared for bed. She is often the first responder in the middle of the night when I need help. Additionally, she is 10 going on 17, so apparently I still have a lot of parenting to do.

Happy birthday, sweet Mimi!

July 21, 2016

The most important thing to survive my ALS is to manage my breathing. I was very blessed to be connected with a kick-ass respiratory therapist named Bethany. She goes above and beyond with managing my four pieces of respiratory equipment. I know how to reach her at any time and this is an enormous comfort considering my life depends on this equipment.

July 24, 2016

Last night was *amazing*! My sister nominated us to be Michael Franti and Spearhead guests through his Do It for the Love Foundation. Franti generously gave us tickets, offered anything to add comfort during the show, took the time to meet and chat with us, and even FaceTimed his amazing wife, Sara, or Mrs. Franti to my kids, so we could meet her as well.

My kids were total soul rockers last night! Jumping, dancing, waving their hands in the air, and singing along. Even though my body is paralyzed, I didn't feel left out because I could feel their excitement and energy.

My favorite part of the night was when he shared with the crowd how his foundation started. Then Michael Franti explained what ALS is, bringing education to the whole audience—which was totally awesome, considering raising awareness is so important to our family. He pointed out our family, which my kids thought was the best thing ever. He proceeded to share with the crowd that Colleen had asked him to play, "Life is Better with You," and my family serenaded me for a second time.

Best night ever!

July 30, 2016

After my quarterly visit a few weeks ago, I had a swallow evaluation done. With ALS patients, the tongue and swallow muscles can become weakened and eventually paralyzed. Eating and talking are yet another basic function stolen by ALS. My speech is still very clear, but softer. My swallow, while still very good, is changing and causing limitations. My tongue has been twitching for about nine months, and the evaluation was ordered so we could see exactly what oral motor and swallow muscles are weakened.

The study was done using several consistencies of food coated with barium, a disgusting, chalky, radioactive dye, which allowed us to watch the swallow muscles react to the food while going down. Let's just say, it was a *really* bad day to have skipped breakfast. Gag!

The results of my swallow study showed my esophagus has weakened and has a hard time pushing down dry foods and those of mixed consistencies. I need to avoid foods such as breads, french fries, and mixed consistencies like cereal with milk. This is not new information as I have already eliminated all of those from my diet because I learned the hard way. The study also showed food still in the front of my throat after I swallowed. It takes me about four swallows and water to get all food down, making it tiring to eat. The good news is I can feel when the food is still there, so I know when and how to clear my throat. When I can no longer feel the remnants of the food, remnants could overflow into my airway, causing aspiration, which would likely lead to pneumonia. I can only take in liquids through a straw since my oral cavity and tongue muscles cannot control a free flow from an open cup or bottle. I always travel with a box of straws. Additionally, my liquids must be ice cold to help stimulate the muscles needed to produce an effective swallow. A nonproductive swallow will result in aspiration, also known as food and/or liquid going into my lungs through my airway. Several ALS patients lose the battle through pneumonia or aspiration, so it is critical we stay ahead of the loss of my swallowing ability. I have another evaluation scheduled in eight weeks to monitor my progression. I will be sure to eat breakfast beforehand since I now know what they will be serving.

I am by no means complaining as many of my ALS friends are solely on a feeding tube—something that could happen to me. So for now, I'll follow doctor's restrictions and appreciate every bit of my favorite foods and flavors, four swallows and one sip at a time.

July 31, 2016

Don't feel bad if you wave to me and forget I can't wave back; don't feel bad if you hand me something and forget I can't grasp; don't feel bad if you offer me a handshake and you forget I can't reciprocate; and don't feel bad if you bring me my favorite hot tea and forget I can't drink hot liquids . . . sometimes even I forget.

Like tonight when I suggested to Eric we rent a limo for our vow renewal as I know our kids would love it. Eric was a fun spoiler when he asked me how I was going to get in. Crap! See, sometimes even I forget.

August 4, 2016

On this day 15 years ago, Eric and I vowed to unite as one. We joined at the altar in a small, white, *Little House on the Prairie*-type chapel. We stood side by side, no bridesmaids or groomsmen, no fancy flowers, no fancy musicians. My dad did all the readings, Eric's dad officiated the ceremony, and we filled the little chapel with our family and closest friends. Having Eric by my side made it a real dream wedding. As we stood at the altar and shared our vows, it would take almost 15 years to fully understand the commitment he made to me.

"I will love you forever and under all circumstances.

I will stand by your side always.

I will have faith in you and encourage you in everything you do.

I will be here to listen to you, to laugh with you, and to hold you.

I will strive every day to make our relationship stronger.

I will love you, honor you, respect you, encourage you, and cherish you, in health and in sickness, through sorrow and success, for all the days in my life."

What that meant was:

I will enjoy all of our friends and family with you, socializing, meeting new people, tailgating, and going to our favorite restaurant with you.

I will join you as your doubles partner in tennis and snow ski down the mountain with you.

I will support you leaving the work force to raise our children as you support me as my career develops.

I will be the behind-the-scenes guy for all of your party-planning adventures.

I will support you with all your volunteer work.

I will give you free rein to decorate our home just the way you want it.

I will travel around the United States for all of your doctors' appointments.

I will remodel our home to make it accessible for you.

I will bathe you, wash your hair, and shave your legs.

I will scratch your head and eyebrows every time they itch.

I will research and investigate our next biggest problem so we will be prepared.

I will learn how to blow-dry and flat iron your hair.

I will gently wash your face every night with the hottest steam towel my hands can stand.

I will clean out your ears and nostrils daily. (I'm pretty sure I have the cleanest ears and nostrils in the world.)

I will brush your teeth, put on your make-up, and wipe your heinie.

I will change your soiled astronaut pants.

I will dress you.

I will hold your lifeless hand.

I will feed you.

I will wake up three to four times a night to help adjust your position, breathing mask, and any other ridiculous need you come up with.

I will be on board for any trips or memories you want to make regardless how much effort it takes to pack or travel.

I will wipe your tears and my tears simultaneously when the reality becomes too much to handle.

I will listen to you nag—I mean teach—how to parent "the right way" when your voice doesn't work.

I will be by your side for every video you make of our children.

I will fill our home with all the durable medical equipment necessary to make your life more comfortable.

I will take over running the household to your standards, a job you treasured.

I will make sure you have 24-hour care, so you are never left alone.

I will follow through with your final wishes (piano lessons and Catholic high school education, hint, hint).

I will investigate and cover all logistical needs before we leave our house to make sure everything is accessible and safe.

I will become your own personal pharmacist, managing all of your prescriptions.

I will put your weak body to bed every night—meticulously relieving all the pressure points with a multitude of pillows—and cover you with your favorite blanket.

I will clean your electrical wires and plastic feeding tube implanted in your stomach.

I will support your advocacy efforts by helping you post your blog and allowing you to share even the most intimate details.

I will lift you, hold you, and help you walk due to your failing body.

I will love you in a way you never knew existed.

As we stand, or in my case sit, at the altar tonight, I look forward to renewing these vows with a new comprehension of our love and commitment to each other and our family.

August 5, 2016

I Still Do

Last night was everything I hoped it would be for our vow renewal. Returning to the small chapel with our parents, siblings, and our little party of five, along with the same minister, who just so happens to be Eric's dad, was perfect. The girls had another opportunity to wear my wedding gown/turned First Communion dresses and gifted us by singing a special song. Ian read the same reading my dad read 15 years ago. We repeated the same vows but with a deeper understanding of what those words really meant. And Eric's dad delivered another amazing homily. I was proud to stand—or sit—next to Eric with our children by our side and be a model of marriage for what I want for them. The same model that Eric's parents, married 59 years and counting, and my parents, married 48 years, have been for us.

I had the opportunity to share special gifts with my little family and sister and pass on traditions and symbolisms, just in case . . . you know. I got to share with them the significance of the cake knife, the ring-bearer pillow, the rope with the knot, the pocket squares, and the pearls.

As our little family crossed the threshold as Eric and I did 15 years ago, our family was everything I have dreamt it to be . . . minus ALS, of course.

August 13, 2016

Well, crap! I fell and hurt my shoulder. We know it's not broken, but I've torn or stretched something to where it's ridiculously painful. *And*, I'm on day eight of nursing an ugly blister on my nose from my breathing machine mask. I can't get anybody to pick the scab off either. I thought my sister would when I asked her to pick my nose and she said yes, only to find out she was willing to pick my boogers but not my scab. I really should be exempt from all of this!

August 15, 2016

My doctor ordered supplemental nutrition via my feeding tube to help maintain my weight. It's not because my swallow is jeopardized. I can still swallow safely with caution, so I'm still able to eat. His concern is that I've lost over 10 percent of my body weight in the last 12 weeks, which is a big no-no when it comes to ALS. *Seriously*, I've tried my entire adult life to achieve and maintain a healthy weight with little success, and then I'm diagnosed with ALS, a disease that is going to kill me, and I lose weight they don't want me to lose.

Anyway, I had my first liquid meal/supplemental nutrients/feeding tube formula—whatever it is they call it. The supplies and setup were delivered last week, and the nurse administered my first one.

I can't say I'm really on board with starting this yet. One thing I know how to do exceptionally well is gain weight. I'm going to try my supplemental nutrition of Graeter's milkshakes as long as my swallow is still safe before I'm all in with doctor's orders. I'll keep you posted.

August 16, 2016

If You Knew What I Knew

Ian starts his first day of middle school today. After my diagnosis, we had a change of plans about our educational priorities. Prior to diagnosis, high academics were the only criteria we had in selecting a school for him. After diagnosis, academics seemed a lot less important. We were very fortunate to have him at Stopher Elementary School, an amazing community-based public school. Stopher and the entire school community knew our family before ALS and really wrapped their arms around our family after we shared our devastating diagnosis. It was exactly where Ian needed to be. The problem is, Stopher ends in fifth grade and we had to find a new school for him to transition to sixth grade. Knowing what we knew was likely to happen to me and our entire family, where did we want Ian planted? Unfortunately, community schools are rare in our public school district, so we had to do some soul searching and prioritizing for where Ian would go next.

Having our children in a public school, I knew it was my obligation to keep them involved in church, be active members of their school community, engage them in service work, and be contributing members in the community. This was my job and I felt devastated I could not continue as planned.

After much discussion and prayer, my heartache was lifted when we chose Saint Patrick's Catholic School for Ian. It feels so strange to not be involved in his new community yet. I feel like I'm handing him over to a community I don't know, but I'm confident St. Pat's will serve his needs spiritually, emotionally, and academically. I literally cried when we made the decision because the burden felt lifted.

Other than the extreme haircut he needed to meet dress code, Ian is anxious but excited about his new school.

August 20, 2016

We lost power a few weeks ago; a transformer across the street failed. My programmed reaction has always been to flick the light switch, check the dinner in the oven, or open the refrigerator and garage door—but that was before ALS. This time, the lights and fridge were not on my mind. I panicked at how much battery my Trilogy ventilator had, how many lifts up the stairs the chair battery had, and what position did I leave my adjustable bed in? Eric sensed my anxiety and talked to the electric company servicing the transformer. He explained I was on a noninvasive ventilator, and an extended power outage would be life-threatening to me. I continued to fear the worst. Not only my ventilator, chair lift, and bed run on electricity, but also my cough assist, adjustable chair, Hoyer Lift, and power wheelchair all run on rechargeable batteries. My anxiety only increased thinking about an extended power outage.

The electric company gave Eric a reasonable six-hour window, instead of a five-day power outage I feared. Eric knew I was still anxious at the potential loss of all of my equipment, and honestly I think he was, too. The power came on about four hours later and gave Eric and I a good what-if conversation and planning we had never considered before.

I later shared my concerns with my respiratory therapist. She said the protocol is when a patient is on life-saving devices, such as a ventilator, they send a letter notifying the local electric company, fire department, and EMS, requesting that the patient be served first in the event of a power outage or natural disaster. I didn't know those letters were on file and honestly, I'm not confident they would be effective if I needed immediate rescuing.

We now have a generator in our garage that hopefully we won't ever need to use, but I won't fear my loss of life over an electrical issue.

August 21, 2016

Call Me If You Need Anything

When I was first diagnosed with ALS, I had an influx of "call me if you need anything" offers. I took these as genuine offers because I extended these words many times to people who have had babies, illnesses, loss of a family member, or other hardships. But when I received these offers, I was so overwhelmed I had not a clue what I needed, and I usually didn't know what gift or support the person could offer. Lots of offers of service and help come shortly after diagnosis, but the need becomes even greater each day as the disease progresses. Over the last 27 months, we have been fortunate to have people put their faith into action, sharing gifts and talents, and lifting burdens to continue to support our family. Whether you are near or far, know the family or not, I created a list of support ideas that people can offer for ALS patients more specific than "call me if you need anything"—and I'm sure many of these apply to other illnesses, as well.

1. Offer to bring a meal or organize a meal schedule.
2. If you have a specialized trade to share (photography, haircuts, electric, home repair), offer your service when needed. Add "feel free to take me up on this offer when you're ready."
3. If you're a near neighbor, send a text the next time you're at Kroger, Sam's, Costco, Target, to see if they have any needs.
4. Hire a housekeeper to help clean the home. (This is a great gift for a group of friends to go in together.)
5. Send a quick hello text and offer to help on a weekly basis.
6. Offer a ride to doctors' appointments. (It gave me something to look forward to rather than dread.) Be willing to take the handicapped van.
7. Offer to take them out for coffee or bring a coffeehouse visit to the home.
8. Send a masseuse to the home for a gift massage.
9. Send a flower delivery. It's nice for a patient to enjoy the flowers while we're living.
10. If you have a book you want the patient to read, don't give them the title, just order it and send it. Better yet, if their arms don't work, buy the audio version.
11. Order take-out and have it delivered or send them a gift card to a nearby restaurant for easy take-out.
12. Let them know you want to be on their on-call list for emergencies and mean it. ALS emergencies happen with no warning.
13. Offer to take your male or female friend out for a manicure or pedicure, considering he or she can't maintain their own nails anymore. If the patient can't go out, provide an in-home simple manicure and/or pedicure.
14. Help the family pack for travel or help pack the kids for camp.
15. If you have airline points to share, help subsidize the cost of travel for medical visits or family trips.
16. Offer to be the point person to help manage care and visitors.
17. If you have a talent to decorate, offer to wrap up any loose ends.
18. Offer to help with yardwork, trimming bushes, raking leaves, pulling weeds, planting flowers, or offer to grow a garden or help maintain an existing garden.
19. Offer to sift through and sort emails, return text messages, and update Facebook.

These daily tasks we take for granted become challenging or impossible when your hands are weak or don't work at all.

20. If you can, contribute to medical expenses, or better yet, set up a fund-raiser. Unfortunately, most ALS patients need a medical fund because of the unrealistic medical expenses that come along with an ALS diagnosis and are not covered by insurance.
21. Gift a fun and cozy blanket.
22. Gift a fun or cute hat or hair accessory. Not being able to wash your own hair means it usually needs to be covered or pulled back.
23. If the patient can still swallow, bring them smoothies from the juice bar or milkshakes. Eating becomes exhausting and eventually dangerous. Losing weight is detrimental.
24. If you are a close friend, offer to help with laundry or dishes.
25. If you have a talent for organizing, offer to come help organize a closet, room, or cabinet. When an ALS patient is no longer able to use their arms, looking at cluttered messes can be overwhelming.
26. Plow the driveway and sidewalk when it snows.
27. Offer to help decorate or take down for Christmas or other change-of-season decor.
28. If you have a connection to help make a memory for the family, help set up that memorable experience (hot air balloon ride, inside connection to Santa Claus, concert tickets, share a vacation home).
29. If the patient is homebound, offer to bring communion to the home.
30. If you have a resource, idea, or product that could help the family, don't just think about it, execute it.
31. If you have a favorite of something you love, send one to your friend (cookies, candy, lip balm, dry shampoo).
32. If the patient's immune system is compromised, send a delivery of hand soap and hand sanitizer.
33. Offer to help with any home remodeling projects that will help the patient transition into their home.
34. Offer to bring a meal outside of dinner, such as a bagels or donuts for breakfast or salads, soup, and sandwiches for lunch.
35. Have a point person to help research clinical trials, grants, or specific medical interventions.
36. If you have an accounting background, financial background, or health care billing background, help manage medical bills. The mailbox stays full of medical bills, and it can become quite overwhelming to keep track of them all.
37. Provide respite care. (This has been a huge help when people offer Eric golfing or my sister and brother-in-law a night out).

38. Gift them with a nice adult bib or apron. When someone else feeds you, there are always spills.
39. Offer legal services to help final documents be completed.
40. If you know of someone who is finished with their medical equipment, please pass it on to another ALS patient. We were gifted with a stairlift chair and a five-foot portable ramp that would otherwise have been out-of-pocket expenses.
41. If you have carpentry experience, offer to build a ramp. This was a beautiful gift.
42. If you are a physical therapist or occupational therapist, offer range-of-motion visits.
43. If you or someone you know has a discount or an inside track to companies that are helpful, please share.

If the family has children:

44. Offer to help with transportation of the kids. Invite the children on a fun outing; include the patient if they're able to go. If you sign up for an extracurricular class or summer camp, share the details and the dates and invite their children to go. That was helpful.
45. If you have a really good gift idea for their children for Christmas or birthdays, share the ideas and offer to help pick it up if they want it.
46. Offer to come in and do a project with the kids, such as cook dinner with them, make a canvas painting or a craft project, or drop off all the toppings for an ice cream sundae bar.
47. Offer to help with birthday party planning or help running a birthday party.
48. Offer to take the kids for a night out so the patient and spouse can have an evening to themselves.
49. Offer to help children with a school project or costume whether you are a parent in the same class or just really good at doing school projects.
50. Offer to help with children's scrapbooks. This is a great task for someone who knows the kids well.

August 24, 2016

Look Mom! No Hands!

My thumb continues to struggle to control my wheelchair. In fact, my thumb, more often than not, has been struggling to move at all. Trying to push the control feels like trying to push 50 pounds of weight with my weak and scrawny thumb . . . just not happening! I knew this would be a loss and I was mentally preparing to take over the controls with my chin, until I found out there was another option, a better option for me. We were able to transition to the foot control because my right foot still has enough strength. Yay, right foot!

My husband and sister, otherwise known as my dream team, were confident enough with my skills to take me out in public today to show off my fancy footwork. It was a bit surreal to be at the pulmonologist office maneuvering around elderly people with oxygen tanks and walkers. I felt like a real badass.

August 28, 2016

Last night I tried to attend our cul-de-sac block party. I felt it was important to go and build community with my street even though Eric and Ian were out of town on a canoe trip. There are several neighbors on my cul-de-sac I hardly know or ever see so I was looking for this opportunity to connect and build community. I didn't make it too long because it was ridiculously hot, and the air felt thick even with my mask on. When I got home, I felt especially weak and was still having a hard time regaining my breathing. My friends Tammy and Nurse Ali were filling in as caregivers, and Suzy was scheduled to come over to "package me up and tuck me in." Suzy lifted me up from my stairlift seat at the top of the steps where I can usually walk the short distance from my staircase to my bed with support, but not this time. I crumbled . . . again.

This is when I say, "Oh shit!" And like intelligent women do, we problem-solved together. Use the Hoyer Lift? Physically try to lift me up? Use a bedsheet? We decided our best, fastest, and smartest option was to grab a handful of men from the block party to be the muscles and move me and lift me on a bedsheet. The muscle gang showed up and bossy Suzy directed traffic. They laid me flat in the bedsheet, slid me to my bedroom, and lifted me like a human taco into my bed. I'm a little sore as expected but not injured, so that's good. So the lesson learned here is—if you can't make it to the block party, make the block party come to you.

August 29, 2016

The Good, the Bad, and the Ugly

I feel pretty comfortable with my honesty, sharing the good and the bad about my journey with ALS thus far. There's not been too much ugly—until this weekend. It's been months since I've had a good all-out cry. I try really hard to live in the moment, which had served me pretty well so far. But this weekend, the moments caught me off guard and I was especially weepy.

I was weepy because I miss my mom and my brother.

I was weepy because I wanted to establish community with my surrounding neighbors, but that was cut short.

I was weepy because my ability to walk a few feet is coming to an end.

I was weepy because my swallowing is becoming increasingly difficult.

I was weepy because I have friends who are disconnected from my ALS journey.

I was weepy because of the thoughts that my amazing husband is going to be a single father of three and have to start over.

I was weepy because I had to have a discussion about my end-of-life directives with Eric and my sister.

I was weepy because of the anxiety ALS causes my children.

I was weepy because my schedule is full of palliative care appointments this week.

I was weepy because I scheduled 36 hours of respite care so Eric could take Ian on an overnight scout canoe trip and that was cut short.

I was weepy because I feel like I've upset a friend.

I was weepy because Ian cut his foot, and I can't help tend to him.

I was weepy because my sister and her husband give so much of themselves to us when I should be the big sister physically helping them take care of their littles.

I was weepy because when I cry, I can't breathe out of my nose and my tears feel like acid burning my eyeballs.

I was weepy because my lung capacity is in the teens and there is no cure or treatment.

So there you go, a glimpse into the ugly—I usually don't go there.

August 30, 2016

Massage Monday

For the past two years, my sweet friend Gina has put her faith into action by providing weekly in-home massages. Sometimes twice a week, depending on what destruction I've done to my body. I am a little hesitant to call them a "massage" because that implies dim lighting, no talking, aromatherapy, and the sound of ocean waves as I melt into a deep, relaxed state. Our massages look more like a three-ring circus! While my friend is moving my weak and paralyzed muscles, she is also managing my phone, giving me sips of water, helping me answer homework questions, and sometimes even breaking up arguments—all while Colleen is scooping her hands into the massage lotions trying to help.

Since Gina started giving me massages two years ago, we've really adapted our technique. At first, I laid on my back, then flipped to my stomach on the table . . . like a normal massage. When I could no longer lay on my stomach after surgery to insert the diaphragm pacemaker and feeding tube, we had to use the table for my front, and she started bringing a massage chair for my back. When I could no longer lay flat, we elevated with a wedge. When I could no longer breath elevated, I had to start wearing my mask during the massage. When I could no longer transfer to the massage chair, we learned to do the best we could while I lay on the table. (Okay, I'll spill the beans. This is how I recently hurt my shoulder.

I fell backward off the massage chair; try not to get a visual.) Gina has learned to adapt the massages and lovingly tailor them to my progression. When we can no longer use the table, we will move to the bed. She knows my body better than anybody else.

ALS has no treatment or cure, but the weekly massages that move all of my muscles and blood are the closest thing I have found to treatment for relief. It's a therapy that is unfortunately not covered by insurance, but in the case of ALS, it should be.

August 31, 2016

Colleen: Mommy, do they have a "key-er" (cure) for ALS yet?

Me: No, unfortunately not yet.

Colleen: But I heard there was a "key-er" across the world in another country.

Me: Colleen, if there was a cure for ALS anywhere in the world, Daddy would take me there.

Colleen: Would I be able to go with you?

Me: Yes.

Colleen: What if it were on another planet? Would you take me with you?

Me: Yes, of course.

Colleen: And we would take a rocket ship there?

Me: Yes.

Colleen: Okay, Mommy.

And she walked away satisfied with my answer.

September 1, 2016

Last week, two mothers from Ian's class reached out to me and offered a meet-and-greet to welcome our family to Ian's new school. They offered to bring breakfast or lunch or drive my van and go out. I told them to please let me play hostess while I still can and accepted their gracious offer to come to our home to greet us. Not only did I accept their thoughtful offer, but I was overjoyed at their extension because I was feeling anxious and disconnected from a school I had just planted Ian in. I still get a lot of "Call me if you need anything" offers and assumptions we have everything under control, but there are still several holes in what I call my safety net.

Yesterday, these two generous mothers showered me with beautiful gifts, specific offers of help, and a promise to be here for our family. They asked how Saint Patrick's could support us. I shared with them my anxiety in not being able to be physically connected with Ian's new community—our new community. I need their help to stay connected, informed, and support Ian. I've known these two sweet ladies less than two hours, and I just wanted to wrap my paralyzed arms around them and tell them how much I loved them. Their gifts and offers were just what I needed, assessing the situation and seeing how they can specifically help our family and fill some holes. After they left, I was weepy because of the love and comfort they provided me through their beautiful demonstration of putting faith into action.

September 2, 2016

Does ALS Hurt?

When I was first diagnosed with ALS, I did a lot of research, which, by the way, I would not advise. The bad news I found was ALS is fatal, no treatment or cure, a two-to-five-year life span after diagnosis, complete paralysis of my body, and likely ending in suffocation or aspiration. The good news is ALS won't hurt—at least according to everything I researched. I'm here to tell you from a patient's perspective, that's complete BS!

Does ALS hurt? My dead motor neurons may not hurt, but the destruction ALS has done to my body hurts.

The deadweight of my arms separating from my shoulders hurt.

The numbness, tingling, and pinprick sensations in my hands hurt, along with the frozen, clenched fists.

My back hurts from trying to support my trunk.

My neck hurts from trying to hold up my head.

The muscle spasms in my legs, feet, and throat hurt.

The blisters from my breathing machine on my nose and inside my nostrils hurt.

Even my tear ducts hurt, producing what some ALS patients call "acid tears."

My elbows hurt from pressure sores.

My tongue even hurts because . . . I don't even know why my tongue hurts.

Oh, and the surgeries and recoveries I've had from feeding tube and diaphragm pacer hurt.

My crumbles and falls hurt.

Honestly, my biggest pain right now is severe constipation. I know that is TMI, but it's an ALS patient's reality. I don't have the muscles to push a bowel movement. Yes, I'm on a stool softener. Yes, I'm hydrated. Yes, I've cut down on my pain meds. Yes, I take fiber. Yes, I've done a suppository and other things that really are TMI.

I'm certainly not trying to evoke sympathy. I just want to call BS. I feel like I've had the crap kicked out of me—not that I've ever had the crap kicked out of me, but if I did I would imagine this is how it would feel. So to answer the question, "Does ALS hurt?"—the answer is *hell yes*!

September 9, 2016

Weaving a Safety Net

When I was diagnosed with ALS 27 months ago, I asked the doctor, "Now what am I supposed to do?" He politely looked at me as though he had heard the question before and said, "Get your paperwork in order and go make memories." I went home and cried in a fetal position for 30 days straight. I had no idea how we were going to make it. I was mourning the loss of my life, Eric's life, and my children's lives as we knew them. I felt all the dreams Eric and I built together crumbled with three letters: ALS.

Somewhere around the 30-day mark, I was able to gather myself physically, mentally, spiritually, and emotionally and gain control of my life—my new life. Now what? The doctor neglected to share what was really most important. I needed to protect my family and weave a safety net in case this ALS thing doesn't work out the way we are faithfully praying, in case the miracle doesn't come, in case ALS forces my family off a cliff.

More importantly than "getting my paperwork in order and making memories," I've used my time to provide my family comfort beyond myself, to investigate resources available for them, to show them a more tender kind of love, to direct them spiritually, to establish long-term emotional support, to create written and video journals, to establish symbolism with them, to share family history and traditions, to teach them faith in action, to show them the importance of celebrations, to continue to model marriage, to teach them to become independent, to educate and advocate for a cure or treatment for ALS with them, to embed lasting memories in their hearts, to finish decorating their bedrooms (trivial, I know, but it is important to me), to build their support network beyond ALS, to alleviate some of the burdens with end-of-life decisions, to give Eric the encouragement to go forth, and to make my final wishes known (continue piano lessons and Catholic high school education . . . I hope they'll thank me for that later).

Many people ask me how I stay positive and strong. The answer is simple—I'm busy weaving a safety net as tight as I possibly can for my family.

September 17, 2016

My sweet Ian turned 12 Thursday! He has asked for a sushi birthday dinner every year since he was six, and we certainly weren't going to break tradition this year.

I remember Ian's ninth birthday clearly. I was getting ready for church and the reality hit me—he was halfway to 18—and I cried. I cried because my baby boy was getting too old too fast. It was halfway over. Little did I know at the time, 10 months later, Eric and I would need to sit our "halfway-to-18 little boy" down and tell him I had ALS, knowing this would change his life forever.

Ian is 12 now and this time I cry not because he is getting older, but because we made it to 12. He kisses me good-bye every day when he leaves and every day when he gets home. He understands. I feel blessed to have gotten my sweet son to 12. I have seen his faith journey get stronger at Saint Patrick's. I have seen him start his middle school years in a place that could not be more perfect. I have seen him follow his passion and join Cardinal Aquatics, a competitive swim team. I have seen him earn the beginning of his Boy Scout ranks. I have seen him become more patient and tolerant of his little sisters. I have seen him become more appreciative. I have seen him show nothing but love and compassion to me. While I may not have the privilege to see this sweet boy turn 18, I am confident many accomplishments are to come. I can see the roots spreading and with comfort I can say, through the sunshine and the inevitable storms that will come, he will continue to grow and blossom into the amazing man I know he will be.

September 18, 2016

Happy birthday to my "little" sister, Elizabeth, Liz, Lizzie, or Sista, as I affectionately call her. She's my little sister by seven years. I'll admit, I wasn't the best big sister to her when we were growing up. (Sorry for traumatizing you by throwing a party when Mom and Dad were out of town and I was supposed to be watching you and for calling you Lizard Breath, but I did pave the path to make you look like a golden child, so I hope you forgive me.) Our friendship has definitely developed in later years.

My sister held my hand through every step of my diagnosis process with Eric and me and hasn't let go. She even took on the heartbreaking task of telling my parents when my ALS diagnosis was finalized. She's gone to every appointment I asked her to and has helped problem-solve along the way. When she said that she wanted to be there for my family, she meant it literally. Elizabeth and her husband sold their home they had been in for a year to move two houses down from our family. Being my neighbor has been such an amazing gift to my entire family. Not only to meet our needs, but we're having a great time together along the way. I get to see her more. I get to see her kids more, and I can always count on her for a gallon of milk. I watched my sister take the medical lead with my mom, ensuring alongside my dad that Mom had a good quality of life. I watched my sister compassionately care for my older brother as he suffered from depression, and now my little sister is caring for me. She holds my hand when I'm weepy. She is my 911 when I fall or get stuck. And she is the first person I go to when I need advice from hostessing to end-of-life decisions.

When my ALS journey ends, hers does not. She and her husband will continue to support Eric and be there for my kids, especially my girls, when I need her. A lot of people have commented that I'm the strongest person they know, but that just means they haven't met my sister. So let me introduce you to the strongest woman *I* know.

Happy birthday, Sista!

September 20, 2016

Taping Tuesday

My sweet physical therapist friend, Angie, comes on Tuesday to tape me back together following my Monday massage. My shoulders are "subluxed," which means the upper arm bone has come out of the socket of the shoulder. The top of the upper arm bone is like a ball sitting in a socket and the ball and socket start to separate—at least that's how Angie explains it. I have at least a one-inch separation and yes, it hurts. The taping lifts my arm back into the socket, providing much-needed relief.

September 25, 2016

So I Fell . . . Again

I know this story is getting old, but it's typical for an ALS patient who still has some slight ability to walk. I only walk assisted from my bed to the stairlift or from my bed to my bathroom, each less than 20 feet. Eric was walking me from the stairlift to our bedroom when my foot experienced a "foot drop." Foot drop is when the muscles in the leg are not getting signals to move so in midstride, my foot does not pick up, causing a fall even Eric could not stop. He says it's because I yelled, "Oh shit! Oh shit!" instead of "I'm falling! I'm falling!" But anyway, foot drop is often one of the first ALS symptoms for people when symptoms start in their lower extremities.

This latest fall means three things:

I got myself a new pair of fancy black PRAFO boots to help flex my muscles, so they're not left in a drop-foot position (not exactly the fancy fall boots I had in mind).

I am no longer walking even a short distance.

My injured shoulder hurts even worse.

We're still all good here. Just like the last 28 months: we're adapting, adjusting, and continuing to move forward.

September 26, 2016

The question I get most is, "How do you write your blogs if your hands are paralyzed?"

In the beginning, I therapeutically tapped at my keyboard, early in the morning, late at night, whenever my brain wouldn't stop.

Then, once my fingers quit working, I transitioned to pushing the microphone button to use voice to text.

Then, when my thumb no longer had the strength to even tap the microphone button, I would sit with one of my assistants and they would push the buttons while I dictated into my phone.

Now, dictation doesn't recognize my muffled voice because I have my breathing mask on all the time, so I voice it and either my assistant or my sister or my friends type. The key is, though, to get an uber texter like my sweet assistant Brittani Dodge—affectionately known as "Brittani Dodgeball"—who can text a gazillion characters in a minute.

September 30, 2016

Anne Marie got to spend her first day of fall break being my personal assistant at the ALS clinic today. Maybe not exactly what she had in mind for fall break, but she has been asking to go with me, so bringing her to this appointment seemed appropriate.

Anne Marie asked great questions, was able to answer medication questions—although she referred to the medications by their shape and color. She was a little bummed when they wouldn't allow her in the video swallow room because of radiation, but my therapist promised to review the results with her. My kids always ask me for updates on the doctors' appointments. Ian even called me on the way to his swim meet to find out what the doctors said and ask if I had to get another shot. Today Anne Marie was able to share the update. As far as breathing goes, my lung capacity showed little decline, so that's a rare, awesome report. And my swallow study showed a weaker swallow but still all going down the esophagus and not entering my airways, so that's good news, too. *And* I was able to maintain my weight—no surprise to me, this is something I've always been good at—so, even more good news!

Today may not have been how Anne Marie envisioned our fall break plans, but still exciting nonetheless!

October 1, 2016

The evidence from an unnamed child unhappy about feeding me lunch . . .

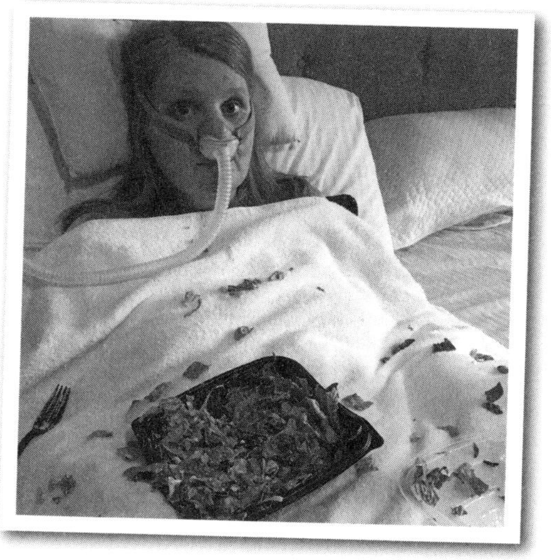

October 6, 2016

My Fancy New Chair

I lost my ability to walk several weeks ago, which meant we had to problem-solve how to get me to and from the bathroom *and* to and from the stairlift. Since my wobbly walk was no longer an option, our solution was to buy yet *another* chair.

So that means I have:

1. a shower chair
2. a manual wheelchair
3. a scooter chair
4. a standing recliner chair
5. a stairlift chair
6. a power wheelchair

And to add to my chair collection:

7. an elevated tilting/potty transfer chair . . . only fancy in my ALS world

My newest chair actually solves several problems. It will transfer me to the stairlift. It will roll over the toilet (there's an insert we can remove for my tushy for potty time). And it reclines so we can wash my hair easily.

Not exactly the type of chair collection I was hoping to accumulate, but I'm fortunate to have "fancy chairs" to make my life easier.

October 9, 2016

Daddy-Daughter Date Night

A few weeks ago, my dad asked me if I knew anyone who would want to go to the Dixie Chicks concert with him. Usually my sister is his sidekick for country music concerts, but she was out of town. Feeling well rested and a bit confident, I thought about it for a few minutes and suggested he take me! He looked surprised and excited all at once. Taking me out means being responsible for my paralyzed body, my 400-pound wheelchair, my breathing machine for life support, my handicap van, and maneuvering me around 15,000 other Dixie Chicks fans. I asked him if he was sure he was up for it, and he said yes! So I put my trust in my dad's hands and made it a date.

My love of country music definitely stems from my dad. I'm proud to say I was born in Nashville, Country Music USA. Country music is stamped on my birth certificate, if not in my blood. My love of the fiddle, steel guitar, banjo, and mandolin have all come from the exposure my dad shared with us.

The concert was awesome, and I only got caught up during one song. My mind took me back to when my life was "perfect"—pre-ALS, of course. Unable to wipe my own tears, I asked my dad if he had a tissue. He untucked his shirt and used the tail as a tissue for me, adding to my teariness, of course.

The only major issue was my daddy-o not being able to hear me. My voice is substantially softened and muffled, and I definitely felt muted during the entire concert.

It was a great daddy-daughter date, and we both agreed that we'll do it again, minus the 15,000 other people.

October 15, 2016

Public Service Announcement and Myth Buster

True: ALS is an automatic qualifying disease for disability.

True: There is typically a six-month waiting period to receive benefits, but with ALS, the wait period has been waived and benefits begin immediately if you are *eligible* for disability.

True: You must earn 20 credits/quarters in the last 10 years to be *eligible* for disability.

True: I have stayed home with my children, led many service projects, spent most of my free time volunteering, but earned zero work credits in the last 10 years.

True: I am not *eligible* for disability.

If you have not worked for the last 10 years, no matter how debilitating your disease is, like ALS; if you don't have the credits, it doesn't matter how many countless volunteer hours you have spent, how many service projects you've led, or your intentions to go back to work. Your disability will be denied—even if you have ALS.

I have zero credits because I have "worked" zero hours for the past 10 years, and I am ineligible for disability even though I have an "automatic qualifying disease."

Just a little PSA for you stay-at-home moms and dads.

October 19, 2016

Hot damn dog! My handicap parking pass expired. No seriously, this is *very* exciting! I remember walking into the DMV a few months after diagnosis to turn in my form for handicap parking. I walked in looking completely healthy and when she read the diagnosis listed, she gave me her genuine condolence and handed me a parking pass that would expire in two years. Having just been diagnosed with faster-than-average ALS, I left the office feeling teary at the possibility I may expire before my parking tag.

So there you have it: three cheers for an expired handicap parking tag!

October 22, 2016

My Newest Problem

I know this story is getting old, but with continued ALS progression comes continued problems and learning how to solve them.

Shortly after losing my ability to walk, I lost the ability to support my neck, and it's very uncomfortable. I finally admitted that we had a problem when I continued to get whiplash in the van. (Eric would like the disclaimer that it was not his driving, but I'm not going to give it to him.) Our short-term solution has been for Eric to physically brace my neck when taking a turn or restrain my forehead when coming to a stop. One hand on the wheel, one hand on my neck qualifies for a little bit more than distracted driving. So now, I have a very fancy head "seat belt" to go along with all my other stylish equipment for my chair. A buckle for my head, one for my body, and four for my chair, and we are ready to roll. I should now be whiplash free.

October 27, 2016

I try really hard not to focus on abilities I've lost in the last 28 months. Honestly, if I focused on everything I've lost, I would be bat-shit crazy. It has served me well to appreciate what I still have and not what I've lost. There is one simple task I did every day without appreciation and sometimes considered it even a chore, if not a fight.

I really miss styling my girls' hair. Brushing their hair, pulling their hair into braids, clipping in bows to perfectly match their outfits, scrubbing their scalps, playing around with new styles. I was never a master of braiding, but I was learning new techniques, and now with Pinterest, I'm sure I would have mastered the Princess Leia braids. But anyway, I miss helping them with their hair. I miss tenderly running my fingers through their hair. I miss what I never appreciated.

Colleen often goes to school looking like a ragamuffin. It's just not a battle Suzy wants to fight. Honestly, I understand. Pre-ALS, I had to pin her down to brush her hair. A few years ago, Colleen's kindergarten teacher even offered to brush her hair when she got to school for me since she knew I couldn't do it and the ragamuffin look wasn't what we were going for. Boy, did I appreciate that offer! Anne Marie, on the other hand, is 10 and old enough to take care of her own hair. She's actually very good at braiding and spends a lot of her free time letting me be her human mannequin as she practices various designs she discovers on YouTube. She's even talented enough to braid while maneuvering my mask, which takes real skill. Anne Marie does tell me she misses me being able to fix her hair; I'm not hearing that from Colleen though.

October 29, 2016

We appreciate Ian's new school, Saint Patrick Catholic School in Louisville, Kentucky, for raising awareness and advocating for a cure or treatment for ALS with our family. Ian has been and continues to be, a huge advocate for research on this disease that has no treatment, no cure, and is 100 percent fatal. Raising awareness inspires him, and he says the more people that know about ALS, the faster the cure will come. I know the rally of support from his new school family will energize him even more. I'm resting today for my one and only day to be a football mom.

November 4, 2016

I have a confession.

I have a confession so deep I needed to attend reconciliation at church. I needed to spill my heart and ask my mom for forgiveness, and I needed to forgive myself. I even brought it up to my dad recently, and he looked at me with sad eyes and said he was hopeful I didn't remember what I had done.

My mom was a mega homemaker and put Martha Stewart to shame. Hot breakfast, nightly family dinners, transportation, laundry. She always looked beautiful; she always looked together; we always had nice pressed clothing. She hosted amazing birthday parties and homemade cookies were always a staple. She never took shortcuts. I'm still not sure how she did everything she did with four children. I was never able to pull it off with three children pre-ALS.

When I was in sixth grade, Ian's age, my mom was diagnosed with cancer. Her survival rate was 50 percent—which was very scary for my whole family. My confession is: I was angry at my mom for being sick. I was angry because my mom was not able to do all the things she had done for us. That weekly casseroles from neighbors had replaced her home cooking. That hot breakfast was now cold cereal. That I lost my personal chauffeur and had to get rides from other people. That I had to do laundry. She was always in bed; her room smelled like burnt flesh from her radiation treatment; her hair was falling out. I was mad at her because she couldn't take care of me the way I felt I deserved, and I let her know. Boy, is that hard to share publicly.

You know how parents say our children are payback for behavior when we were younger? I feared that one of my children would react in a coldhearted, lack-of-empathy manner toward me. Honestly, I felt I deserved that from my children because that's how I treated my mom. I would be devastated if one of my children treated me the way I treated her. The pain I endure knowing how my health will bring a lifetime of sadness with a loss of my physical presence. My children have ALS just as much as I do, and they have *almost* always shown me a type of love and compassion I didn't know was possible from a young child. They're not embarrassed by what I usually call my rolling freak show. They advocate with me. They take care of my basic survival needs such as feeding me, helping me brush my teeth, helping me with bathroom needs, helping with my transfers, my breathing machine, getting me in the car, wiping my tears, and massaging my numb limbs. Whatever it takes, my three are, without resentment, all in.

November 9, 2016

How Are Our Children?

[Giant lump in my throat and tears in my eyes . . . wait a minute while I try to regroup]

I cannot mentally put myself in my little ones' hearts; my mind will not take me there. I cannot imagine their heartache watching ALS progress in front of their eyes—watching my body slowly fail and caring for my growing needs.

I can share that my kids have been working with an amazing therapist for over two years. Sometimes they discuss normal kid problems and sometimes extraordinary kid problems—like living with ALS.

Several months ago, we added in family therapy with an art therapist who works with palliative care families. These sessions have allowed us to share openly as a family and discuss what none of us want to talk about. I am at the point in my progression where I can go downhill quickly, very quickly. I'm trying to take away their fear but keep their faith.

The family therapy has been very helpful, and we have made some special artistic keepsakes. My children are used to me being involved in all aspects of their lives. They are used to me being a lunch-time volunteer in their preschool. They are used to me being their classroom parent. They are used to me being active in their school. They are used to me being a regular in the PTA office and giving me proud smiles and waves as their class would walk by. They are used to me knowing all of their classmates and knowing most of the parents. They are used to me being involved in service projects that they can participate in with me. They are used to me physically being there and being connected to their friends and parents. They are used to me being active in our church community. They are used to me being their Girl Scout leader. ALS has painfully stripped these things away not only from me but from each of them.

Each one of my children are struggling in different ways. Ian tries to stay really busy with Scouts and swimming and school and would bury himself in a video game if we allowed it. Anne Marie feels a complete loss of control and expresses that in ways we're parenting. Colleen struggles with so many people in and out of the house helping me and often resents my caregivers because she feels she could take care of me herself—which she probably could until she needed to lift me up.

My kids are good; my kids are compassionate; my kids are doing well academically, but they are all three struggling in their own ways.

We feel incredibly blessed to have them planted where they are with families that either know us well or new families we share a faith with. I am still here fulfilling my life dream of mothering my children, it just happens to be from the comfort of my own bed.

November 14, 2016

Thank you, Two Chicks and Company for hosting Team Dewey for your Shop for a Cause. Boy, do my friends know how to shop! Two Chicks and Company has generously offered to keep the benefit open until Friday. So, if you're a late shopper, just mention Team Dewey and 20 percent of the sales will go to us; however, we are excited to share we will be paying it forward by passing the proceeds on to two very worthy causes. We'll share more when we know the total.

November 17, 2016

Am I Receiving Hospice Services?

My health care is covered under my husband's private insurance, we do not have secondary insurance, and I am not eligible for Medicare. Hospice gets a little tricky for ALS patients under the current company providing hospice services in our area.

Both palliative care and hospice care provide comfort. But palliative care can begin at diagnosis and at the same time as treatment for symptom management such as pain. A physician must document that, with normal progression of the terminal disease, the patient has six months or less to live. Hospice care begins after treatment of the disease is stopped.

We definitely need all the resources and support to provide comfort, expertise, and relief. We did not consider hospice services when I was receiving alternative treatments. These alternative treatments were private pay and did not slow down my ALS progression. I was also receiving physical therapy and occupational therapy, but I was discharged from both because I was not showing improvements. *Hello*, ALS patients don't improve. If I accepted hospice care, we would also need to discontinue participating in the ALS clinic, which would really be no loss. I could still see the neurologist and respiratory therapist; those are the specialists I attend the clinic to see anyway. Once we came to this point in our journey, we thought we were ready for hospice care.

We met with Hosparus, the local company providing hospice care in our area. I obviously met all the criteria to enter into the hospice program except for one—I would need to relinquish my Trilogy breathing machine. I would need to downgrade to a BiPAP, which is the breathing machine I started with early in my diagnosis. Hospice does not cover life-saving measures and currently my Trilogy breathing machine is a noninvasive ventilator saving my life.

We considered entering hospice care and keeping the Trilogy via private pay, but the rental rate is $1,500 a month per unit and I have two of them!

Hosparus was piloting another program for palliative care patients. It's similar to hospice care but works as a private pay à la carte program. This new program allows me to keep my insurance coverage and pay for the hospice services we need at this point. This is definitely the best option until I am ready to downgrade my breathing equipment.

November 21, 2016

A Reason, a Season, a Lifetime

Shortly after my diagnosis, a woman named Deb with ALS reached out to me to offer support and advice. Her very first words were to be prepared to lose friends. I thought this was a bit odd to receive this advice at the top of the list. She warned me that Eric and I would lose friends I would never expect to lose. I remember thinking poor Deb, she doesn't have the kind of friends that Eric and I have.

Eric and I have actually gained hundreds of friends since diagnosis. People who have chosen to go into the fire with us, knowing full well the outcome of this story. We are inspired by the outreach, by complete strangers putting their faith into action, and by the support we've received from many parts of our lives. But unfortunately, Deb was right. Eric and I have lost friends we never expected to lose. The percentage of friends we have lost has been very small. But there are still a few who have chosen to disconnect.

My friend and caregiver Suzy, who often hears me complaining about the same friends who have stepped out, shared a good life lesson with me. She explained that not every friendship is meant to last forever and that's okay. That's because God brings people into our lives for a reason, a season, or a lifetime.

We often hear "you find out who your true friends are when you fall on hard times"—or in my case, when ALS invades your family. This is true for me as well. We've also learned that while some friends have moved into the shadows, new friends have come into our lives after my ALS diagnosis. I never anticipated how much these new friends would bring to my family and how seamlessly they fit with our strong established friendships. I understand now that God has the people in our lives right where they should be.

We are ridiculously blessed with the amazing support that has circled our family.

November 26, 2016

Thanks and Thanksgiving

One of my many blessings is the gratitude that has filled my mind, heart, and spirit.

It's been hard, really hard, this past year. I lost my mother. I lost my brother. I lost my ability to walk, stand, pivot, hold my body up, breathe on my own—basically, I lost all physical abilities from the neck down. But as my dad continues to say, "Be thankful for what you have and not resentful for what you don't have."

Gratitude to my husband and kids who take such good care of me and allow me to still be the mother I want to be.

Gratitude toward my sister and her family for being here for us. And when I say "here," I mean physically picking up and moving two houses from us, making a long-term commitment to Eric and the kids.

Gratitude toward my dad and sister who have modeled the epitome of extreme caregiving.

Gratitude toward my friends who provide respite care known as "Carrey Care" for my family.

Gratitude toward my caregiver and friend, Suzy, whose job description is never ending and almost comical.

Gratitude toward my assistants, Brittani and Karlee, who patiently let me boss them around and who continue to be my "hands," carrying out detailed tasks.

Gratitude toward my community led by Mike and Dawn Ansert, rallying an amazing fund-raiser and establishing my medical fund to provide financial relief and added comfort.

Gratitude toward our Stopher Elementary School and community to whom I entrust my girls to every day.

Gratitude toward our community of Epiphany who established Team Dewey and assured our family that a village of support would be there for us.

Gratitude toward Saint Patrick's community, which has embraced our family without knowing us.

Gratitude toward my faithful prayer warriors who pray for our family's specific needs.

Gratitude toward Team Dewey for their loud cheering section and generous acts of kindness.

Gratitude toward our friends, both old and new, that are the fibers in my safety net, which brings me confidence for my family long after ALS has run its course.

How can I not feel anything but overwhelming gratitude?

We are thankful for what we do have. Happy Thanksgiving from our little party of five to yours.

November 28, 2016

A year ago today, I was excited to host a surprise birthday party for Eric. I had so much fun. I had an incredible time planning and celebrating. This year is quieter, but I'm very grateful to be here with him and celebrate with the type of husband I didn't know could exist. Happy birthday, Eric. I love you now more than ever!

November 29, 2016

We missed Black Friday, Small Business Saturday, Cyber Monday, but we're all in for *Giving Tuesday*. Can I suggest three very worthy nonprofit organizations if you would like to participate in what this season is all about?

Inheritance of Hope provides Legacy Retreats that give parents who are terminally ill resources, tools, support, and memory-making to move forward during what could be dark times. They have been a true blessing since our IOH Legacy Retreat with them in January.

ALS TDI is the world's only nonprofit research lab focused solely on finding a treatment or cure for ALS. I feel confident the cure will come out of this lab. If you want to fund the cure, this is where to donate.

Team Gleason is an organization that directly supports people with ALS with advocacy, donations of speech-generating devices, and providing family memory-making trips. (A list of additional resources is provided in the back of the book.)

December 1, 2016

My dad's side of the family, the Robinsons, get together the Saturday after Thanksgiving. Everybody lives in St. Louis, but my dad moved away after college and eventually settled in Louisville, Kentucky, so we are the out-of-towners. I have wonderful childhood memories of traveling to St. Louis to stay at my grandma's house and visit my extended family for Thanksgiving. The Robinson family has been very supportive; in fact, many of them came to Louisville twice in the past 12 months for my mother's and brother's funerals. Since my diagnosis, my extended family has shown their love and support in many ways. Many of them either participated in or were represented at the comedy night auction; they formed a Team Dewey in the St. Louis Walk to Defeat ALS; and several of them have contributed to my medical fund. But, the ultimate display of support came this past Saturday when I couldn't travel to St. Louis for a family gathering and *24* of them came from St. Louis to Louisville to celebrate Thanksgiving with us.

Thank you, Robinson family, for your continued love and support. Always.

December 2, 2016

Forty-five and Still Alive

Yep, that's right; today I'm 45.

Eric and I are waiting in the car until they are ready for me to enter my surprise/not surprise party. I mean, I know about the party, but I don't know *any* of the details. I'm super excited to celebrate this very special birthday with friends old and new who have chosen to be part of the safety net!

December 3, 2016

Forty-five Plus One Day—Eric's Post for Carrey

Carrey really wanted to do a Facebook post today from her surprise/not surprise birthday party and about her birthday, but today was filled with activities she'd been planning to do for a while, and she is exhausted. So, I'm stepping up to help her out with this one, a surprise post. We had back-to-back events today, a cheer competition and swim meet.

Watching the kids do things they enjoy really brings a smile to her face. The kids were both thrilled that Mom was there to watch and cheer them on. They know the energy it takes to get out on a normal day, much less a day after a late-night party that included them as well.

After those events, we got home and Carrey got comfortable in the big brown chair, where she will be for the night. Papa Joe stopped by for a visit and some time to reflect and remember Ellen, Carrey's mom, marking the one-year anniversary of her death.

ALS sucks the energy out of you. Usually after a night like last night, Carrey would stay in bed the next few days to recover, but schedules don't always permit that full recovery time. She put on her rally hat and made it to see our kiddos in action.

December 5, 2016

A great big *thank you* to Cardinal Aquatics families, coach Amy Albiero, and all competitors at the Cardinal Christmas Classic swim meet for contributing to Inheritance of Hope. Your extremely generous contributions totaling more than $8,200 have allowed eight children, whose parents are terminally ill, the tools to leave a legacy and to make memories to last a lifetime. Thank you for embracing IOH and making them your charity of choice this year on our behalf. Your financial gift has just given two families the tools to guide them through what feels like dark days and to allow them a beautiful array of memories to last a lifetime. Thank you!

December 6, 2016

Huge *thank you* to Two Chicks and Company for supporting Team Dewey during their holiday shopping. On the Tuesday after Thanksgiving, newly named Giving Tuesday, we chose to pay the majority of the proceeds forward by contributing to Inheritance of Hope and to a local ALS family who lives eight miles from my house and does not have the overwhelming support we have.

The remainder is being used to move my chairlift from the back staircase to the front staircase. This will allow for safe transfers, as my ability to move my feet, even a short distance, has been lost.

Thank you, Team Dewey shoppers, and thank you, Two Chicks, for your generosity.

December 7, 2016

Everyone knows I love a good party, planning all the details to make it perfect.

Last Friday, I had the tables turned and was surprised with an amazing birthday celebration, led by my dear friend, Lisa Wilson.

My friends have tried to convince me to have at least a half-birthday since March, but I said, "No, I'm going to make it to December."

Even when the discussion rolled around in November, I wasn't sure I wanted to have a party because I'm always tired, things were a little chaotic in my family at the time, and I was a little uncomfortable being the center of attention. She told me to just give her a "Yes" and not ask any other questions. And that's how it became a surprise/not surprise party.

I could not have planned a more beautiful celebration with so many personal details that were obviously done with much love. It was clearly *my* party. The drinks were flowing, including my pink signature drink, the food was amazing because it was all my favorites, and the caterer let them bring in two of my absolute favorites—a Cheddar Box cheese torte, and the green chili wantons from the Bristol, which explains why there was no veggie tray at *my* party.

The details included my favorite musician, Bob the Singer—I'm sure he has a more professional name, but that's what I call him—who came from Ohio; "Carrey's Favorites" table; framed photos from throughout my life, which was a nice trip down memory lane; a trivia game (I only got two wrong); a word board; an amazing video of my life; gorgeous hot pink floral centerpieces; signature monograms everywhere; and a gorgeous cake. We had the most incredible party favors ever.

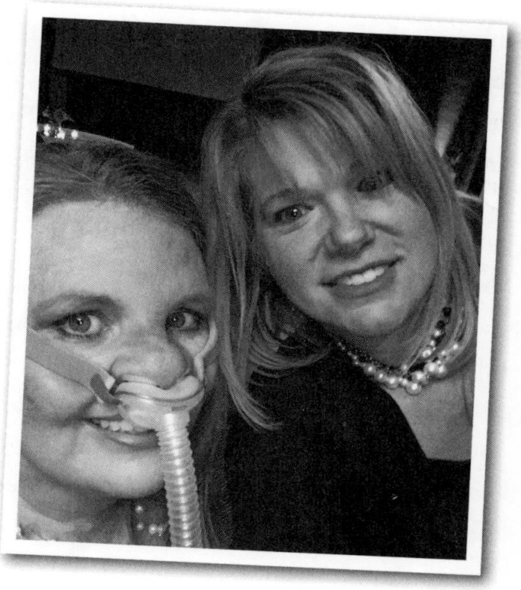

Sometimes I'm disappointed that I know I won't be there to attend my own visitation or funeral, and I felt so full because it was a celebration of life that I got to participate in with my family and friends.

To Eric, the entire PPC (Party Planning Committee), and my friends: I can't thank you enough for giving me the most special birthday gift I've ever received.

December 11, 2016

My Little Family Apartment

I am very fortunate to have a space in my home I absolutely love. It's by no means fancy or showroom-ready. It's spacious, has a beautiful view, and an office connected to it. It's the first room I decorated when we bought our home. I love everything about my bedroom.

Over the last six to nine months, my bedroom has transformed more into a family apartment than a bedroom. You may notice most photos taken inside my home show me in my bed because I spend more time there than in my chair. For two reasons: one, my bed is way more comfortable than my chair; and, two, it takes *a lot* of effort to transfer me downstairs where my power chair is—three exhausting transfers, to be exact. We talked about moving my bedroom to the first floor, but I just couldn't bear to leave this space I love so much. We eat family meals in my room—heck, we had Eric's birthday dinner and cake and ice cream in my bedroom! That was nine people. Family games, lunch dates with girlfriends, math homework . . . lots of math homework. We draw—I mean they draw—play board games, do puzzles, play card games, do hairstyling, have family therapy, practice gymnastics, referee arguments, enjoy social visits, and I do all of my shopping, from school supplies to Christmas gifts to space pants and wipes. My bed turns into a pirate ship when my nephews come over, and we have a little TV time thrown in there. We've even started our Christmas wrapping up here, and tonight we're planning on decorating our annual gingerbread houses upstairs in our little family apartment.

I feel as though I made the apartment official by moving our family Advent calendar and Advent wreath from their designated spots in the kitchen to our family apartment upstairs, and my girlfriend brought me a little Christmas tree for my little apartment. Plus, we converted our adjoining home office into a medical supply closet to house my bedside potty and transfer chair, massage table, Eyegaze, Hoyer Lift, Afflo vest, and feeding tube supplies (which, by the way, I'm still boycotting). So, the only sign of ALS in my bedroom is my nightstand full of breathing apparatuses. I have ALS pretty hidden in my little family apartment.

December 12, 2016

We finally decorated our family Christmas tree last night. I was exhausted (I'm not sure why, since I've spent the last seven days in bed), but I knew this was something I had to push through. They were excited to have me come downstairs, where we gathered around the fire to do our traditional Christmas tree decorating, and I did not want to miss it either.

I had a few special things planned for them, like the book my friend Sally made for me, cataloging all of the ornaments with their histories. We started this project last year as we packed up the ornaments at the end of the season.

I'd like to say it was a magical night for us, hanging the stockings, playing Christmas music, and displaying our favorite ornaments, but somehow it turned into a painful disaster.

I want these special memories and moments with my family so much, and it's painful when we have "normal people problems," and everything blows up.

I even said to my youngest, "If this is my last year decorating the Christmas tree with you, is this how you want to remember it?" Yep—I said it. I know I shouldn't have, but I really wanted her to know that she was destroying the moment.

So, after losing my temper and letting a few profanities fly, we finished the tree and took the picture (at least four of us had fake smiles), then sent one child upstairs with her telling me I was ruining her Christmas!

It's hard to navigate between normal people problems and ALS problems. Last night was a big crash between the two worlds, and our Christmas tree decorating was anything but jolly. But, we got all the ornaments hung and took the picture and sent one unhappy child straight to bed.

December 19, 2016

I had my quarterly ALS clinic appointment Friday, and I usually follow that with a physical update. I invited Ian to miss his half day at school before Christmas break to join us.

I've been on the edge of holding on to many abilities, and the physical strength I've lost in the past three months has made a substantial difference in who is able to transfer me and how I am transferred. I have very few working muscles left in my body, and what working muscle I do have left is overcompensating and being strained, causing secondary problems. For example, sometimes I quit eating because my jaw is too tired, or I often opt for liquid meals because I know I don't have the energy or strength to finish a meal.

The good news is my breathing did not drop substantially, so that's great news! My lung capacity is at 17 percent. That may sound really low, and it is, but it's enough to take shallow breaths for about 30 seconds off the machine, and enough to still have a voice, so that is miraculous news I am thankful for. Usually, at this point in someone's progression, their voice and swallowing would be extremely compromised or depleted altogether.

Physically, my body is a rag doll. When Eric, my sister, or one of my trained caregivers lifts me up, I cannot support my head, I can't move my feet, and my arms just dangle. I can't assist with dressing, and my potty is now bedside—it's even worse than it sounds.

Our last appointment was just that, our final appointment with the ALS clinic. Most of our final appointment was making sure we're prepared when the storm hits. Making sure we have all the ammunition if congestion settles into my lungs. Making sure we know all the warning signs of CO2 build-up in my breathing. Making sure we have all the tools in the event I begin to aspirate on food or my own saliva and making sure we have medication to provide "comfort" for me if the need arises. Ian didn't have too many questions, but he was definitely listening, which is typical for Ian.

ALS can move so quickly physically, mentally, and emotionally, and I think it has done that in all respects over the last 12 weeks with me. I am not alone; I'm just done with clinic.

December 22, 2016

I was not only proud but blessed to be at Ian's Boy Scout court of honor where he personally pinned me with his rank advancement. This pin was the second of seven I am confident he will earn. Ian and I have a special box holding Eric's Eagle Scout award and my mother's pins in the event I can't be there to receive them myself. Two down, five to go!

December 29, 2016

Merry Christmas!

Merry Christmas and happy holidays from our party of five to yours. I know it's late, but that comes along with having ALS. Everything takes longer, everything takes enormous effort, and lots of tasks I once deemed high priority don't get done . . . like our family Christmas card this year. I removed my own pressure about sending out Christmas cards so I could enjoy the greetings and photos we were receiving. I certainly had intentions for our annual family photo with perfectly coordinating outfits and the equestrian backdrop, but I let go of that pressure, too.

Christmas was definitely different—the physical abilities I have lost, the equipment I have gained, and certainly the loss of my mother and brother were all felt. Our family made modifications and continued to adapt, adjust, and move forward even with our holiday traditions. As we roll into 2017, our family wanted to take the opportunity to wish all of you who have chosen to follow and support us down the ALS path merry Christmas and happy holidays.

Whew! And with this post, I can say our greetings have been sent. Not neglected, just modified.

2017

January 3, 2017

New Year's Day Tradition on Hold No More

Our little family has spent several years celebrating New Year's Day at Great Wolf Lodge in Ohio. I was able to squeeze out my first year with ALS when I could still walk up the steps and ride the water rides, but last year was just too much. I couldn't walk safely; I was predominantly wheelchair bound; and I needed help getting lifted out of a chair. Keeping our family tradition of celebrating New Year's Day at Great Wolf Lodge just seemed impossible. I gave in to the fact that it was a tradition of the past and my little family could reinstate the tradition after ALS had run its course. Well, I must have forgotten our motto: "adapt, adjust, and move forward" because with the generosity of a friend and the support of Karlee, my assistant, somehow I was able to rally my body for the two-hour drive to Great Wolf Lodge this year. A trip my kids always expected turned into a huge surprise full of excitement!

As Eric and Karlee lifted my sore body out of bed into my wheelchair on the last day, I looked at Eric and said jokingly, "Whose bright idea was this?" He replied, "Yours . . . and the kids had an awesome time and they were so glad *you* were here. Thanks for making the trip for our family." Somehow his answer made most of my aches and pains go away.

So cheers to a season of adapted and adjusted traditions and 2017—boy, am I glad to see *you*!

January 13, 2017

What I Miss Most

My friend asked me, with all the abilities I've lost so far, "What do you miss the most?" I try not to think about what I've lost because I still have so much—specifically my voice and ability to swallow. But I do often find myself yearning for a few abilities ALS has stolen from me.

At the beginning of my journey, I would have assumed the obvious answers would be eating independently, bathing, and dressing myself, or driving. I guess because I have friends who can help me with those tasks, I don't have a true sadness at those lost abilities. If I could wave a magic wand—or I guess I should say *you* could wave a magic wand for me—I would really love my handwriting back. I miss being able to pen my own letters, cards, and love notes or at a minimum, sign my own name on a signature line. I would really love to be physically connected to my children's schools. I miss being familiar with their classmates and families, being able to see my children throughout the day, being a familiar face to their class and teachers, getting to know Ian's school routine and being able to make personal connections at his new school. Also, I liked the kids knowing that I was physically invested in their schools. I would also really love the ability to hold my children and husband closely.

I miss being able to run my fingers through their hair, give them tight squeezes, hold them when they get hurt or feel bad, and rub their tummies to sleep (well, maybe not Eric's). These are by far my greatest losses.

January 17, 2017

A Slight Scare

Who would have thought little ol' Jell-O could cause such havoc?

Last night I was enjoying time with my family and watching a Bruno Mars interview (we *love* Bruno Mars!) while Ian spooned Jell-O into my mouth. I must have been too entertained by Bruno to think about how I was swallowing, and the next thing I knew I was choking on Jell-O!

My family rushed into action like pros. Eric quickly turned on my cough assist machine and stuck the mouthpiece between my lips. Colleen knew to take my nose hose off. I can't use both at the same time because both force high air pressure into my lungs. Fortunately, the cough assist machine did the trick and the Jell-O made its way up or down or maybe both. I saw big, concerned eyeballs and a sense of urgency, but when my choking escapade ended, my big-eyeballed children rubbed me compassionately and told me everything was okay, and they were so sorry. Somehow I felt I needed to console them for the fear I saw in their eyes.

My cough assist machine is another fancy piece of durable medical equipment that sits next to my Trilogy breathing machine on my nightstand.

Its function is to force air deep into my lungs and then sucks it out with force to help me stimulate a cough, which I am no longer able to do on my own because of my weak diaphragm. The cough assist helps bring up phlegm as well as break secretions or pull up what's lodged in my airway.

My big lesson learned is I need to remember to focus on swallowing with every bite, even if it's just Jell-O!

January 19, 2017

My three-and-a-half-year-old nephew said to me, "Joey wears a diaper and I wear a pull-up at night, but you wear astronaut pants!"

It's legit, folks!

January 20, 2017

Being Married to, I Mean with, ALS

Being married with ALS is very complicated. I'm sure every patient's experience with

ALS is different depending on whether young children are involved and the strength of a marriage before the diagnosis. I would say Eric and I have a strong faith-led marriage and complement each other. I always knew everything would be okay with him.

The first year we were married with ALS was actually pretty good. I lost some physical abilities, but I was able to compensate, and our marriage stayed unchanged. Emotionally, we truly believed a cure would come before ALS destroyed my body. The second year, we spent a lot of time and energy flying around the country seeking potential treatments. My body had weakened enough that I depended on Eric's physical strength to lift and hold me. Now that we are in the middle of year three, our marriage has completely shifted. My love for Eric is definitely deeper than it has ever been before. I've experienced a side of compassion and true love I didn't know existed in "real life" and for that, I am grateful.

But it's hard. And it's sad. We worked hard to build the life and marriage we have, it didn't just happen . . . and once ALS invaded our marriage, Eric was faced with the reality of being a single dad of three and I'm on the polar opposite end of the scale. Slowly relinquishing both my short-term and long-term mothering privileges and preparing a safety net for the love of my life and my three beautiful children when the time comes I have to say good-bye. Being planted in polar opposite circumstances changes our openness and communication. I can barely process my own fate—I can't bear to think about or discuss with Eric what he is facing or vice versa. Our "date night" conversations have transitioned from planning our next vacation or the next party we're hosting to his legitimate questions: When do I want him to give my children the gifts I have purchased for them? Where have I left all the final instructions? Where have I left all the letters and videos I made for my kids? How do I want my jewelry divided? (That's not too hard; I don't have much.) What are the most important "final wishes" I have for my children? If given the choice, would it be in the best interest of our children for me to die in our home or with palliative care in a hospital? Where do I want my ashes spread? Seriously, these are the conversations we're having now. It's hard. And it's heartbreaking, and it doesn't get easier as time passes. Believe me, there is no one praying harder for a miracle than our family. But we feel we would be irresponsible if we didn't consider our reality.

Unfortunately, our marriage has shifted from more of a husband-and-wife relationship to a patient-and-caregiver relationship. It's something neither one of us wanted to happen, but somehow it did. Maybe because of all the needs I have, and I'm most comfortable under his care. He's the one who can physically lift me. He's the one who puts me on my bedside potty chair, then wipes my tushy. He's the one who gets up in the middle of the night to pull phlegm out of my throat and care for my every need. We worked really hard not to come to this patient-caregiver relationship, but my body is failing me, and he is transitioning into taking over my responsibility.

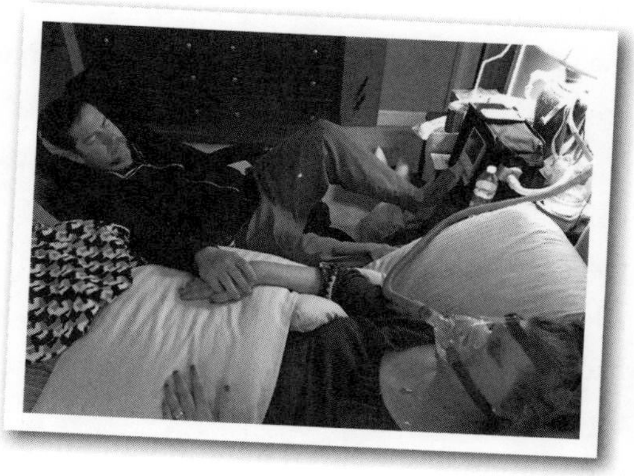

There are definitely still intimate moments between us, but certainly not as I would have imagined. He scoops me up like he's carrying me over the threshold to put me in bed. He kisses me nightly on the forehead. He lifts me out of my wheelchair and holds me tightly and we call that our own dance. He lays next to me in bed holding my hand, facing me, at the end of the night.

While ALS has definitely invaded our marriage, it certainly won't end our marriage.

January 24, 2017

The Sound of Music That Was Almost Silent

I was excited to have the opportunity to take my little family to see the Broadway Series production of *The Sound of Music*. We love this musical, and everyone in my family can play at least one song from the musical score; even Eric can play "Do-Re-Me." I called the ticket office to secure our tickets, and to confirm they could accommodate my needs in a big, 400-pound wheelchair. As it turned out, there were definitely seats available, but not handicapped seats. I am clearly at the point physically where I cannot sit in an "able-bodied seat" any more.

When I called the ticket office, they said, "Sorry, no handicapped seating available." I knew that was absurd and asked out of curiosity just how many handicapped accessible seats they allot.

Seven.

That was complete BS and ridiculously unfair. It was really the first time I have ever felt discriminated against for having ALS. I couldn't take my children to see *The Sound of Music* because I could not sit in an "able-bodied seat."

My girlfriend Lisa told me her family was going to see *The Sound of Music*, and I explained why my family was not. She was also shocked by the number of accessible seats the ticket office quoted me. Seven? Five minutes later, she came back and said, "As it turns out, seven seats are not within ADA [Americans with Disabilities Act] compliance." She estimated the venue should have approximately 20 accessible seats and promised to investigate this in the morning.

The good news is, the fifth person my friend talked to was able to secure the one handicapped seat and four companion seats needed for our whole family to sit together. I am so glad we were not separated, because I enjoyed watching my children's facial expressions as much as the talent on the stage.

Yet another family memory was made with and through *The Sound of Music*.

February 1, 2017

Just in case there are any questions . . .

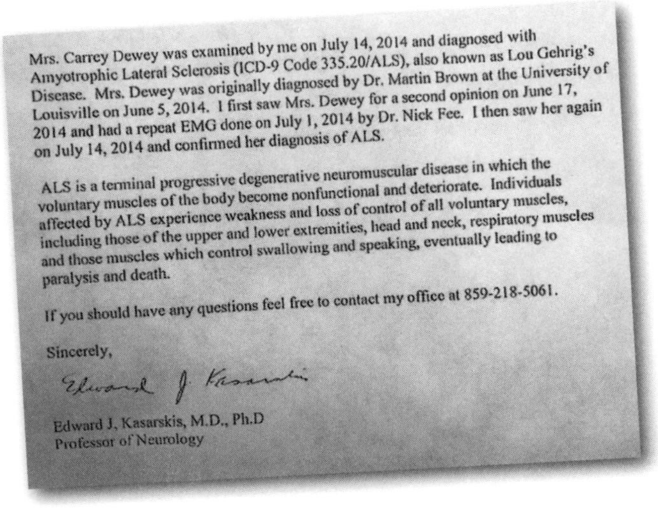

Mrs. Carrey Dewey was examined by me on July 14, 2014 and diagnosed with Amyotrophic Lateral Sclerosis (ICD-9 Code 335.20/ALS), also known as Lou Gehrig's Disease. Mrs. Dewey was originally diagnosed by Dr. Martin Brown at the University of Louisville on June 5, 2014. I first saw Mrs. Dewey for a second opinion on June 17, 2014 and had a repeat EMG done on July 1, 2014 by Dr. Nick Fee. I then saw her again on July 14, 2014 and confirmed her diagnosis of ALS.

ALS is a terminal progressive degenerative neuromuscular disease in which the voluntary muscles of the body become nonfunctional and deteriorate. Individuals affected by ALS experience weakness and loss of control of all voluntary muscles, including those of the upper and lower extremities, head and neck, respiratory muscles and those muscles which control swallowing and speaking, eventually leading to paralysis and death.

If you should have any questions feel free to contact my office at 859-218-5061.

Sincerely,

Edward J. Kasarskis

Edward J. Kasarskis, M.D., Ph.D
Professor of Neurology

February 4, 2017

February 10, 2017

Both girls wanted me to attend their class Valentine's Day parties today. They *really* wanted me there. I have to be careful in large crowds due to germs. I wear my full-face mask whenever I'm around a lot of people, especially when I'm at the kids' school and there are a bunch of petri dishes walking around. I reminded the girls if I came I would have the big mask on and I wouldn't be able to help, or participate, or even talk. They didn't care. They just wanted me physically there. Colleen even reminded me this morning to wear my mask, so I wouldn't get the "yucky school germs." I love that my girls are not embarrassed by the way I look. I was definitely an observer, not a participant, but I loved being there with both of them today.

February 11, 2017

My kiddos understand I can't come to all their activities. A few months ago, I asked them which activities are most important for me to join them. Ian said swim meets and Boy Scouts court of honor, Anne Marie said her cheer competitions, and Colleen said class parties. Today was an extra busy day starting with a cheer competition followed by Ian's swim meet. I feel very blessed to make it to both. Now I'm home resting in my big brown chair with hopes I can squeeze out a wine-tasting party tonight, even though it is a stretch. Then I'll use all of next week to recover.

February 12, 2017

Will You . . . Please and Thank You

Will you please . . .
Hold my neck?
Scratch my head?
Give me a sip of water?
Answer my phone?
Uncurl my fingers?
Clean out my belly button?
Wipe my face?
Elevate my elbows?
Brush my teeth?
Suction my mucus?
Wash my hair?
Sign my name?
Shave my armpits?

Straighten my legs?
Turn my neck?
Help me go potty?
Read and reply to my text messages?
Wash my girly parts?
Help me type my blog?
Shave my legs? Never mind, I gave that up a few months ago.
Lift my head up?
Put my hand in my lap?
Wipe my eyes out?
Move me off my pressure points?
Move my feet?
Feed me breakfast . . . lunch . . . dinner?
Put a blanket on me?
Take a blanket off me?
Lean me up?
Change my space pants?
Charge my phone?
Clean my ears?
Wash my face?
Pick my nose?
Give me a drink of water?
Give me another bite?
Scratch my eyebrows?
Push up my toes?
Rotate my feet?
Get me dressed?
Adjust my breathing mask?
Pick the food stuck in the back of my teeth?
Get my mouthwash?
Adjust my boobs? (It could be worse. The men have to ask to have their "nuts fluffed"!)
Brush my hair?
Clip and paint my nails?
Put on my mascara?
Put lip balm on me?
Strap my legs together?

Bend my knees?
Open my wine?
. . . Please and thank you!

February 18, 2017

My Biggest Fear

This may sound absolutely ridiculous, but my biggest fear is throwing up—seriously! I can't sit up, I can't roll over, I can't lean my body, I can't lift my head up, I can't turn my head, and I definitely can't release my mask. My inability to do any one of those would cause me to choke and suffocate on my own vomit. The only thing I can really do to prevent this scenario is to avoid the flu bug.

February 27, 2017

I'm a Little Teapot

The left side of my body is much weaker than the right. When I was evaluated for my diaphragmatic pacer, the doctor video X-rayed my lungs and breathing muscles. Even the left side of my diaphragm was weaker than the right, which I didn't even know was possible.

Now that I'm pretty much paralyzed from the shoulders down, the weakness is noticeable in my neck, which slumps to the left. We even named this position "teapot" because I feel completely tipped over. I usually tell someone I'm "tea-potting," and they know that means I'm tipping over and to center me back up. Just for giggles, sometimes I sing the "I'm a Little Teapot" song from childhood as a polite request to push me up.

It's really quite a nuisance when I'm stuck in a slumped-over teapot position. Sometimes you may see me or other people with ALS in a neck brace or with a neck pillow on—not because we have injured our necks, but because ALS is stealing our neck muscles as well.

February 28, 2017

Medical Victory

A few weeks ago, there was a serious concern with blood clots in my arm. I had all the symptoms: hot, rashy, and swollen upper arm. It was also very painful, but my arm always hurts since I tore my rotator cuff falling off the massage table. I didn't know who to call.

I've decided to call upon my primary care physician whom I have not met before. She did not have the capability to give an ultrasound in her office and directed me to the ER—the absolute last place I wanted to be! I had an ultrasound in both arms, and I am currently clear of any blood clots. The lesson learned here was that we needed to find a medical solution that worked best for me and my unique needs.

March 1, 2017

Keeping with our family tradition, we invited a family over last night to celebrate Fat Tuesday in preparation for Lent. I told Eric I wanted to come downstairs early to "boss people around" and make sure dinner was made right, and the decorations were done right, and the table was set right. Eric said, "No bossing around allowed" and made me wait. I'll admit, the kids did a great job decorating, Eric and Colleen did a great job cooking, and I did a good job of letting go. I love that my family carries on our family traditions without needing my direction.

March 3, 2017

My wheelchair drove right through the living room french door, leaving a nice gaping hole. But as my kids always say, "It's not my fault!" I pushed down on the foot pedal to accelerate, my foot dropped, and I couldn't release. "Foot drop" is a common ALS symptom. For many patients with ALS, foot drop is their first sign or symptom of the disease. It's not really a significant symptom for me until I try to control my wheelchair with my foot. Even after I plowed through the door, the wheels kept spinning and I literally burnt black rubber on my living room carpet. But again, it's not my fault!

The significance is much bigger than the hole in my door or burnt rubber on my white carpet. I am having a hard time controlling my wheelchair with my foot. The foot control was a perfect solution for independence, but Eric and my sister Elizabeth said the time is here where I need to give up my foot control. Not only do I experience foot drop, but I am unable to turn my chair left or push my heel down to reverse. I find myself doing a lot of U-turns or turning 350 degrees to the right when I only need to go 10 degrees to the left. When I'm in my chair using the foot control, I always need somebody nearby to help maneuver me—especially when I almost took out a china display at Home Goods last week.

So now what? I had a new control installed to steer my 400-pound wheelchair using my chin. It's not as easy as using as my foot. In fact, it sucks. I think I'd rather run into the door and claim it's not my fault than use the chin control. I'm still practicing with it, and I am hopeful I can roll it out to you all soon and write an illuminating blog to show how practice makes perfect. But don't hold your breath. I am nowhere near even being able to navigate a straight line.

It's not my fault!

March 5, 2017

Yesterday we joined our University of Louisville Cardinals for the last home game of the year against Notre Dame. U of L friends and staff generously offered us handicap and family seating to accommodate our needs. After pulling out a win, we had the opportunity to meet the players, Coach Rick Pitino, and the coaching staff—they called me their lucky charm.

Two takeaways:

I cannot believe how gracious and polite every single player was. I mean every single player!

I loved watching my dad introduce each player to the kids by name. Seeing my family's excitement, especially Dad's and Eric's, during our team meeting was truly priceless.

Certainly another awesome memory for the books.

March 10, 2017

Sacrifices and Accomplishments

I went to bed with my heart full of love and peace, a great start to a good night's sleep. I was trying to drift into "la-la land," Eric bedside rubbing my hand as he often does. I was thinking about how much I loved him, how I knew early on he was my soul mate, how good he's been to me, how lucky I am to have him taking care of me, how proud I am of Eric, and how blessed our children are to have him as a father. These feelings took me back to the beginning of our marriage and our hopes and dreams we set: one day we could have children and grow a family; one day we would be in a position where I could stay home with our young; we would be able to move into a home our family could grow into; we could expand our circle of friends; we could continue to grow our marriage; we would find a church we could call home; Eric would continue to develop his career; we could find a school for our children where I would be involved on a regular basis.

All of these thoughts really should have brought peace because that is exactly where we are 15 years later. I know I should follow the saying "Don't cry because it's over, smile because it happened," but that's more difficult knowing what's ahead.

It made me sad that here we are. We did it. And now ALS is going to foil the second half of our plans. The plans we had for me to go back to work in some capacity and use my master's degree in instructional technology. To send our kids to Catholic high school. To build a pool and be the home where kids wanted to hang out under our supervision. To travel. To take our kids on wonderful senior spring breaks so they wouldn't have the kind of senior spring breaks Eric and I had. We wanted to take our children to Ireland and show them the "old sod." We planned to take all of our children and grandchildren on an annual trip.

I know I should be grateful for the first 15 years of accomplishments we achieved through dedication and sacrifice. And I am, but I'm also sad. And then I began to cry. And Eric gently wiped my tears as fast as they fell, and since I don't have the muscle strength to blow my nose, he elevated my bed. I tried to quit crying because it's difficult to breathe when I can't blow my nose and it drains down my throat and someone has to extract or I'll choke on my own sad snot. It's not just me; it's thousands of other people whose plans are being cut short as well because of the lack of a cure or even a treatment for ALS.

Eric went from rubbing my hand gently to caressing my head and dealing with his own sadness as he continued wiping my tears. I finally drifted off to sleep.

I wholeheartedly believed after the momentum of the Ice Bucket Challenge, a cure or treatment would come in my own lifetime. I'm not counting it out and still praying for a miracle, but that cure or treatment better come quickly because I'm running out of time.

March 17, 2017

Progression

I usually give an update of my progression after my quarterly ALS clinic appointment. However I'm not attending clinic anymore, but that certainly does not mean my progression has stopped—quite the contrary. My condition continues to worsen because that's what happens with ALS. Every part of my body has gotten weaker. Every transfer is harder. Every outing has to be well thought out to accommodate my growing needs. There are no "big losses" in this update, other than my ability to control my wheelchair with my foot. Eric has officially withdrawn my foot control. My neck would be the most noticeable muscle loss, as I explained in my previous teapot post. But it's what's inside the neck that is most concerning—the esophagus and epiglottis. The ability to swallow and open my airway is becoming increasingly difficult. I know my breathing has dropped. Mask changes are done in three seconds or less, unless you're Brittani Dodge. She is a ninja and can do them in two.

ALS is a real energy sponge. Fatigue is a common symptom, but in the last few months, I have felt ridiculously fatigued. I have too much to do to sleep as much as my body is forcing me to. Some of this is because of my decreased oxygen levels combined with the minimal muscle strength working triple time. I've had a hard time staying awake this week. But at night, I'm laden with shallow breathing at the fear that I may go to sleep and not wake up.

Equipment wise, we've added the suction machine to suck out secretions from my mouth and nose because I don't have the muscle strength to blow out or suck up mucus. We have also added the AffloVest, which is used to vibrate my lungs and break up secretions; fortunately, I have not had to use it yet. But when the time comes to wage war, I'm ready.

I'm no longer able to put my legs together, so I wear a gait belt or scarf to keep my legs closed, making me feel a little more lady-like. I'm still working on the chin control. But I feel like I have made more road rash on my chin than progress, and it is incredibly frustrating to be stuck in my wheelchair, unable to move at all.

I spend most of my time in bed in our master bedroom, affectionately called our "family apartment." I still take outings, but they have to be impactful to my family to be worth the strenuous transfer process. I'm physically and mentally comfortable in my room, and I can get an enormous number of things accomplished from my bed. Some people call it command central up here.

On that note, I'm getting ready to transfer downstairs to celebrate our big fat annual family St. Patrick's Day dinner. We go all out and let our Irish fly!

March 23, 2017

Hello, Tubby Time

My friend Erin told me she was thinking about me while she was taking a bath.

She asked if I was a bath girl. Without trying to reminisce too much about my love for taking a "tubby" and letting my muscles soak and melt in the hottest water my body could tolerate, I said heck yeah, I *was* absolutely a bath girl. She asked when the last time was that I was able to get in a bathtub, and I told her it had been about six months. We explored several options to safely transfer me into and out of the tub, but there were logistical roadblocks with every option, forcing me to bathe tub side while tilted in my rolling shower chair. Like all other losses ALS has stolen from me, I try not look back at what I have lost and appreciate what I have and keep looking forward.

My friend took getting me into the bathtub again as her logistical challenge. After some slight modifications to the bathtub floor she was able to find a bathtub lift that could get me back into my soaking hot water.

Erin was so excited for me to take my maiden voyage she rolled out a spa-like bathtub warming party for me. Sure is nice to say hello again to what was once known as my "tubby time," plus my littles have repurposed the shower chair as a pedicure spa chair! Side note—don't drink champagne through a straw when thirsty.

March 29, 2017

Happy birthday to my dad, affectionately known to all, big and little, as Poppa Joe although he prefers "The Poppa Joe." I'm excited to celebrate with my dad this year. With the loss of my mother and brother so quickly and the reality of what my diagnosis means to him, I don't take celebrating his birthday for granted.

Many have the privilege to call him "like a dad"; I have the privilege to call him *my* dad. He has led our family in faith by example. He has taught us our actions not only represent us individually but our entire family. He taught us the importance of taking the high road. He has mirrored the good Samaritan every time the opportunity arose. He's modeled for our family and others what a marriage should look like. He taught us to appreciate where we come from. He taught us to say I'm sorry. He taught us how to forgive and move forward. He puts everybody else first—almost to a fault. He has never met a stranger. He's always ready to give a hug. He compliments young men who look him in the eye and give him a firm handshake. He is genuinely interested in other people, which typically leads to a peppering of questions, not because he's being nosey but because he truly cares about other peoples' stories. He has shared his love of

sunshine and snowy mountains with us, and while I did not inherit his mad basketball talent, I did end up five foot, ten inches, which, believe it or not, makes me the shortest of four siblings. My favorite advice from him is "Always appreciate the good, because there is always more good than bad." Advice we both remind each other of daily. He loves ice cream, peanut M&Ms, and all things chocolate. He can't get enough country music, college basketball, or news of the day. He taught all his grandkids how to say "Black-Berr-*eees*" and "Sweet wa-*terrr*" just like he always has. The party is more fun when he is there. I definitely inherited his love of nicknaming. And his nose.

Happiest of birthdays to my dear friend: my dad, Poppa Joe!

March 30, 2017

Just when I thought I had maxed out on all the equipment I would need to live with ALS, I have added one more valuable piece to my collection. The bad news is my oxygen-saturation levels were dropping pretty considerably from my norm. So we've tapped oxygen into my breathing machine, forcing in room air and pure oxygen.

The good news is this seems to have helped considerably with my fatigue.

Oh the joys . . .

April 1, 2017

Yes, ALS is painful. Every part of my body hurts, but I can tolerate the pain. It's the choking and suffocating that are hard to accept. This ALS party is really starting to kick it up a notch over here. Now that my entire body is like a rag doll, this cruel killer is homing in on my breathing and swallowing. I've choked twice this week on my own saliva. The lesson learned is, I can never be left alone. There were times when there was a short time gap, and I was completely comfortable with the TV on to "babysit" me. But not anymore . . . those days are over.

The good news is I still have my voice—but not while choking.

April 2, 2017

Woo-hoo! Spring Break 2017

Spring break 2017 is full of realities for our little family. This is the first year we've not taken a family trip over the break. I don't feel sorry for my kids because we're not going anywhere. Honestly, our children shouldn't expect a spring break trip every year. Unfortunately, we've set a standard of vacationing over spring break every year.

Spring break 2017 is the harsh reality for my family that my ALS progression has taken away my ability to travel, at least comfortably and safely. It's too much equipment; I require too much physical attention; I'm uncomfortable outside of my bed; we always need a caregiver, resulting in an additional car; and ultimately, I don't have the physical strength.

Our kids will be busy this week enjoying the time with our favorite neighbors, affectionately known as my sister and nephews, and finding new ways to have family activities within our family apartment. It's going to be a great week, but it is a harsh physical reminder that part of my life, our family life, is over.

April 14, 2017

As part of my Good Friday observance, I attended service with Ian. His class reenacted the Passion Play during the service, which is always powerful to see, even more so when your son plays the part of Jesus.

April 15, 2017

Easter Parade

I never intended to be the face of ALS. Really, the last thing I wanted to do was put my "rolling freak show" out for public display—not because I'm embarrassed by my disease but because of the extreme anxiety it causes. But when the ALS Association asked my family to join them in the annual Louisville Easter parade, I said yes because: (1) my kids don't see me as a rolling freak show, it's their norm and they would have fun, and (2) most importantly, you understand ALS a little better when you see it—for just a glimpse—among a ton of candy.

Happy Easter!

April 17, 2017

We did it!

And by we, I mean Andy, Kathy, and Coach Kris Krohn successfully completed the Boston Marathon, and I was alive today to cheer them on. When Coach told me a year ago he was gonna run Boston in my honor, I was worried it would end up being in memory of me, because statistically I didn't have 12 more months to live. A huge accomplishment for all four of us today.

Kathy sent me a message after the race: "I had written on my shoulder, 'I love you, Carrey,' and people thought my name was Carrey at a glance. The crowd would yell, 'Go Carrey! You've got this Carrey!' as I would pass in pain. It was almost like you were running for me. I wouldn't want it any other way. I would much rather them cheer for you than me because that is what this race was all about."

I know it was a God moment that our friend Philip (Boston College student), wearing his Team Dewey shirt, was able to catch Coach Krohn at the top of Heartbreak Hill.

Congratulations Andy, Kathy, and Coach Krohn for completing the Boston Marathon in my honor and advocating for all ALS patients!

April 21, 2017

Change

We've been really busy the last two weeks. All really good stuff, but it also comes with a big step in progression. Nothing overly obvious unless you're with me on a daily basis, but it's definitely progression that's been mixed in with our last two weeks of fun. I'm losing strength in my mouth; my lips can no longer form a seal around my cough-assist mouthpiece. I'm having a hard time moving food around my mouth with my tongue. I'm choking on my own saliva, and I have a very slight slur in my speech. I'm no longer able to swallow my pills with applesauce; the grit gets stuck in the back of my throat. We are transitioning to yogurt or pudding, something with a thicker consistency. My children and caregivers are needing to suction me more frequently than before.

The added oxygen has definitely been helpful—I call it my Red Bull. My lung capacity has declined. I don't know the exact number; I'd guess in the upper single digits. I'm starting to have some whack-a-doodle side effects or symptoms; I can't distinguish between the two. My hair is starting to fall out, flavors are more potent, and my short-term memory is definitely compromised. I don't know if these are symptoms of ALS, side effects of medications I'm on, or my brain is just on complete overload. Either way, these are the least of my concerns right now.

It's crazy, even though my body is failing me, I still feel really good and definitely consider myself living with ALS, not dying from ALS.

April 25, 2017

My Newest Problem

When you spend most of, I mean, *all* of your time lying in bed or sitting in a wheelchair, your skin starts to get pissed off. Places on my body where pressure is constant, such as on my heels, elbows, palms, and even my tushy, are vulnerable to extremely painful spots called pressure points. If untreated, these pressure points can turn into an open wound called pressure sores. Pillows and lamb's wool have become my new best friends—hence my fancy "quarter Ugg boots," as we call them.

And since my tushy crack never moves, I have a slight open wound where the sun don't shine. No, it's not humiliating being rolled on my side and a wound care nurse inspecting and photographing my butt crack; it's just a pain in the ass, literally. I'll spare you the photo.

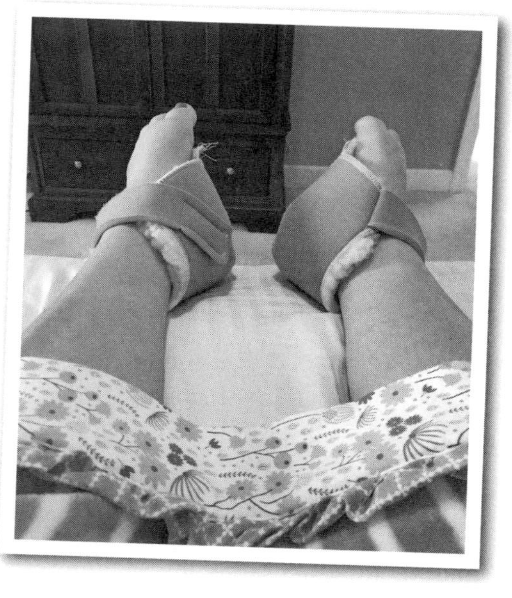

In addition—more TMI coming—I developed a yeast infection on my chest, underneath my breasts. I had *no* idea a yeast infection outside of girly parts was even possible. Since I rarely wear a bra nowadays, there is constant skin-on-skin contact. It feels and looks like a raging army of fire ants. I've since learned to keep a barrier between my breasts and skin, and I'll spare you this photograph as well.

Yep, those are my newest problems.

April 29, 2017

Normal People Problems

Through our Hosparus family therapy, we've been working with a wonderful therapist. It became apparent during counseling that our biggest issues were "normal people problems." Our family therapist was honest and told us she specialized in bereavements and not normal people problems that had become our biggest issues such as siblings arguing, kids pushing each other's hot buttons, talking in a disrespectful tone, not listening to directions the first time, abusing screen time, not treating each other with respect, on and on and on. So we will be transitioning to a new in-home family therapist who hopefully can help us with our normal people problems while we're living with extraordinary circumstances.

I know, I know . . . kids are resilient and it's probably a bigger issue for me than it is for them. As always, we will adapt, adjust, and move forward as we transition and rethread the safety net.

May 4, 2017

It's Been a Really Shitty, Full-of-Tears Week

Since my diagnosis almost three years ago, our family has done everything possible to live a life with ALS. My eight-year-old understands that ALS is fatal, but what does that really mean? For the most part, while my body may be growing weaker each day, I have remained mentally, emotionally, and spiritually strong . . . but not this week.

This week my frustrations and irritations have run high, and my confidence in what is to come for my family has been low. I am frustrated not being able to parent the way I want to, frustrated there is no substitute. I am frustrated listening from my bedroom to our family's "normal people problems." I'm not able to physically get involved, or yell, or shake my finger at them when they've crossed a line I have clearly set for them. I am frustrated by the toll my deteriorating health is taking on my husband, and his realistic fear of what is to come.

This week the frustrations have come out in the form of harsh words, lots of tears, and constant snot suctioning. This is the first week I've really yearned to get in my car that I haven't driven in a year and a half, or to take a run or even take a walk around my neighborhood. I need to air out my head, yet I am stuck in my bed or my wheelchair for someone else to control for me. I have discussed with my caregiver the notion of having her slam the door for me. Would that help? I want to lash out, physically, emotionally, in whatever way I can, and I can't—but all I can do is lay in my bed. I have written about the good, the bad, and the ugly of ALS before, and here's more ugly for you.

I really feel this week is the first time ALS has been bigger than me. It has interfered with my friendships, my parenting, my marriage, and especially this week, my emotional state. I've done a lot of talking, or crying really, to my family and close friends. I just need an outlet to purge my frustrations, disappointments, and angers. I know I'll be better—probably after I hit the "publish" button, and I can get back to living each day to the fullest. But this week all of that has been much easier said than done.

Thank you for listening to me purge!

May 9, 2017

My cough-assist machine is used to help evoke a cough. It forces air deep into my lungs and then pulls the air out. When I first began using the machine, my respiratory therapist asked me if I wanted the mouthpiece or the mask.

"The mouthpiece, of course. Why would anyone want the mask?"

In recent weeks, I have grown to understand why the mask is offered. My lips have weakened and can no longer hold a seal around the mouthpiece. The good news is I now have the mask.

May 12, 2017

My Priorities

When I was first diagnosed with ALS, being a mom with three young children, I knew I would be known as "the mom with ALS." What I did from that point forward would, to some people, define who I was. My diagnosis day was a huge flashing red light on my life's time line. We reference "before diagnosis" and "after diagnosis" all the time. I had to figure out how I was going to use being diagnosed with ALS in a positive way.

Was I going to start a foundation or charity? Was I going to raise money for research, scholarships, education, patient care, or even my own medical care? Was I going to be an activist, knocking on the doors of the FDA, our local and state representatives, and members of Congress? Was I going to be an educator, sharing the truth of ALS? Was I going to be an innovator, developing new ways to live disabled in an enabled world?

The first priority I devote my time and energy to is my family, trying to be the best mother, wife, sister, and daughter my family deserves. My second priority is to use my energy to educate in real time in a real ALS world. It's something I definitely do by choice, it gives me some bit of purpose for my diagnosis—if you can call it that. I have to stay focused, though, because there are so many injustices I want to advocate against. In doing so, I have to walk away from urges to get involved. Screaming on soapboxes.

I want to scream how unfair and unjust the minimal amount of money dedicated to ALS research is.

I want to scream how unfair and unjust it is I'm not eligible for disability because I haven't worked in 10 years.

I want to scream how unfair and unjust it is insurance won't cover the cost of my care unless I'm in a hospital or a nursing home.

I want to scream how unfair and unjust it is my state has not legalized medical marijuana even though it's been proven to help ALS patients with their symptoms.

I want to scream how unfair and unjust it is I now have a pre-existing condition.

I want to scream how unfair and unjust it is I can't enter hospice care unless I forfeit my Trilogy breathing machine . . . well, technically I can keep it if I private pay $2,400 per month.

I want to scream how unfair and unjust it is 100 percent of the ALS Ice Bucket money didn't go to research and patient care.

I want to scream how unfair and unjust it is insurance doesn't cover the cost of durable medical equipment needed for ALS patients to continue living inside their homes.

I want to scream how unfair and unjust it is that handicapped parking doesn't come with a driver's test (i.e., those lines next to handicap spots are needed for the ramp of a van, not because you're handicapped and don't know how to park).

I would be completely exhausted, even more so than I am now, if I began to take a step on any of these soapboxes. Like many diseases, not just ALS, there are so many things that are unfair and so many injustices. I'm choosing to use my time wisely and stay focused solely on my family and continuing to educate. With that, I canceled our reservation to the ALS Association Conference and Advocacy Day in Washington, DC, this weekend. It's not best for my family, certainly not best for my body, and I am looking forward to spending Mother's Day at home for the first time in three years.

May 18, 2017

Great turnout Saturday for the ALS Association Kentucky Chapter Walk to Defeat ALS. We absolutely felt the love from our community, including my ALS community. The bad news is, we had to make more "in memory of . . ." signs because ALS is not letting up and my ALS friends are continuing to die. The good news is, Team Dewey showed up loud and proud, and extra motivated to keep kickin' ALS. We will not let up!

May 20, 2017

Mother's Day 2017

I'm delayed on my Mother's Day post. It's not because we celebrated a week late; it's just taken me several days to process. If there was a possibility, a very real possibility this could be your last Mother's Day to celebrate with your children, imagine how you would want the day to look. Yep, mine didn't look anything like that. Quite the opposite, actually.

Ian spent the majority of his day at a swim meet—which, by the way, I didn't know he was signed up for. The girls bickered nonstop through lunch and argued all through crafting a memory tree, which was supposed to be my Mother's Day gift, as I sat completely paralyzed and helpless. It was a perfect storm for a complete meltdown on my part. I wanted to make the day really special, not for me, but for their memories, their keepsakes.

On a positive note, they stopped arguing sometime last week. *And*, I also got a $350 portable suction machine for my wheelchair, so my children won't have to clear the secretions out of my mouth with a tissue when we are in public. What more can a mom with ALS ask for? Belated happy Mother's Day!

May 25, 2017

Do I Still Feel Touch?

There are two types of nerves: motor nerves and sensory nerves.

ALS affects motor nerves which send signals to the muscles. With ALS, the motor nerves die, causing atrophy and eventually paralysis to the patient's body. Motor nerves control movement, diaphragm breathing, tongue, and swallowing. The atrophy of these motor nerves has caused my paralysis.

ALS does *not* affect the sensory nerves, which send sensations of touch, pain, and temperature to the brain. So the answer is yes, I can and always will be able to feel. Especially my kids' squishy hugs . . . I just can't reciprocate.

June 1, 2017

ALS invades so much of a patient's body. Not only does it destroy the nerves and muscles inside, ALS simultaneously alters physical appearance. My face is swollen—although honestly, that's probably from medication. My legs are so slender that my shin bone sticks out. I have what's known as an ALS tummy, which means I look nine months pregnant . . . with twins. My hands and nail beds often look white and corpse-like because of lack of circulation (a good hand massage usually can fix that). And last night while Eric and Anne Marie were putting on my night mask, Colleen got a glimpse of my nose and exclaimed, "Mom! Why are your nostrils so big?" I explained to her when you have two plugs sticking up your nose all day long, they get stretched out. I can't believe it took her this long to even notice. It's difficult to feel different physically, look different physically, but nothing in my mind has changed.

June 5, 2017

Happy Year Three to Me!

Today marks three years of being diagnosed with ALS. Every year as I approach this date, June 5, I feel bittersweet and I am filled with mixed emotions. I find myself wondering how other people with a fatal diagnosis view their diagnosis anniversaries.

When I was first diagnosed, I was told I had a faster-than-average progression, so making the three-year point is a milestone for me. I really thought I would still be able to walk because my legs were so strong, but that didn't happen. Now, I'm just like an oversized, heavy rag doll. On the other hand, I thought for sure I would lose my voice by now and have all my meals through a feeding tube, but neither of those have happened yet. *Hallelujah*!

On my first anniversary, I was filled with anxiety as I approached the date. I wasn't sure if I was supposed to be mournful about my impending future or joyful to hit one year. Eric even asked if he was supposed to buy me a gift.

On my second anniversary, I was again happy to see year two, but so much had changed in the previous year that I was terrified as to what destruction was coming next. Year two was spent finishing my bucket list and making memories, most of which were done from home.

Recently, I had clarity as to how I wanted to commemorate this third-year milestone. I really wanted to throw a big-ass party and include everybody who had chosen to shine their light on our path or contributed to helping me be here today. There is absolutely no doubt the financial resources we received from our community to our medical fund made all the difference. It helped provide all comfort measures, equipment, and caregiving we needed. It also removed the added stress that often comes with this disease in regard to financial hardships that almost all ALS patients endure. I believe that if I had included everyone on the guest list it would have exceeded a thousand people.

The alternative was to host a smaller, intimate dinner with my regular caregiving team, including Brittani (affectionately known as BTD), Bossy Suzy [I, Suzy, reject this title BTW], Karlee (also known as Karlee Fries), my sister Lizzy, my dad, and of course, Eric, and their behind-the-scenes support. We celebrated last night at a 'special occasion' restaurant and our dinner was full of laughter, stories, toasts, and cheers! It was a perfect way to say, "Bring on year four and many more!" While my body may be failing me, my spirit and desire are stronger than ever.

Happy year three to me! Year four is going to be filled by continuing to strengthen my safety net, loving my family, and appreciating the beauty in all the little things.

June 9, 2017

Bucket List

When I was first diagnosed with ALS three years ago, I was advised to get my paperwork in order and "go make memories." The confirming doctor added, "Your ALS is progressing faster than the three-to-five-year average lifespan," because weakness was being shown in my second limb already. *What*? Where do we even begin with that information? It was the first day of summer break for my babes, and all I wanted to do was make a summer bucket list of fun, not a crash list of life experiences I wanted to accomplish with my kids.

After eight weeks of nonstop tears and swollen eyes hidden under my sunglasses, we checked off our easiest trip from the ALS bucket list. For the next two years, we were aggressive in marking travels off the list, doing everything we could while my weakening body was still able. We started with Chicago. We went to Disneyworld. We went on a Disney cruise. We swam with the dolphins. We went to Colorado to snow ski (it stills blows my mind I was able to snow ski with ALS). We took our family to Washington, DC, not only to advocate for a cure or treatment for ALS but also to see the nation's capital, monuments, and tour the White House. We had a festive weekend during Christmastime at the Gaylord in Nashville. We did the whole Pigeon Forge/Dollywood/Gatlinburg get-up the following fall. We took our kids out of the country; I know Cancun hardly counts, but they did get their passports stamped. I went to Costa Rica with my beloved couch ladies. And I even made it back to my beloved Sanibel Island last summer.

My list included more than travel memories. I wanted to renew our wedding vows with our children at the church we were married in. I wanted to be part of the girls' First Communion sacraments. I wanted to be the hand the girls squeezed when they got their ears pierced. I wanted to gift each child with a surprise bedroom makeover (more on that later). I wanted to take them to their first concert. I wanted to see Ian earn his Boy Scout rank.

As I got closer to year two, I realized as things were getting crossed off my bucket list, new things were being added. I wanted to be a part of the Boston Marathon when Coach Krohn, Kathy Klopp, and Andy Nussbaum and crew were running in my honor. I wanted to see Ian off on his sixth-grade trip to Huntsville, Alabama, the same NASA trip I took my sixth-grade students on when I was a teacher. I wanted to see Colleen ride her bike. I wanted to see Anne Marie nail her back walkover and then her back handspring. I wanted to get to plant a rose garden with my family, mixed in with all of my mom's flowers. All of these seemed so farfetched when I put them on the list. Now I know I can keep adding to the list because I don't really know how much time I have left. But then again, none of us do.

The whitewater rafting trip and Alaskan cruise aren't going to happen in my lifetime, but I'm okay with that. Honestly, I'm most comfortable and happy at home. I still have an ongoing bucket list. I'm definitely not done yet. We have a dear friend's wedding in July as well as the Bubble Run my kids are going to participate in with my high school classmates. I want to celebrate our 16th wedding anniversary in August, and I want to settle the kids in their next school year. And of course, Bruno Mars is coming to see me in September—or maybe it's the other way around. We continue to make memories all the time even from my own bed. I still have more living to do.

June 15, 2017

I went to sleep the other night with labored breathing; it felt like every inhale of forced air needed extra effort. I had Eric disconnect my breathing machine from the humidifier to help me get direct air, but that didn't seem to work. I was really terrified to fall asleep and not be able to help my body consciously inhale and thought maybe this is it, this is how it happens.

The good news is I woke up the next morning! We figured out that my mouth was opening as I was falling asleep, causing my air supply and oxygen levels to drop to dangerously low levels. From here on out, I'll sleep with my mouth strapped shut. That should also help with my sleep talking, which I'm sure is gonna disappoint all my caregivers.

June 22, 2017

I knew from the beginning ALS would affect my mouth. Not because ALS often steals the ability to speak and eat, but because I knew the nerves to my tongue were being compromised during the onset of my diagnosis. I had the lovely pleasure of having a long EMG needle stuck underneath my chin up into my tongue muscles. If it sounds like it hurts, multiply the pain by one hundred. The results showed delayed nerve signals to my tongue.

Therefore, here I am three years later, and the effects of the nerve loss are becoming evident. First and foremost, it is a miracle I have maintained my speech and swallow until this point. So everything that follows is without complaint.

My tongue muscles have grown noticeably weaker. I'm starting to slightly slur my speech. I'm having a hard time moving food around in my mouth with my tongue. Additionally, I have excessive saliva pooling in my mouth because I have a hard time swallowing it. Thank God for the fancy portable suction machine I got for Mother's Day; it goes everywhere I go. Little did my kids know, they would become constant suctioners. I'm trying different homeopathic remedies to dry up my saliva—I'm aiming for self-induced cotton mouth.

I'm definitely grateful for the voice and swallow I do still have, but I have to be honest—the thought of losing my speech, swallow, or choking on my saliva is utterly terrifying. It's twisted fate how my mouth would get me in trouble when I was younger and it's now the cause of concern when I'm older . . . a bunch of BS if you ask me. For now, I'm appreciating the voice and mouth movement I still have.

June 25, 2017

My New Giddy-up

I've spent the last several months paralyzed without any ability to control my chair. Eric, my sister, and Ian can control my chair with the attendant controller behind me. Other than that, I'm stuck.

I started to control my chair with my thumb until my thumb gave out. Then I moved to the foot control, which was fairly easy to use. I felt great freedom with the foot control. The bad news is it cost $7,000, and unfortunately, my foot gave out faster than we expected. We next moved to the chin control, which under my circumstances was complete crap. You have to be able to move your chin from left to right and I didn't have that type of control with my neck muscles. Which brings us to my new giddy-up.

My newest control is a combination of slight head movement and a ton of patience. I slightly tap the headpiece attached on my chair and navigate with the screen on my chair one of four directions. It works wells considering that I have been completely stuck the past two months. It works for now, but my neck is growing weaker by the day and I teapot to the left. This sometimes makes it impossible to tap my headpiece. I am a much better driver earlier in the day when my neck muscles are well rested. Eric issued me my permit after I passed my driver's test at Costco. He only had to take over the attendant control once in the refrigerator section because I had a long line of people stuck behind me as I waited patiently for my screen to toggle to the direction I wanted to go.

So for now, giddy-up, wheelchair!

June 30, 2017

Sanibel Island 2017

Our annual Sanibel Island trip with family and adopted beach family will be remembered as the year ALS grounded us. In my late stage of progression, ALS requires too much equipment, too many logistics, and too much physical strength to take this show on the road. I said good-bye to my Sanibel paradise last year. I had closure with many years of memories and comfort knowing my children and Eric will continue to experience the same joys and family bonding I had for 40 years of my life.

However, Sanibel 2017 did come with intense anxiety. Not anxiety for being grounded, but anxiety for how my kids, who expected this trip every summer, would react. The anxiety at how they would react toward me because of my health interfering with our annual trip. I knew they would be disappointed because they consider it a constant in their summer break.

"We've been to Sanibel every summer my entire life," Colleen explains.

I fully expected my kids to beg us to go. I fully expected them to not see beyond the obvious obstacles. I fully expected them to try to be stowaways with my sister or Dad so they wouldn't miss out. I was prepared to defend our decision to all stay home as a family—I couldn't bear to be away from them for the week.

Sanibel 2017 is the year my brother Ryan and sister-in-law, Michelle, shipped us an over-the-top beach in a box to decorate our "family apartment." Most importantly, it will be remembered as the year my kids showed compassion and extreme selflessness. Not once did any of them make me feel guilty. Not once did they try to problem-solve how they could get to the beach without me. Not once did they complain about being home this week while our family sent us constant photos (at my request) from the beach. When my sister came to give us a tearful good-bye, I was sure they wouldn't be able to help expressing disappointment or jealousy, but they didn't.

Last night, our beach family FaceTimed from the resort bar, surprising me with a mass amount of Team Dewey love. They all earned their shirts last year, making my last beach trip possible. Chris, the bartender, earned his shirt by years of having Colleen as a barfly.

July 3, 2017

If I had to do "it" all over again and by "it," I mean ALS, I would definitely do a few things differently.

I would get the superpubic catheter. It's a catheter implanted into the bladder to eliminate the need for consistent help when tinkling. It's just a real pain to have to ask for help every time I need to pee.

I would journal in my own handwriting. I loved my handwriting; it was curly, curving, and artistic. I knew I would lose my handwriting early because of the loss of movement in my arms and hands, but I guess I was in denial. I have very few personal writings in my own handwriting.

I would establish myself under the care of a pulmonologist immediately and not wait until I was breathing on a noninvasive ventilator.

Most importantly, I would provide Eric with the same support I desperately researched and put in place for my children three years ago, such as personalized therapy, support groups, and respite care.

I definitely know Eric and I have done more right then wrong, but for the sake of educating, especially those diagnosed with ALS following my journey, it's important I share what I've learned and would do differently if I had to do ALS all over again—thank God I don't.

June 14, 2017

Finally feeling back to my normal ALS self. Somehow I ended up with double pinkeye—how the hell someone whose arms are paralyzed gets pinkeye is beyond me—plus an ear infection, which I haven't had since I was 12 years old, and some other virus that made my throat hurt like a raging inferno with blisters. On top of getting my butt kicked by my current ALS progression, I got an extra dose of feeling like crap. I've been pretty healthy the last three years, aside from ALS, which is a holy miracle. Last week was a raw awakening of how compromised my immune system is and the need to keep any possible virus carriers away from me. I am finally feeling better, but not without some pretty pathetic crying, which, by the way, does not help heal pinkeye.

July 16, 2017

Brian and Colleen's [family friends] wedding has been on my bucket list for a while, and we made it!

July 18, 2017

Happiest of birthdays to my favorite middle child, Anne Marie. I'm pretty sure you already knew that it was her birthday, because it's marked on your calendar as a national holiday, or at least that's what she thinks! We've always told Anne Marie her birthday means the most to her dad and me, because she is our gift from God. Anne Marie is creative, stylish, compassionate, smart, emotional—I guess that comes with being 11—and above all, she is an amazing caregiver. She helps with space pants, can reposition me in bed, suctions, pushes the feeding tube, and she used to be in charge of evening pills, when I took them orally. She says taking care of me makes her feel better. There is no doubt that when ALS has run its course and these acts of love toward me are no longer needed from my sweet Anne Marie, she will share her caring and compassionate heart in other ways.

July 21, 2017

How is Eric?

First, I offered for Eric to share this blog from a husband and caregiver perspective, but he politely declined, and I understand—plus he said I usually speak for him anyway. If you ask him how he's doing, he'll say one of two things: "We're doing the best we can" or "Hangin' in there." Since he is my husband, best friend, and caregiver, I can explain what he means.

When he says he's doing the best he can, what he really means is that it takes an enormous amount of strength to transfer me. He transfers me from bed to wheelchair and three physical transfers to get me into my power chair. All the while making sure my arms aren't flopping, my neck doesn't get whiplash, and the ports in my stomach aren't pulled. He means he's absorbing all of my household responsibilities I had as a stay-at-home mom. He means he is managing therapy appointments for our three children and himself. He means he cannot ever leave the house without making sure I'm cared for at all times. He means he's my pharmacist, managing what I take, when I take it, and how much to take. He actually became buddies with the pharmacist because he's such a regular, which if you knew my husband wouldn't surprise you. He is in charge of all of my medical equipment logistics and being prepared for the progression that is right around the corner—losing my voice and my swallow. Additionally, any time we go out, he must scope out the location ahead of time to figure out logistics for my point of entry and what ramps we need to travel with.

When says he's hangin' in there, he means he is subjected to constant bickering I can no longer help with. He means not only does he have the role of preparing to be a single father—and I know there are single parents who do this themselves all the time—but he's in a unique situation of managing the three kids and watching me deteriorate.

He means he attends a lot of functions solo because it's too much of a physical and emotional toll on me to join him. He means he is exhausted from getting up three to four times in the middle of the night to suction, change space pants, adjust my body, and make sure I'm still breathing. He means he is experiencing a type of pain that only those who have lived through it can understand where he is physically and emotionally.

He means he is struggling not to crack because my life literally is in his hands. He means that he is stressed, not only physically but emotionally watching his spouse deteriorate and the reality of what's to come is breaking his heart.

He means he misses the dream life we had pre-ALS and is sad that we won't be able to fulfill our hopes and dreams together as planned.

He means he continues to be the sole provider for our family. And while he has transitioned to working from home so he can be on call in case of an emergency, that comes with additional isolation from the positive work environment he's used to. It takes an immense amount of internal strength to face each day with the best attitude for the situation. When the tough days hit, they can be completely draining and difficult to refuel. I know he keeps a box of tissues in his Jeep because he contains his emotions until he's in the car. He is angry because we have ALS. He feels cheated because we have ALS.

So how is Eric? He's doing the best he can and hangin' in there.

July 28, 2017

Special Moment

Guest post by Suzy Mackowiak

I think most of you know that for the past two years I have been a primary caregiver for Carrey. She has been a sassy, determined fighter of ALS for the past three years.

I have many thoughts and experiences I could share about all the wacky, funny, sad, difficult, or intense times we've shared. Carrey has told me many times that I am free to share whatever I want, from my unique perspective, and I've started many blog posts in my head. But I feel most drawn to share an experience that happened last month.

One morning, I was with Carrey doing our usual morning routine. I woke her up and changed her breathing mask, and we chatted and got the day started. Her three children were out of school for summer vacation by then. So after a little time, here comes eight-year-old Colleenie Bear bouncing into the room with a smile on her face and climbs up onto the bed and flops on top of her mommy and stretches her sweet little arms around her mommy's arms. Carrey asked for a big hug, so Colleenie squeezed with all her might.

"Can you feel that, mommy?" she asks.

Carrey sighs and says, "Yes, I sure can!"

I'm standing by watching this adorable scene and I thought wait a minute; we can do better than that! I went into action. I picked up each of Carrey's paralyzed arms and wrapped them around Colleenie's back and propped them up with small pillows so they wouldn't slide off.

And there it was . . . this precious moment where mommy and daughter got to indulge in a long-missed hug that has been robbed from them since ALS came along.

The smiles on each of their faces and the love that passed between them was beautiful. I hadn't seen a smile on Carrey's face like that maybe ever. Colleenie just buried her head in her mommy's chest and absorbed the feeling of her mommy's heavy arms wrapped around her. She looked up and gazed into her mommy's eyes and they connected. Colleenie was telling her how much she loved her and how she was the best mommy. I grabbed my phone and quickly captured this precious moment. I got caught off guard and got choked up, so I quickly left the room to allow them this special time and pull myself together.

You see, I am with this family almost every day. I have been through it all with them, in the trenches as they say. I've seen it all, so nothing really fazes me; it's just our everyday life at the Deweys. But once in a while something unique stands out, and I'm so happy to have played a part to make this one a reality.

July 30, 2017

Bubbles for Carrey

My sweet Oldham County High School class of '89 friends organized "Bubbles for Carrey" in my honor. One of my favorite things about my high school years was I had tons of fun, I mean, a *ton* of fun—grades not so much. Almost 30 years later, these fun faces and big hearts haven't changed. I'm glad my kiddos had the opportunity to meet many of my classmates from middle and high school. Thanks for organizing and sharing; my kids said they'll be back next year!

August 1, 2017

Tuesday Tubby Time with Tamika and Eric and Suzy

My lips are weak; it's my best attempt at those stupid duck lips. That's okay, Tamika has enough attitude for both of us.

August 3, 2017

Sweet 16

Tomorrow Eric and I celebrate our 16th wedding anniversary. I can hardly say that without a lump in my throat and tears in my eyes. Not tears of sadness, I guess tears of appreciation because my health has held out long enough to celebrate another year with the love of my life. I know 16 isn't a milestone anniversary, but for us it's pretty significant.

Last year we had a beautiful vow renewal service in the tiny church we got married in with our children by our side. The night was perfect and honestly I thought our 15th would possibly be the last anniversary Eric and I would share. So the emotion of celebrating our 16th wedding anniversary comes with more emotion than last year.

When Eric and I married, there was no question we would celebrate our 25th silver anniversary together. He was the kind of husband I didn't know existed in the real world. We were perfect partners, and the commitment, loyalty, faith, foundation, and friendship was solid. We had both just come out of very hurtful relationships, and we also knew we would be each other's protector "until death do us part." I did the math, and if our health held up and we lived to 80, we could make it to the golden fiftieth. I had no idea that "in sickness and in health" meant I would be rejoicing to celebrate 16 years of marriage with Eric.

However, it is also bittersweet. As in any marriage, we have our ups and downs. When ALS joined our family, things changed. At first, we were a solid team, searching for treatment options and figuring out how to live with ALS. We simultaneously continued our beautiful life with our children while planning for the inevitable destruction that ALS would do to our family. Somewhere in year two, when my physical needs began to progress, so did our stress. It became a balancing act to try to maintain as much normalcy within our family along with the overwhelming obstacles and caregiving that needed to be considered to make our little party of five as strong as possible. As the past year has progressed, there is a realization that neither one of us have an endless supply of patience or answers or energy. There are plenty of times when both us are physically, mentally, and emotionally exhausted, to the point of serious breakdowns for both of us. As a result, our communication suffers, but we've definitely maintained our love, commitment, and support of one another in good times and in bad.

This year, I've watched several close couples celebrate 20, 25, 50, and even 60 years of marriage (Eric's parents). I selfishly find myself a bit bitter; we won't have that "Hooray, we made it!" moment because ALS is stealing it from us. I see these celebrations of marriage more as a celebration of life: "Hooray, you lived long enough to celebrate your big anniversaries."

Sixteen years may not be bronze, silver, or gold, but it will definitely be sweet: Bittersweet 16.

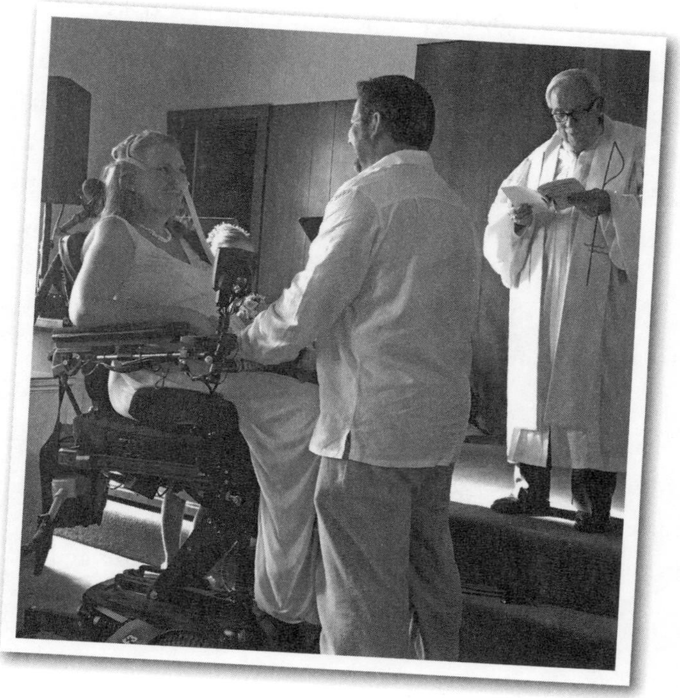

August 8, 2017

I'm considered to be in the final stages of ALS, but I am definitely not done yet! I am busier now than I've ever been, getting everything done with the help of many hands from the "comfort" of my bed.

August 11, 2017

Bedroom Bucket List Project

I've spent a lot of time making our home a place of comfort, functionality, personality, and design that reflects our family. I love to decorate! Picking out the perfect fabric, chair, or wall decor makes me happy. I take great pride in the spaces I created that reflect our loving home.

With my love of interior design, I could hardly wait until my children turned 12 so I could gift them their "big boy" and "big girl" rooms, bedrooms they would keep through high school.

I started on Ian's room a year after my diagnosis; he was 10, almost 11. I was still able to drive (well, sort of) and I shopped for the perfect pieces by myself. He went away to summer camp, and I had an entire week to put in place his "extreme bedroom makeover." I was able to shop and put together everything for his room by myself, with a few helping hands from friends to make the bed and assemble the futon.

Anne Marie had pretty high expectations. When I began her room, getting out was very difficult. I wanted to design and shop from home, but I could no longer drive or walk. Lucky for me (and Anne Marie, too), Wendy, one of my dear friends, is a brilliant and talented designer. Everything Wendy touches is amazing. She helped me select fabric, furniture, paint colors, and accessories all via text and online shopping. During Anne Marie's "reveal," she repeatedly squealed, "I didn't even know my room could look like *this*!" Those sweet words still make me smile.

Colleen, the youngest, had been trying to plead her case for me to expedite her makeover because she didn't like pink anymore. What?

Wendy and I worked quickly together along with Debbie, a talented home décor seamstress, to (1) design, plan, and order ensuring my vision for Colleen's room was in place and (2) complete the project in case ALS took me first.

I feel fortunate to have the opportunity to gift my children these spaces. Their rooms are also a representation of friendship and generosity given to me. Lots and lots of love in those bedrooms!

August 16, 2017

As of today, I have a third, fifth, and seventh grader back in school. Ian waited until the 11th hour to get his back-to-school haircut and be in compliance.

I wasn't up to get the girls fed and ready, but Suzy took care of that for me. My sister and Eric transferred me from bed to bus stop in under 11 minutes, which is usually a 30-minute task, so I was able to physically send my girls off this morning. I don't think anyone noticed I didn't have on space pants, shoes, or my dress was on backward.

August 21, 2017

Honestly, I could really care less about the eclipse today, but I didn't want to miss an opportunity to make a memory with my family. So, we joined the girls at their school today for the eclipse viewing. Been there, done that.

August 28, 2017

Overdue Physical Update

I know I am delinquent sharing a physical update on my progression of ALS. My delinquency is not because I have been too busy, too stressed, or too forgetful. My delinquency is because my ALS progression has taken a frightening turn in terms of my breathing, swallowing, and oral muscles. I could never before wrap my head around what life would be like. Now that I'm here, there are no words to adequately describe my progression, but I'll do my best.

From the neck down, I cannot move my body. I am five foot, ten inches and no idea how many of pounds of deadweight. My swallowing has slowly been compromised over the last year. I was able to manage eating by staying away from mixed consistencies, using extra swallows, taking smaller bites, and staying away from tough foods that I can't mash down. Eating has not been a problem until a few months ago, when I began choking consistently on foods. Big red flag here!

My palliative care doctor stressed to both Eric and me the importance of beginning to use my feeding tube on a regular basis, especially if I wanted to see Bruno Mars in September . . . and so we have. I can still eat, but only soft textured foods that I can basically puree in my mouth or moist foods that are not gritty or grainy, and definitely no dry foods. No more dairy, because it creates too much mucous, causing me to choke. I have to concentrate intensely when I eat. To help force food into my esophagus and not my airway, my head and chin must be in a "chin tuck" position when I swallow. The hardest part of all, for me at least, I cannot talk while eating. I know you are not supposed to talk with food in your mouth anyway, but when it takes me two minutes to puree and swallow one bite, I usually have something I want to chime in. I am absolutely not complaining because I can still eat some foods, but only my absolute favorites. Otherwise, it's a can of feeding tube formula poured in a bag, dripped through a tube and into my stomach. Many, or even most people at this stage in their ALS progression, are depending entirely on the feeding tube for nutrition and hydration, so I can't complain.

I am 100 percent dependent on the Trilogy machine to breathe and have been for a little over a year now. My face and head have developed a rash from constantly wearing a mask 24/7. Again, how could I complain when the Trilogy is literally keeping me alive by breathing for me? It is definitely a love-hate relationship.

My speech is changing daily. I talk like I'm drunk, slurring my words most of the time. So, I guess if I were drunk, you wouldn't really know. If I am tired, you will likely have a hard time understanding me. But if I am well rested, I have a slight slur and sound nasally and quiet.

Emotionally, being physically stuck is increasingly frustrating. I am either stuck in my bed or stuck in my wheelchair. I can't do the things I would like to do, like everything you would do with your hands, legs, or feet. Forget it! Even the simplest of tasks, like adjusting my foot in bed, turning my neck when I want to look away, or wiggling my body just enough to divert a bug crawling off me. When I ask for help outside of my caregiving team, people often do not understand what I am saying, or they will just look at me, smile, and politely shake their head. My family, along with my caregiving team, continues to do a kick-ass job of trying to keep me comfortable and not on the brink of a complete meltdown, but sometimes there is nothing they can do, except wipe my tears and suction my snot.

Every patient progresses differently, so all things considered, if I had to choose my course of progression, having my speech and swallowing go last is not so bad.

September 4, 2017

My high school squad—some girls I've known since elementary and middle school. They know all my secrets, bad decisions, every boyfriend I've ever had . . . and they still love me. For our girls' trip this year, it was sangria and a sleepover in my bedroom.

Thanks, ladies, for coming into town and spreading the love!

September 6, 2017

Photos are not going to do this priceless gift justice. My friend Batt's mother, Mary, is truly the Queen of Quilting. I turned over nine of my favorite Lilly Pulitzer dresses to Mary and in return, she gave me the most beautiful and detailed quilt imaginable. The girls will have to figure out later who's going to own the blanket, but for now it's all mine. I'm enjoying the labor of love and warm memories that comfort me with this quilt, and the girls are enjoying pointing out their dresses in the quilt.

September 14, 2017

It's been an infirmary over here at the Dewey household. Between my stomach pains and intermittent fever, Anne Marie developing something that resembles appendicitis (a full day of testing in the hospital ruled that out), and Eric's gallbladder attack Sunday night with minimal recovery, it's been a real shit show over here, to say the least. I finally called Eric's doctor, and his parents to take him to the doctor, and guess what? He won the award yesterday as most severe: "Do not pass Go. Go straight to the hospital for immediate surgery!" This is a surgery we knew Eric needed, but we were trying to wait until he was no longer caring for me. Surgery went well with no complications, but his recovery may take a little longer due to the size of the stones. The good news is our children are very well trained in caregiving, and Eric and I will be spending a lot of time together in bed.

September 16, 2017

I now know why I haven't felt well and why I've run a fever for five days; I have pneumonia. It doesn't sound serious, but pneumonia is a leading cause of death in ALS patients. Any respiratory infection at all for a person with ALS is life threatening. We caught my pneumonia early, due in large part to a concierge medical group that I transitioned to as my primary care physician six months ago, allowing me access to in-home diagnostic testing, like chest X-rays.

I started strong antibiotics yesterday morning and feel better already. Eric declined the doctor's offer to stay another night in the hospital and was home to celebrate Ian's birthday with us. He's moving slowly, but definitely on the mend. Ian had a great 13th birthday yesterday, and we're still planning to see Bruno Mars on Tuesday with some accommodations.

September 20, 2017

Bruno Mars was awesome last night and not just because it was Bruno! Last night was *way* more than seeing him perform live, it was about the date on the ticket. I purchased our tickets in November—which is an eternity ago given my prognosis. I knew whether I was here or not, my family would know I bought the tickets for them. Last night was no doubt an awesome show and Bruno even got my toes to wiggle a bit, but it was even more awesome because I made it to the date on the ticket!

September 22, 2017

Seven days after I was diagnosed with ALS, our dear family friend, Ryann Tewell, was struck and killed by a cement truck in a pedestrian-vehicle accident. Her death was a painful and gut-wrenching reminder that we don't always have a heads-up when our time is near. My mom came to celebrate my birthday at my house and the next day died of respiratory failure. A few months later, my brother lost his long, hard-fought battle with severe depression. Two months ago, I received a care package from my aunt, and four days later, she went to bed and died in her sleep. There were no good-byes for anybody, and lives were left shattered. The reality is unfair and heartbreaking. I guess I have a unique perspective because I know what is going to end my life. These heartbreaking losses are a deep reminder that we don't know when we will be called home, not even me.

September 27, 2017

Hello and Good-bye

Adios, space pants; hello, catheter. I always try not to look too far ahead so I really didn't put much thought into when or if I would need a permanent solution to my tinkling issues. After numerous sheet changes, leaking space pants, and not wanting to ask "sitters" to help me with my girly parts, I knew I was getting close. It wasn't until the Bruno Mars concert when I sat in my soaking wet, urine-saturated space pants for the entire show, I realized it was time—probably past time. The "Why Dewey Run" was my inaugural outing with my newest equipment, a catheter. I know it's going to make caring for me easier on my caregivers and more sterile for me, but the thought of having a tube shoved up my girly parts the rest of my life is a mind-blowing reality of the destruction ALS continues to do to my body. Eric's mom quickly made a catheter cover for me to hide my urine bag, so I hope you'll never have to see it.

Now when we transfer it's: "Watch my feeding tube port!" "Watch my pacer wires!" "Watch my catheter tubing and pee bag!" The good news is I'm able to stay more hydrated through the feeding tube and out the catheter.

September 28, 2017

My doctor ordered a second round of antibiotics when my follow-up X-ray showed my lungs were not completely clear. Nurse Stacey came five days in a row to administer my second antibiotic by injection. Colleen held my hand tightly in case the shot hurt; little did she know I already had four injections. Her concern was heartfelt.

I have a feeling Nurse Stacy and I are going to become good buddies because she's managing my catheter, too.

Side note to the ladies—you know what two rounds of antibiotics back to back get you? Yep, I got it.

September 29, 2017

And they are off! Ian and Anne Marie and Poppa Joe are headed to the Hope Loves Company, Inc. retreat. Poppa Joe is their escort but will also be chaperoning at the retreat as well. I am excited for them to have an adventure and bonding experience with other children who are going through, or have been through, a unique life-changing ALS experience with their parents. Colleen is staying home with me because she just "can't bear to be gone that far away" from me. Prayerful for a good weekend for everybody.

October 3, 2017

Team Tuesday

Eric's recent surgery has put him on the bench in terms of lifting me. Eric and Liz were the only two who could lift my deadweight. Not just because they're strong, but because they understood what they had to maneuver around. You can't lift under my arms because my shoulders and arms are separated. You have to watch out for my feeding tube port and my pacer wires. You must make sure my air supply doesn't get knocked off, and now we have to watch out for the long tube coming out my girly parts. Lifting me really is a logistical nightmare. It's long overdue, but we started transitioning to the Hoyer Lift. The Hoyer Lift is like a human crane, only I feel more like a beached whale. It definitely takes some getting used to. We've certainly had our near disasters that put two of my friends in tears, but I think we're starting to figure it out.

October 4, 2017

I was feeling really puny yesterday; everything hurt. Infections were not cleared up yet. My friend was visiting with Colleen in my bedroom and she asked, "Who's the boss of your family?"

Colleen replied, "My mom."

Yep, I still got it!

October 6, 2017

The big kids came home Monday after a fun-filled weekend retreat with Hope Loves Company, Inc. My dad traveled with the kids and volunteered at the retreat as a chaperone, which meant I got nightly reports and lots of pictures, and people old and young got a loving dose of Poppa Joe. Ian and Anne Marie really had a great time, they met a few people they heard me talk about before and connected with some families that we had met through the DC advocacy and Inheritance of Hope Legacy Retreat. Ian and Anne Marie appreciated connecting with other children who have experienced the same emotions and unique situations they have had while sharing in a fun-filled, high-adventure, action-packed weekend. Hopefully my kids, including Colleen, will return to another retreat. Thank you, Hope Loves Company, for your priceless gift to our family.

October 7, 2017

Following my bout with pneumonia three weeks ago, I continue to be abnormally tired and experience pain in my left side underneath my rib cage and on my side. Lying flat on my back is excruciatingly painful, as well as being turned or rolled on my left side. After two rounds of heavy antibiotics and three X-rays over three weeks with minimal change, we—as in my sister and Suzy—knew we were dealing with more than pneumonia.

At my sister's urging, we requested more blood work. The blood work came back with an elevated D-dimer level, and I needed testing beyond X-rays, specifically a CT scan to eliminate any concern of a blood clot in my lung or a collapsed lung. The scan could not be done at home, only in the hospital. At this point, we reached out to my pulmonologist. His team was able to schedule a CT scan immediately and have the radiology report read urgently.

The process was fairly painless but imagine transferring a paralyzed person with a ventilator and a catheter to lay flat on a CT table. Of course, Eric and Liz helped with the transfer, which definitely eased my anxiety. I wanted to get a group photo for my blog, but nobody, including Eric or Liz, was agreeable while they transferred me.

The doctor walked in and said, "Well, you were right. You have bilateral pulmonary emboli." My sister replied with the f-bomb. I'm a dumbass and don't know any medical verbiage, so I asked what that meant. He explained, "Blood clots in both lungs." To which I replied with the f-bomb. The results took my sister by surprise because she thought we may be dealing with the possibility of one clot in the left lung, not multiple clots in both lungs.

Honestly, this is the first time since accepting my ALS diagnosis that I've been scared. The clots are little, but many. He said we are really lucky we caught the clotting early, and he put me on a new blood thinner to hopefully avoid any further clots and allow my body to absorb the little clots. Knowing my wishes and desire to stay out of the hospital, he allowed me to go home. At this point, there's really not much more I can do other than take the medicine and pray it works.

The results took me off guard because I'm worried about CO2 poisoning, aspiration, aspiration pneumonia, suffocation, equipment failure, a big drop down the steps with the Hoyer, or my lungs being over-ventilated and just giving out. I had aspirin in my cocktail of medication, so I never considered a blood clot. The good news is we caught the clotting early, I'm able to rest in the comfort of my own home with my own caregiving team, and my pulmonologist has great confidence in the new drug . . . and he lives right around the corner from me.

October 11, 2017

After three weeks, I'm finally starting to feel a tad better. My body seems to be absorbing the small clots in my lungs. It's a good thing I have a catheter because I can see exactly what is being excreted from my body. It was kind of scary at first because the urine was dark and bloody. But we closely monitored it and were sure to push a little extra water through my feeding tube.

When Colleen first came in and saw how abnormally dark and red my urine was in the catheter bag, she lectured me on making sure I got enough water in my feeding tube, followed by, "Dad, did you see mom's tinkle bag?" Even Colleen was concerned.

The next step we are working on with my doctor is getting the new medication covered. It was denied by insurance and will cost $600 out of pocket if not appealed. Hopefully, jumping a few hoops and some documentation will take care of that, and we'll keep moving onward!

October 12, 2017

Why Colleen Runs

The week following the "Why Dewey Run?" fund-raiser, Colleen had a cross-country meet that neither Eric nor I could attend. Colleen has great form and no shortage of energy, but she lacked motivation in her cross-country career. She would often hang in the back so she could chit-chat with the slower runners, deeming her a slower runner herself.

Not last Saturday! Colleen was so excited to earn her first medal of the season. I received lots of photos and compliments about her performance, and I was so proud of her for her amazing effort. And she was proud of her medal.

That night, we finally lay down together and when we were both almost asleep, Colleen quietly chanted, "When your legs hurt, what do you say? I'm running for mommy 'cause she can't run. When your lungs hurt, what do you say? I'm running for mommy 'cause she can't breathe."

I looked at Eric with confusion, wondering where this verbal pep talk came from, and he replied, "If you have cramps in your side, what do you do?" And Colleen mumbled, half asleep, "You breathe deeper and keep moving, 'cause mommy can't."

I was so moved and taken aback by my Colleenie's authentic inspiration to run for me. I would never have known if it weren't for her quiet chant in bed with me before we fell asleep.

October 14, 2017

Why Dewey Run?

"Let us pray. Oh, God, this is indeed the day you have made. And by inspiration, others have been moved by the meaning and purpose of this event, and many have made the decision to be here in this moment. Bless them. May the walk and the run be one that touches their hearts as they realize that what they are doing is an act of compassion and care for the Dewey family in their journey that has altered their lives and their hopes and their dreams. This is the day that you have made, and we will rejoice and be glad in it. Amen."

—The Reverend James Dewey, Eric's father, September 24, 2017

And what a beautiful day it was to rejoice and be glad. Boy, did we rejoice at the love and support that circled us! Eric and I waited 100 yards before the finish line to cheer, give high fives, and listen to people shout why they were running. Such awesome moments! We felt so blessed to be lifted by the many loving communities who joined together to make this inaugural family run an unbelievable success.

Huge thanks to Kathy Klopp, who not only ran the Boston Marathon in my honor last April, but came home and said, "I want to put a race together for you: 'Why Dewey Run.'" It definitely sounded like a huge undertaking, but I agreed because it sounded like fun, which is what we are all about. Boy, did I underestimate the power of her determination.

Thank you to the 600-plus registered runners and walkers, I don't know how many leashed dogs, 40-plus volunteers, our sponsors, our numerous financial donors, our in-kind donors: Chick-fil-A Middletown Commons, Kroger, Derby City Timing/Races, Jack Tiesing Graphic Design, Louisville Water Company, Walmart Middletown, DJ Mike Ballard, and photographer Becky Ennis. Most of all, I want to thank Kathy Klopp, Coach Krohn, Krista Bradon, Steve Brown, and the many Team Dewey members who helped with the details and execution. Hopefully next year's race will be for ALS survivors celebrating the cure.

October 15, 2017

Worship for Why Dewey Run 3K Race

Led by Reverend James A. Dewey

"This is the day that the Lord has made; let us rejoice and be glad in it."

Welcome to the Why Dewey Run 3K event. This run/walk is to honor Carrey Dewey who has been battling amyotrophic lateral sclerosis (ALS) for over three years, to raise awareness and raise funds for Team Dewey and Project ALS. Walkers, runners, leashed dogs, and strollers, you are all welcome here today, and we are absolutely delighted that you have chosen to be here in support of Team Dewey and Carrey. We give our thanks to the planners, organizers, and sponsors of this event. And too, we give thanks for Team Dewey and their constant, compassionate, and caring support of Carrey and her family. They are remarkable.

Why Dewey Run 3K event? The funds raised for this event today will be shared with Project ALS, which continues to research and seek a hoped-for cure for this devastating disease. And the fund will also be shared with Team Dewey in support of medical expenses for Carrey. By Carrey's and Eric's invitation, I have been asked to share with you some worship moments before the race and walk begins. I'm deeply humbled and honored to be standing here this morning with all of you.

From the beginning of humankind's adventure on this earth, people have been running and walking for some purpose and event in their lives. Whether it was to gather food for survival or to bring messages from battlefields of the news of defeat or victory to their villages and towns. Then too, the ancient Greeks, long ago, created sporting events, which included all matter of running and walking and now have evolved into what we know as the modern-day Olympics. The human race has been racing for a long time. Today, we are aware of many, many weekend races and walks that are focused around all matter of causes, cares, and concerns. There are events for heart disease, cancer, mental illness, and the races go on and on. A number of you here today have participated in those events.

The Dewey event today is no different in some respects to other races and walks, but in others it is unique. As shared earlier, funds from this race will be given to the research arm of Project ALS. As every family and every person in this very moment of suffering and living with ALS knows, there is no cure; they know the devastating and crippling power of this terrible disease firsthand. It's ending is non-negotiable.

Let's reflect on this for a moment. Do you remember a number of years ago when Martin Luther King gave his "I have a dream speech?" Well, every day in a person's life with ALS and in every moment of a family walking this terrible road, they too have a dream. A dream that one day, as a researcher is looking into that high-powered microscope and sees the enemy ALS swimming around in that slide, they see something never seen before—a breakthrough. They discover the cause and how this disease is given birth. They rejoice. Now they know how to begin to work for a cure, an actual life-saving cure. That is their dream. And today the money that is donated by you and your sponsors for this research may hasten the day when this dream of a cure comes into reality. Our dream, my dream, the Dewey family dream is that a cure will be found, and someday soon, there will be runs and walks for the survivors of ALS. What a dream that is . . . and our prayer is: O God make it true, make it true.

Now the unique part of this walk and race is that Team Dewey will receive the other half of the donations made to help Carrey with the mounting medical expenses. Each new day for her is also another day of special need and care, which these funds will help provide. And another unique reality about this race is the life, the witness, and the sharing of Carrey Robinson Dewey.

When this life-threatening disease entered her life, she made a determination that she would not just wait for this disease to take its course. She made many decisions. She would be an educator about this disease as it affects her life, and she would be a spokesperson to people in government and other places about the need for money for research and development of a cure and the production of medication.

She also, with her husband, Eric, worked on their bucket list and wanted those experiences for their family before the disease became too advanced. She chose to write about her feelings, her emotions, her wrestling in both mind and heart with what was happening to her daily. She knew the course before her, but she has never stopped fighting, she has never given in to its power.

Her spirit has soared, touching the lives of all of us and many more through the Internet and her writings on Facebook, which reveal her true self in raw emotions and a deep abiding spirit. She has never lost faith in the future going past what others thought impossible . . . from doctors' predictions, even to buying tickets last November to the Bruno Mars concert that she and her family attended last Tuesday evening.

Carrey, you have been and continue to be an inspiration to more people than you ever imagined. A little over 16 years ago, when you stood before me and shared your wedding vows with each other, not one person there ever dreamed that where you are now would have been your journey. But there is no doubt in any of our minds that when you and Eric said to each other: "I give myself to you, to be your wife and your husband. I promise to love you and sustain you in the covenant of marriage from this day forward, in sickness and in health, in plenty and in want, in joy and in sorrow as long as we shall both live" that your life together would you lead you to this place this morning.

Eric and Carrey, by your love for each other, your constant care and support of each other, you have raised very high the meaning of these words. They are not empty phrases but the beautiful fulfillment of your commitment and love for each other. You have laid a very meaningful foundation of what marriage is even in the midst of this terrible disease.

Rabbi Kushner a few years ago authored a book entitled, *Why Bad Things Happen to Good People*. One of his main conclusions was that, "at times life is unfair." It has been unfair in your life, Carrey, for you, Eric, your children Ian, Anne Marie, and Colleen, and your immediate families and extended families. You and your family have become the beautiful expressions of three specific verses of scripture: From the Hebrew Bible, the Prophet Isaiah says, "How beautiful upon the mountains are the feet of the messenger who announces peace, who brings good news, who announces salvation, who says to Zion, 'Your God reigns.'"

From the book of Acts 20:24: "But I do not count my life of any value to myself, if only I may finish my course and the ministry that I received from the Lord Jesus, to testify to the good news of God's grace."

And, from the letter II Timothy 4:7: "I am fighting the good fight, I am finishing the race, I have kept the faith."

The Dewey family, their faith, their endurance, their sharing of life with so many has been an inspiration and has lifted the lives and touched the hearts of more than we can count. They have been a family of good news in the midst of their difficult journey.

Now runners and walkers, it's your turn to begin the Why Dewey Run 3K race. Know that every step you take and every pace you set to run, is your gift of compassion and care for the Dewey family. Your presence here today is your witness of knowing the beauty of life and love that is being expressed by the Dewey family. So run and walk with joy. And as it is said in Hebrews 12:1, "Therefore, since we are surrounded by so great a cloud of witnesses, let us also lay aside every weight . . . that clings so closely, and let us run with perseverance the race that is set before us."

This the day the Lord has made, let each of us rejoice and be glad in it. Amen.

October 17, 2017

The only heartache worse than having ALS is to watch your own child slowly lose their hopes, dreams, and life to this disease.

A little over a year ago, a reader named Jennifer reached out to me through Facebook. She shared her ALS story with me as many readers do. Once you have ALS in your family, you instantly share a bond with other ALS families. Jennifer's daughter, Katherine Grace, had ALS and she shared with me qualities her daughter and I had in common. I could hear her sweet mom's heartbreaking pain through her words.

Today would have been Katherine Grace's golden birthday—17 on the 17th. Jennifer's courageous daughter was no exception to the reality of ALS. Her beautiful, once very active 16-year-old passed away last week from juvenile ALS, a year and four months after being diagnosed. Katherine Grace's mysterious symptoms started almost a year before her diagnosis as a tiny limp that was thought to have been from a dance injury as she danced three days a week for several hours at a time. But in the end, she was dealt the heartbreaking reality of a rare form of juvenile ALS.

There are no exceptions with ALS, not even age. As her mom said, it's a "brutal, relentless, non-discriminating beast of a disease."

Happy golden birthday in heaven, Katherine Grace.

October 20, 2017

Big Decision

I have enormous anxiety right now sharing so publicly what will be my most personal and private post. Since I signed on to educate and advocate for a cure or treatment for ALS through my Facebook blog, I would be doing other ALS patients an injustice not to share the big decision most of us have to make.

From the very beginning of my journey, before I even knew much about the fatal disease I had been diagnosed with, I said all of my decisions will be made in the best interest of my family. I choose to be cared for at home with my family, which means we must pay for care privately out of pocket; insurance only pays for caregiving if I move to a nursing home. Due to the generosity of our community, we believe we can sustain this as long as I'm able to breathe on the Trilogy machine, which is a noninvasive ventilator doing all of my breathing for me through a mask I wear on my nose. Once the airway is no longer clear, ALS patients have to make a decision if they want a tracheotomy, an invasive ventilator that is surgically planted into the windpipe. When this happens, patients lose their voices, if ALS hasn't already stolen that ability. They need a higher skilled level of care, and most significantly, emergency trips and stays in the hospital are more common than not. Fewer than 10 percent of ALS patients choose to have a tracheotomy.

There's nobody that doesn't want to live life more than me. To be around to mother my children through life's celebrations and inevitable heartaches, to guide them down their paths to adulthood. To continue my dream life and love story with my husband of 16 years and watch my children grow up living on the same street with my sister and her family. But I also just watched my sister and dad care for my mom through multiple hospital stays where we always had a family member or caregiver stay with her. I watched the physical and emotional toll it took on both of them. Although I know they would do it all again without complaint, that's not what I want for my family. So I have chosen to forego the tracheotomy surgery, the surgical life support.

There are lots of patients with ALS, even ones reading this blog, who would say they have a full life on a trache. My decision is based on my own personal experience; it's not what I want for my family and I certainly don't want to live in a nursing home. I hope this decision won't affect the near future because I am in the middle of some big projects, though with ALS, things can change overnight. As always, I appreciate everybody's love and support in this very personal and private decision.

October 26, 2017

ALS from the Outside

ALS is a mean, ugly, destructive disease. Not only has ALS destroyed the insides of my body, it has been physically destructive on the outside, as well.

Since I lost my ability to walk, my toes have become locked in a curled position. My stomach has lost all of its muscle wall. Because I am ventilated 24/7, a lot of air is trapped. We've had my stomach X-rayed several times, and the number of air pockets inside me is surreal. And a lot of the distention is from chronic constipation. It hurts. My stomach can become so stretched and hard that it is painful, and not only causes ugly stretch marks, but they protrude and hurt. I call them big fat worms—I know it's gross, but that's really how they look and feel . . . or so I am told because I can't touch them. I have hair loss and even blisters at times on my scalp from where the strap on my mask rubs. My face and fingers are always swollen, but that may be from medication. There is no muscle or fat on my shins—they are literally skin and bones. My fingers look like that of a corpse because the webbing between them has atrophied. I know this is trivial, but my nasal mask has stretched out my nostrils until they are as large as a raging bull's. But it doesn't hurt. I usually have some sort of red mark or blister on the bridge of my nose from my night mask.

These physical changes have not occurred all at once but have taken their toll over time. Honestly, I don't look in the mirror anymore. I got my hair cut two inches on Friday and I've yet to see it. I'm okay with that, because I know what is really me is in my heart and in my mind. ALS can't—I mean won't—destroy either.

The one physical benefit from ALS I have inherited is soft hands and strong healthy nails. I guess that's the one perk, if you can call it that, from being paralyzed by ALS.

P.S. I'll spare you the photos on this post!

November 5, 2017

We've been really careful about maintaining the integrity of my skin: making sure to elevate my heels off the bed, change positions, place a mountain of pillows under my arms, and put protective barrier cream on my tushy. Eric has said, "There will be no pressure sores on my watch!" Although I've had a few, we have caught them early through the daily skin checks. When my tailbone started hurting, I started sleeping on my side (which isn't the most comfortable since my shoulder is separated from my arm). Pressure sores are very common with any disease that keeps someone in bed or in a wheelchair. So, we've been keeping a close eye on my heels, tushy and elbows, but the thought of a pressure sore on my ear never crossed my mind. But sure enough, a nasty pressure sore on my ear cartilage has yielded yet another side effect of ALS.

I found the perfect solution. I was able to purchase an ear pillow—who even knew those existed? So the good news is now I have this awesome pillow that looks like a PacMan ghost! It's my new best friend.

November 15, 2017

I've been out of the house a few times in the last two weeks and the biggest difference I've noticed is not a change with me but a change with my peers. The lack of eye contact or even a simple greeting. I know not to take this personally. People don't know how to act around me or the amount of equipment I travel with can look overwhelming. I know I look funny, talk funny, walk funny . . . oh wait, I don't walk anymore. I get it.

My mind and brain are exactly the same. It's hard enough not being able to contribute or participate as I had done so passionately before ALS. I know you're uncomfortable, I understand. But when you avoid looking at me, I notice. When you don't say hello to me, you make me feel different. I know it's not intentional, but it still hurts.

So my public service announcement from all disabled people is: Please don't fear me. Please don't ignore me. Please don't treat me like I'm invisible. Please see beyond all the equipment and oddities and help me feel normal by at least acknowledging my presence as I would do to you.

November 25, 2017

I'm not gonna lie. November has been a difficult month physically and emotionally. As my breathing becomes shallower and my speech becomes much softer and slurred, my anxiety levels are heightened. There are times I wake up and I have tears rolling out of my eyes before they're even open, *but* I am able to calm my anxiety by focusing on my blessings. While ALS has robbed me of so many abilities we all take for granted, "There is still more good than bad," as my dad always says.

I am thankful to still have my voice, even though it is softer and a bit slurred.

I am thankful for my breathing machine, which truly is my life support.

I am thankful for FaceTime allowing me to be virtually present with my children.

I am thankful for my ultra-patient, passionate, MacGyver husband; there is no doubt I am still alive today because of his care.

I am thankful for our communities who have held our hands, and at times, have carried us in our journey—Stopher Elementary, Saint Patrick Catholic School, Epiphany Catholic Church, Saint Patrick Catholic Church, Lake Forest neighborhood, Cardinal Aquatics Swim Team, Stopher Cross-Country Team, and Oldham County Alumni.

I am thankful for my medical team who have allowed me to manage most of my medical care from home.

I'm thankful for my nurse case manager who helps me navigate ridiculous insurance roadblocks.

I'm thankful for my sister and her sweet family for moving right next to me so she can be right there by my side, tending to both my physical and emotional needs.

I'm thankful for my Carrey Care friends who cover a daily portion of my caregiving needs, even as my progression takes an emotional toll on them.

I'm thankful for my dad who will drop everything and do anything for me and his unwavering commitment, not just to me, but to my family.

I'm thankful for my faith allowing me to trust, to accept God's gifts, and walk without fear.

I'm thankful for my caregivers Brittani Dodgeball, Bossy Suzy, Karlee Fries, and Becky Tiptoe, who far exceed their job descriptions.

I'm thankful for the ALS community, which continues to provide unique friendships, problem-solving, and support.

I'm thankful for the many gifts and donations of time and talent we have received: from meals to quilt making, family photos to scrapbooking, and teddy bear making to baking with my girls.

I'm thankful for my Hosparus team, who provide medical consultation, therapy, bathing, and hand-holding.

I'm thankful for my medical fund, which allows our family to focus on living and not the overwhelming financial burden that comes to all people diagnosed with ALS.

I'm thankful for my spacious bedroom, also known as our family apartment, with a beautiful view that allows me to be comfortable and see God's beauty from my window.

I'm thankful for my three healthy children who show compassion toward me I didn't know was possible at their ages.

I'm thankful for Facebook giving me a platform to share our journey with ALS authentically. This gives me purpose in the midst of my devastating disease.

I'm thankful for *you*, my Facebook followers, who have taken the time and interest to become educated on ALS.

When I run through my blessings, I'm able to settle my anxiety and be grateful for all I still have because there is still more good than bad.

November 28, 2017

Help me wish the happiest of birthdays to this guy! I've always called Eric my dream husband. I've never taken for granted his love, compassion, intelligence, ultra-patience, work ethic, faith, leadership, determination, friendship, and humor—even though it's on the geeky side. Eric wears an ALS awareness bracelet that reads "(A)lways (L)ove (S)trong," and that he has certainly done.

Happy birthday, Dewey. I love you!

December 1, 2017

Since Eric's surgery in September, we have been transferring solely with the Hoyer Lift—basically a human crane. The Hoyer is obviously big, bulky equipment, and I was not looking forward to the transition. I don't like change, which by the way, ALS is a disastrous disease if you struggle with change. Anyways, the transition was long overdue. I think we finally worked out the kinks, so the fear factor is removed.

December 3, 2017

Yesterday I turned 46. I can't tell you how good it was to wake up and to have aged one year overnight! It's a birthday I prayed I would see, but honestly, the odds have been definitely stacked against me, so it made this number even more beautiful. My friends wanted to host a party for me, but we did that last year, and it was perfect. My party days are over. I have anxiety with crowds. If there are more than four people in a room, you can't hear me, and I'm always uncomfortable unless I'm in my bed. I told them no party, no open house, but if anyone wants to stop by and wish me happy birthday, my bed will be open . . . as it usually is.

With that, "I don't want a party or an open house," Lisa and Krista decorated my room like a magical winter wonderland, stocked it with delicious cocktails, and helped me roll out the welcome mat. I thought maybe five or ten people would stop by, but it was a few more than that. Yesterday was the most amazing "I'm *not* having an open house or a party" birthday I've ever had.

Forty-six plus a day feels *so* good!

December 7, 2017

Best Gift Ever!

One of my biggest problems right now is my speech. I have been diagnosed with dysarthria. Sounded kind of scary, until I learned it was just a medical word for good old-fashioned slurred speech—another perk of having ALS. For the most part, you can usually understand most of what I am saying—but you have pay close attention, and you have to be right next to me with no background noise because my voice is definitely soft. Crowds, even small crowds, give me anxiety, which makes me feel I am not getting enough air . . . a real problem when breathing on a mechanical device.

So what do get your friend who talks like she's a quiet drunk? A microphone and speaker like Lady Gaga has, of course, so she can talk like a loud drunk. I first used it on Saturday, and it was such a blessing. I could ask for help and be heard, I could be part of a conversation, and I did not have any anxiety with my birthday visitors. It doesn't take away the slurred, drunken speech, but that's okay, I have a good excuse.

December 11, 2017

Damn, Sam. My handicap van has a total jinx on me. Three weeks ago, we were out, and I almost suffocated to death in my minivan because my breathing machine was almost out of power—more on that one later. Last week we went out to get our Christmas trees, and they fell off the top of our car in the middle of the expressway. Last night, we went out and a damn deer head butted the side of the handicap van. My last three outings have all been jinxed. I wonder if God is sending me a message I should stay home where I am comfortable and safe with all of my needed equipment.

Now I am officially without transportation. I am a true shut-in until my handicap van gets fixed. I really don't have anywhere to go but the thought of being stuck at home makes me a tad anxious. Damn, Sam!

December 13, 2017

My speech has changed significantly within the last month. My tongue and lips are muscles and they are growing increasingly weaker because of ALS. My lips can no longer form a seal around a straw and my tongue has a difficult time moving food around in my mouth, even the smallest of bites. Those are the things you won't notice though. What you will notice is my slurred, drunk-sounding speech, thanks to my weak tongue and lips.

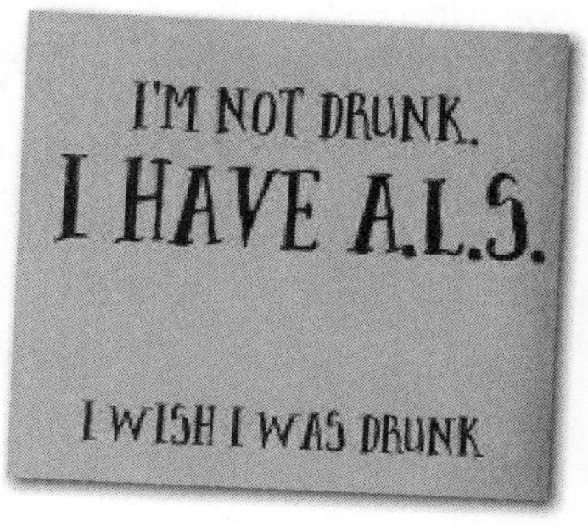

December 25, 2017

My best Christmas gift was hearing all three of my babes in the bell choir on Christmas Eve alongside their church friends they met in the nursery. They've been playing together the last several years. Colleen was too young last year, so I especially considered this year a miraculous gift I'm so thankful to see. Merry Christmas from our little party of five.

December 30, 2017

I've had a bit of anxiety the last few days over the scheduled loss of a fellow ALS patient who lives eight minutes from my home. He was diagnosed with ALS a year before me, but my progression has been faster than his. We were both paralyzed, but I know my breathing, swallowing, and speech were more compromised than his.

So what exactly does scheduled death mean? It's actually more common than you would think. ALS patients, usually under the care of a hospice medical team, are medicated to induce a coma and then the breathing machine mask is slipped off, letting them die peacefully on their own terms without feeling the reality of suffocating. I can't imagine making that decision, but I certainly understand why patients would choose that option. ALS is brutal, its relentless, it's painfully destructive and can take an extreme toll on your mental and emotional state. Not just a toll on yourself but on your family and caregivers, as well. The difference between me and my neighbor is the support our family has received. We have an abundance and always tried to share with him. I was personally touched when my friends and family put their faith in action and saw ALS beyond me: sharing a massage, donating restaurant gift cards, making him a meal, donating to his fund-raiser, helping with his broken van, and sharing any virtual resources we uncovered. I was very proud when Team Dewey reached out to him without knowing him.

I've lost several ALS friends, but his loss hurts a little more because I knew him personally and felt I was taking him under my wing, sharing my abundance. In the end, ALS was bigger than any support we could provide.

2018

January 2, 2018

Yep, you all were right! I have a very painful case of shingles. What started as blisters on my scalp has now also become blisters in my mouth and throat and on my neck.

I need all of my energy to fight ALS, not shingles. I'll keep you posted.

January 5, 2018

What I Don't Share about ALS

In my efforts to advocate and educate I have chosen to be very public about the good, bad, and ugly of ALS, even though sharing too much information makes me feel vulnerable. Honestly, for as much as I share, there is just as much I don't share because the reality is horrific and really is *way* too much information.

What I don't share about ALS because it's TMI is:

How I hang in the Hoyer Lift over a bucket to have a bowel moment.

Or how when I'm in bed, I'm wearing a cut tank top and nothing else for potty purposes.

Or how Eric has had to manage my menstrual cycle, which started a few months ago once I started taking blood thinners.

Or how the saying "you can pick your friends, you can pick your nose, but you can't pick your friend's nose"—does not apply with ALS patients.

Or how Eric and my sister, Liz, maintain the hygiene of my girly parts.

Or how the intimacy between my husband and I has drastically changed.

Or how we manage a real mess in my bed when I took too many laxatives after 10 days of no BM.

Or how my hemorrhoid problem has gotten out of control.

Or how my devoted husband or sister have to manually stimulate or retrieve my bowel movement because I have no push muscles.

Yep, way TMI, but these are just some of the harsh realities of ALS.

January 9, 2018

Hip, hip, hooray! I made it to both girls' cheer competitions on Sunday. Just as we were ready to roll out the door, I had the need for an urgent bowel movement, making me not only late, but a little traumatized by having my first bowel movement in my wheelchair. The good news is, my chair reclines in all sorts of crazy positions making it possible . . . not pretty, not comfortable, not easy, and definitely no dignity, but possible.

I promised my girls I wanted to be at the competition. I promised I would try my hardest to be there. I just can't promise my kids anymore I will be somewhere. I can only promise my children I'll try. By the looks of their sweet, sweet faces, they were happy I gave it my all . . . or maybe their smiles are from taking first place and grand champs!

January 11, 2018

I am preparing to lose my speech. Twenty percent of ALS patients lose their speech first. It's called Bulbar Onset.

So how can you actually prepare to lose your speech? Many ALS patients record thirty or more hours of their spoken language to get a computer to generate a synthesized version of their own voice. I've tried this, but after two hours I was done. So, step one for me was to write down all of my needs in current phrases into my Tobii Dynavox. This computer has eye tracking, allowing me to type and communicate with my eyes. I always thought speech loss was far off in the future and didn't want to think about it.

The good news is I'm still here. The bad news is I have to learn to communicate with my eyes, now, not later. My IT department assembled and set up my Eyegaze and helped me program my needed sayings.

Looks like ALS might steal my speech, but it will never steal my voice.

January 12, 2018

This photo came across my Facebook feed yesterday, giving me a glimpse back in time to six years ago.

Usually when these photos appear, I smile and appreciate the goodness, and usually the cute clothing they still let me dress them in. But this photo felt different. I loved this time in our life: I really felt like our little family of five was just getting started. Ian was in first grade, Anne Marie in preschool, and Colleen attended one day a week at a Mother's Day Out program. It was a time when I hired a babysitter every Friday so I could volunteer in Ian's classroom. A time when putting Colleen in a Mother's Day Out program once a week allowed me to volunteer at Anne Marie's preschool as a lunch monitor. I knew I wanted to be an active parent, not just in my children's education, but with their school as a whole. I wanted to set the tone right away with my children that I would be a presence in their classroom at school, starting in preschool.

This photo is a reminder of where Eric and I thought we knew our journey was headed, and the plans we had for these three little people. The plans we had for us. Little did I know that two and a half years later, a bomb would be dropped on our family, forever changing our lives.

I know I need to look at this photo with great memories, but this one just got me. It made me sad to see how ALS could just barge its way in and reroute our family plans.

January 17, 2018

Happy ninth birthday to my teeny-weeny Colleenie Bear! She's definitely the fireball of our family. Colleen knows my ALS is not getting better, but any timeframe is inconceivable to my new little nine-year-old. She wants to know what my name will be when I'm a grandma.

Happy birthday to my:
Messy bun wearing
Punky Brewster styling
Constant cartwheel flipping
Inquisitive thinking
Back-stroke swimming
Conversation starting
Messy bedroom living
School loving
Wild and ruckus raising
Little sister pestering
Daddy's sidekick helping
Mommy's cuddling
Fair freckle face smiling
Little cousin protecting
Party girl in training
Angelic voice singing
Hilariously funny and entertaining
Homebody being
Carrey care checking
School teacher in training
Strong willed insisting
Eight-count cheering
Louisville Cardinal loving
Cross-country running
Compassionate and caring
Boundary testing
Hopeful and always praying
Spicy food eating
ALS advocating and educating
"That's not fair" shouting

Passion for cooking and baking
Adele and Michael Franti loving
Extremely outgoing Teeny!

And, as her uncle Mickey says, "If she had a Twitter account, I'd definitely follow her." I'm so relieved to get Colleen to age nine and to plan her ninth birthday party—Eric and my friends just had to execute it. And I told Colleen, my grandma name will be Gigi.

January 19, 2018

Despite some of my positive posts the last few weeks, there have been some real low ones I haven't been able to share. Some because of time and energy, and some because of emotions.

My shingles are getting better. I guess it's good my arms are paralyzed, and I can't scratch. But holy flipping fireball, do they hurt. I live with an ice pack on the back of my head. I did call in for a big-gun pain medicine I probably wouldn't have been able to get without ALS, so I guess ALS with shingles has its perks, if you want to call it that.

While I'm training to use my Eyegaze, I grow increasingly frustrated and anxious when people are sitting right next to me and don't understand what I'm saying. I can add interpreter to the growing job description for my caregivers.

I had a medication change that knocked me on my ass for four days. Apparently it was pretty scary, and my caregiving team wasn't sure if it was medicine related or just ALS taking its natural course. They thought it may be time. I was asleep through most of it, so it didn't affect me too much, except I lost four days of whatever life I have left.

I'm struggling parenting a young teen, a pre-teen, and a wannabe preteen. It's hard for me to pick and choose how I want to spend my emotional energy on parenting, and I don't want to leave it all up to Eric. I really wanted to have things in order with their behavior, making things easier down the road for Eric. That's not how I feel; we've taken a step backward. (Don't worry, I'll feel better about it tomorrow.)

I am tired. I am very tired. I am definitely sleeping considerably more, giving me fewer hours of the day to get my long list of things done. I'm too busy to sleep, but ALS has another opinion on that. I spent all day on the phone with my new insurance company, trying to figure out what's covered, what's not covered, what forms need to be submitted—for hours with an interpreter repeating what I said.

January 22, 2018

Oh my gosh, shingles are incredibly painful. My meds are good, but they make me crazy constipated and completely out of it. I have bought all the ice packs from my local drugstore. The only real relief from the shingles on my scalp is ice. Thank God for ice!

January 25, 2018

After much Facebook stalking, my Friday caregiver, MC Hammer, and her talented mom, Amy, made this fun and one-of-a-kind artwork for our family. I've always admired the hand-stitched state pillows, but the sticker shock of them allowed me to just enjoy them at boutique stores. This gift is a thousand times better. I love it so much I wanted to share it with you all, too!

January 26, 2018

Friends. Friends. They're good for your heart; the more you have, the more you don't want to be apart!

More girly time, and it couldn't have come at a better time. If you think I'm uplifting and always positive, I've strongly misled you. It's been a difficult month, both physically and emotionally.

My BFF since first grade, Susie, came to town from Florida to visit me. She's a busy mom, with a busy business, and I always appreciate and feel comforted by her frequent visits.

My friend Sally and I have been friends since sixth grade when we were all awkward. Sally and I have literally grown up together, raising our three children at the same time and seeking advice from each other on a daily basis.

And of course, Wendy is my high school friend who has helped me with my "extreme bedroom makeovers."

I'm blessed with many friendships, new and old, but this trio of girls are some of my lifelong friends. They know all of my secrets and love me anyway. Boy, we've had a lot of fun the last 30 or 40 years, even though they are rusty at Jell-O shots.

January 29, 2018

Thank you very much, ALS, my Christmas tree is still up, and I don't even care. Okay, maybe I do care a little.

February 1, 2018

About six months ago, I started using my feeding tube for supplemental purposes. Insurance provided one option for feeding tube formulas. Basically, the formula was soy everything in a can, and I have a soy sensitivity. Then we tried another formula. Just reading the contents of the second formula made me justifiably nauseated. I would be fueling my body with these ingredients I can't even pronounce while fighting to extend my life.

My resourceful and generous friend Kristin introduced me to Liquid Hope, an all-natural formula my stomach was able to tolerate. Kristin rallied some of our senior church friends to cover the expense at $600 a month and assured me they'd figure out a way to keep it coming. That's when I got busy on my end figuring out how to get insurance to cover the cost. With the help of my kick-ass medical team for their consistent documentation and adjustments with the crappy stuff, we had enough documentation for my insurance to approve Liquid Hope as a medical necessity. (FYI: the guidelines we used on documentation requirements paperwork can be found on functionalformularies.com.) So for breakfast and lunch today I've had garbanzo beans, green peas, carrots, whole-grain brown rice, whole-grain brown rice protein, flax oil, sprouted quinoa, sweet potato, broccoli, almond butter, kale, garlic, turmeric, rosemary, ginger and wakame. And Liquid Hope . . . that's what's for dinner!

February 3, 2018

I rarely get out of my bedroom because all the fun usually comes to me (woo-hoo!) and I'm most comfortable in my bed where all of my equipment is nearby, but both of my girls had cheer competitions today. Actually Anne Marie had two back to back at two different locations.

It takes *at least* ninety minutes of physically maneuvering my quadriplegic body to get dressed, down the stairs, and Hoyered into my wheelchair, and gather medications and all that other crap but if you get a text from Colleen begging you to come and you know this may be the last opportunity to see them cheer because you know your ALS journey is coming to an end, you take the beating and appreciate your quadriplegic body still has a heartbeat and can breathe on a ventilator sitting in a wheelchair to proudly watch both of your girls. So yes, I made it to both Anne Marie's and Colleen's competitions. To top off my efforts, Anne Marie's team won grand champs at both competitions, and Colleen's team received first place at her competition.

I'm now tucked into bed, completely wiped out but extremely grateful to have had this opportunity to see their hard work come to life on the cheer mat!

February 6, 2018

I don't usually talk like a slobbering drunk foaming at the mouth but on days when I'm really tired, my "talker" gives out and I can't close my jaw. Usually a muscle relaxer, a jaw massage, and a chin strap help relax the muscles, and I can talk like a normal drunk person versus a slobbering drunk-drunk person.

February 11, 2018

Bucket List

When I was first diagnosed with ALS, I made a bucket list of things I wanted to do with my family. The list was aggressive because I was still able to walk and move and travel with minimal to no difficulties. We took the girls to the American Girl Store in Chicago. We went on a Disney Cruise. We swam with the dolphins. We took our family to Colorado to go snow skiing. We spent Christmas at the Gaylord in Nashville and saw the Rockettes. As time passed, there were a few things we weren't able to do because of my progression, and I was totally okay with that.

I wanted to see my girls receive their First Communion and renew our marriage vows. I wanted to take my family to see the Broadway Series *Sound of Music* and Bruno Mars in concert. I was grateful to be able to share all of those with my family as it would have been heartbreaking to have had an empty seat.

As my body continues to give out and I feel ALS closing in on me, my bucket list may sound simple, but it will take a lot of effort, prayers, and the energy will be focused solely on my children and Eric.

I wanted to see my girls' cheerleading competition and I was able to do that last weekend—hip, hip, hooray!

I want to go to my first school-wide Mass with Ian, and I'm planning to do it this coming Wednesday, Ash Wednesday. I don't usually wake up until eleven, so prayers needed I can be at Mass and reverent by eight a.m. In addition, Ian earned a part in his school musical in mid-March.

My teeny Colleenie auditioned for a part in *Beauty in the Beast*. I have to see Colleen be the cutest and most animated napkin that *Beauty and the Beast* ever had!

This list may sound simple, but it really is monumental, and I appreciate the continued prayers to help me fulfill my bucket list.

February 12, 2018

Thank you, ALS, for another pain in the ass. Well, not my ass. This time it's a bedsore on my scalp. Yes, it hurts, and I apologize if this post is too graphic. This sore has been covered with a heavy scab for weeks, but today that scab got loose and came off! Along with a wad of hair. I'll save you that graphic image.

February 14, 2018

I made it to Ian's school for Ash Wednesday Mass this morning. This cool 13-year-old held my hand through most of Mass. Can't wait for him and his sisters to get home so I can shower them with Hallmark love!

February 15, 2018

A Valentine's Day Love Story: One Family's Courage and the Light It Shares

I have held onto this story until Valentine's Day, because I don't know of a better love story to share. It's not a Hollywood kind of story. It's less romance than reality. But love is weaved through every line, love of life, love of family and friends, love of a husband and wife. The following speaks to the difference love can make, in corners of the world you never imagined it could reach, if one has the courage, even amid astounding difficulty, to express and share it. —EC

By Eric Crawford

Louisville, Ky. (WDRB)—The deadline for this story was not set by an editor or a producer. It was set by a disease, and it is a hard deadline, in every sense.

Carrey Dewey has some things to say before she can speak no more. She is battling amyotrophic lateral sclerosis (ALS). It has stolen her ability to walk, to breathe without assistance, to cough without help, to sit up, to wipe her own tears, to stroke her children's hair. One by one, every little thing we take for granted, every little thing she took for granted in those days that now float up to her periodically in Facebook "Memories" photos, has left her.

She was diagnosed in August of 2014, nine months after her first symptoms. She was 42 years old, her children aged five, seven, and nine. The doctor who confirmed her diagnosis told her to get her affairs in order, then go make some memories. Her life expectancy was set at three to five years. Doctors told her the form of ALS from which she suffers is more aggressive than most.

That was three and a half years ago. On a frigid January afternoon, in the Deweys' living room, Carrey and her husband, Eric, sit in front of a fireplace, beneath a mantel still decorated for Christmas. She asks Eric to move her hand into her lap, and he does, then leaves his hand on hers. Let's do this soon, they suggested not long ago, because now, ALS is gradually taking Carrey's ability to speak.

For Carrey Dewey, this is no small thing. In the years since her diagnosis, words have been her weapon against this "beast" (her word) that has befallen her. A teacher before her diagnosis, she has spent her years with ALS on an assignment she gave herself—to write, poignantly, of her experiences. She has shared details, heartwarming and heartbreaking, graceful and gritty, through a personal blog on Facebook that has grown to more than 5,000 followers around the world. It has inspired, comforted, and enlightened countless people of all ages who suffer with the disease or are touched by it.

When she began to notice the changes in her speech last fall, she took to the blog with characteristic humor and defiance. She posted a picture that says, "I'm not drunk. I have ALS. I wish I was drunk." But this is a difficult blow. She also writes, "ALS might steal my speech. It will never take my voice."

Carrey Dewey has a voice. She will always have a voice. She wants to speak. She has a message. Listen to it.

"I guess it's good that I'm losing my speech last," she said. ". . . I really, honestly, did not think I would lose my voice. I thought something else would take me. The good news is, I'm still here. The bad news is, I will lose my speech. I can't swallow completely. So I'm learning to communicate with a computer with my eyes. We've got phrases typed in there. Ian (her oldest child, now thirteen) typed in phrases for me, my needs and basic things. So that will give me a start. But to learn to type each letter with your eyes, when you're a blogger, seems a little overwhelming. But we're going to do it. I'm anxious to show people how we have to communicate."

Making Some Memories

These are not the general responses to calamity you may be used to hearing. "I guess it's good" or "I'm anxious to show people."

They also are not responses that will surprise anyone who has spent time with Carrey Dewey over the past several years, not family, not friends, not the numerous medical care professionals.

Make some memories, the doctor told her. Two days after the diagnosis, she started checking items off her bucket list. The family went to the American Girl store in Chicago. In the coming months, they would go on a Disney cruise, skiing in Colorado, swimming with dolphins in the Atlantic Ocean, to meet runners competing in the Boston Marathon in her honor. She wanted to throw her husband a 50th birthday party. She settled for throwing the huge bash when he was 45. They also threw a big bash for her on her 45th birthday, video on a big screen in a large reception room. We partied like it was her last. It wasn't. When ALS settled on this person, it chose a determined adversary.

The bucket list used to have a lot of ambitious travel. Now, the list includes items that are more simple, but no less difficult. On this Valentine's Day, she hopes to get up early and see her son sing in a schoolwide Mass. Her youngest daughter, Colleen, has auditioned for a role in a school play, *Beauty and the Beast*. Recently, she made it to cheerleading competitions for both Colleen and her older sister, Anne Marie. After this interview, they were heading to a birthday party. It's a major effort. It's an effort she wouldn't miss.

"My children are going to remember how I handled ALS, so I want them just to view the strength," she said. "Not saying I don't cry. They've all three wiped my tears many times, because that's the hardest part. I've tried to prepare them with the love notes, letting them know that I'm always in their hearts. They all know that. I told them that before ALS. But I emphasize it now. The young kids, they all understand it on a different level. My oldest can explain it to you pretty well. My youngest wants to know what I think I'll do when I'm a grandma. So there's a wide range of understanding and acceptance. But we also started therapy right away. And we have a lot of cuddling in Mom's bed. A lot of blankets and cuddling."

Make some memories, the doctor told her. For her daughter Anne Marie's First Communion, Carrey knew it was a potential memory milepost. She wouldn't get to shop with her daughter for a wedding dress. She scouted out places all over town at which to find dresses. She braced herself not to cry the whole time. Then Anne Marie asked, "What did you do with your wedding dress?" And she had her answer. A friend crafted two First Communion dresses out of Carrey's wedding dress, one for Anne Marie and one for her younger daughter, Colleen.

In June, a blog post: "Yesterday was Anne Marie's birthday . . . When she was blowing out her candles, she said every time she makes a wish it's always the same and looked at me with her sweet smile. She has wished for it, prayed for it, cried for it, advocated in DC for it, written letters for it, dumped ice for it, sold lemonade for it . . . it's truly heartbreaking."

And inspiring. Let's not forget, inspiring. These are not saints. They have their difficult times. The whole thing becomes too much for each of them and all of them. They are on edge sometimes. One of the phrases Ian had to program into his mother's speaking apparatus was, "No fighting in my room."

But this is life. I can't tell you how many times, just while writing this, I've had to get up to take a break, as much for emotional reasons as any other. They can't take a break.

Adapt, Adjust, Move Forward

Their motto has been, "Adapt. Adjust. Move forward."

Things don't get easier. Eric had gallbladder surgery in September. Carrey battled pneumonia. Amid the struggles, light. Colleen wandered into the bedroom and performed Lady Gaga's "Million Reasons."

November was a difficult month. She started to notice a change in how people interacted with her. She wrote about it:

People don't know how to act around me, or the amount of equipment I travel with can look overwhelming. I know I look funny, talk funny, walk funny . . . oh, wait, I don't walk anymore. I get it.

My mind and brain are exactly the same. It's hard enough not being able to contribute or participate as I had done so passionately before ALS. I know you're uncomfortable, I understand. But when you avoid looking at me, I notice. When you don't say hello to me, you make me feel different. I know it's not intentional, but it still hurts.

So my public service announcement from all disabled people is: Please don't fear me, please don't ignore me, please don't treat me like I'm invisible; please see beyond all the equipment and oddities and "help me feel normal" by at least acknowledging my presence.

A couple of weeks later, on Thanksgiving Day, she was back, noting how much good there was. Caregivers who massaged her permanently clawed feet long enough that she could fit back into some old boots just for a while. Friends who brought her children a large book filled with letters, pictures, and newspaper clippings from people all over about their mother.

Not long after, she came down with shingles. All around her are friends who have helped her. Meals without fail for three years. Visits. They come to clean her house. Her medical caregivers are astounded by her. These people, too, are heroes in their own right. I can't name them all here, and I don't want to distract from her story. But one anecdote is instructive, of the heart of her support group, and of her ability to inspire action.

Eight minutes from the Deweys lived another ALS patient, diagnosed a year before Carrey. When her friends and family found out about this man, they reached out. They took meals, restaurant gift cards, supported him financially where possible, helped with his van repairs. Though Carrey's disease progressed more quickly than his, she still struggled this past December with his death, which he had scheduled in advance. Yes. Some ALS patients, she writes in her blog, make the painful decision to be medicated, have their breathing apparatus removed, and give up the fight.

"I've lost several ALS friends, but his loss hurts a little more because I knew him personally and felt I was taking him under my wing, sharing my abundance," she wrote on December 30. "In the end, ALS was bigger than any support we could provide."

Everyone who helps, who brings a meal, who writes a note, who helps with children, she says, is "sharing the light."

What Love Looks Like

So here it is. When I asked her, what it was she really wanted to say on this day, with her voice perhaps growing short, it was to all these people, and to all of us, that she spoke. She doesn't want that light to go out.

"I have been incredibly fortunate to have a host of friends and family," she said. "We have so much. Don't take any of it for granted. But I would like to see the same love and help and support for other patients, even if you don't know them. Bring them a meal. Offer to clean their house. I think that taking whatever light that I shined on people to carry that light. This is not going to end when ALS is done with me. I would like to see people continue to put their faith into action. It's been just a beautiful gift that I've received."

I met her husband, Eric, when we lived in Threlkeld Hall at the University of Louisville. I looked back for some pictures of us the other day and I couldn't find any in which we weren't both, how do I put this, in a pretty festive mood. Eric was a fun guy. He was a rolling party. Everybody liked him. We all knew him to a be a good guy. Even so, I don't think any of us would've picked him, of all the people we knew, to be the best father and husband we would know.

That's what he has become. Through her blog, just as many relatives and caregivers and friends of those with ALS have been interested in things she has shared about him. And when the talk turns to this little family, that's where it gets tough. Today is Valentine's Day. This is what love looks like.

"I could talk all day long about ALS, but it's difficult to talk about it in terms of my children," she said. "The good news is, Eric is awesome. If anybody can do it, he can do it. So that brings me, definitely comfort, knowing it will be hard, but he'll be great. Right now it's a lot on Eric because I can't physically do anything. So it's harder than being a single dad, because he's doing all of that, and he's caring for me, and working full time. The care for me is a lot. So he's got a lot on his plate and he's still doing a great job."

Then she looked at him next to her and said, "How's that, Dewey?"

He smiled. Just when you're about to cry, she'll say something funny.

"One of the things I've learned from this is that the disease is a progression, so the stuff we go through today didn't go from zero to today, it has built over time," he said. "And then we've had an outstanding support system. There's someone here when I'm at work. There's someone here if I'm working from home. But if you were to go from zero to where I am today, it would throw anybody for a major loop. But being able to gradually get into it, you understand it's a progression disease, and you're going to be constantly changing the way you get things done. Our motto has been adapt, adjust, and move forward. With schedules, and where Carrey can go and can't go, to taking care of running the household."

As we're talking, their youngest, Colleen, now age nine, is lying back in a chair watching and listening. She has brought from her room all the love notes her mother has given her. They started in Carrey's own handwriting; now she dictates them to others. Colleen understands her mother has a deadly disease and that there is no cure. The timeframe, however, is a bit sketchy. In her blog, Carrey wrote about Colleen asking if she were going to sell their house once all the kids moved out.

So many friends she connected with after learning she had the disease now are gone. She was contacted by a woman who lost her daughter at age 16 to the disease, and said she's thankful, despite everything, not to have to endure that. But recently, when a medication change left her sleeping for the better part of four days, she mused, "I lost four days of whatever life I have left."

Time, borrowed or otherwise, is the most precious thing there is. In the time since our interview, she is using an interpreter more, because her speech is becoming more difficult to comprehend.

"I am tired. I am very tired," she wrote. "I am definitely sleeping considerably more, giving me less hours of the day to get my long list of things done. I'm too busy to sleep, but ALS has another opinion on that."

Carrey described recently her latest "best gift ever." It was a clip-on microphone with a small amplification device that helps others hear her and understand her more clearly.

Carrey Dewey has a voice. And she has a message. She doesn't need a writer or a camera or anyone to communicate any of this. Goodness, her last post is not just heartfelt, but wonderfully written, one letter at a time. But she does, at long last, I suppose, need a microphone and an amplifier. So let us listen carefully.

"Knowing that this would be how I would be remembered—I definitely didn't want this platform," she said. "But being young, I felt I had maybe more of a voice. People that are our age can see that it's not an old person's disease, as once thought."

Donate money for research. Get involved with families affected with this disease and many others. Read her words, at this Facebook page. And hear the words of someone who is using what words, and life, she has left to demonstrate how indefatigable love can leave an indestructible legacy.

February 20, 2018

Valentine's Day

After marking "attend school Mass with Ian" off my bucket list, I came home to be showered with love from a host of people. Our sweet friend Julie Crawford spearheaded the showering. She coordinated decorations, family friendly games, flowers, candles, playlist, and a quiet lunch with Eric and I, as well as a big family festive feast full of our annual Valentine's Day traditions. My kitchen kind of looked like a bakery fit for a king. Julie's like a calendar. She shows up with some sort of display of love each month. Additionally, Julie and her journalist husband, Eric Crawford, posted the Valentine's Day article and video about Eric and I, which was a complete surprise. Thank you to Suzanne McHugh, Lori Hall, Two Chicks and Company, Stopher Elementary School PTA, Mike Flynn, Shannon Hill Zickel, Tommy Smith, Julie Dunn Crawford, Henry Crawford, Amy Stewart, Eric Crawford, and *WDRB News*.

February 24, 2018

Hello Hospice, Nice to Meet You!

Under the Hosparus Health programs, I transitioned from their palliative care program to hospice a few months ago. I was uncomfortable and fearful of giving up control and the stigma hospice sometimes carries. But it became obvious to my entire medical team, family, and me, that now was the time I should transition over to hospice care. We needed more help with pain management, faster medical turnaround time, management of my medications, and continuing in-home therapy. Once I entered hospice care, I actually felt better, both physically and emotionally. It has been a relief to all of us to add a doctor and nurse to our team who follow my care weekly, if not daily, and are considered experts in what my family is experiencing. I love my hospice doctor, nurse, social worker, and therapist, and my CNA comes to get me tidy twice a week in exchange for a handful of chocolate hidden under my bed.

Hospice has been incredibly helpful refilling my medications, which means no more last-minute pharmacy runs. As part of their service, they provide all needed supplies, and show up faster than Amazon Prime or even *I Dream of Jeannie*! I knew I wanted to use hospice for end-of-life care, allowing my family and caregivers the bereavement therapy benefits that come with hospice services. But once I got shingles, that was the final straw. After having bed sores, pneumonia, blood clots, staph infections, and the pain that comes along with being on my tushy 24/7, it was time.

I'm in a good spot, but not finished yet. This Momma has to see Ian in his middle school musical in March and my teeny-weeny Colleenie as a singing napkin in her role in *Beauty and the Beast* in April, plus I have so much more to share about what ALS looks like beyond the bucket of ice. We are happy with the added care and peace of mind that comes with knowing that no matter what comes up, hospice will be there for my entire family.

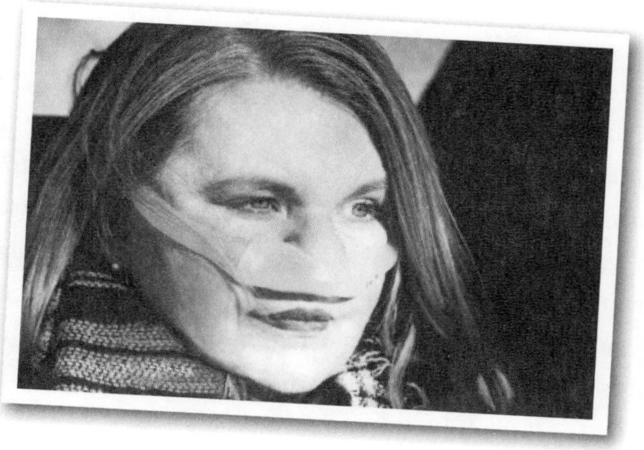

February 28, 2018

My sweet girls. This is how they fall asleep most nights. Anne Marie is in my "pocket" and Colleen is snuggled in my "pouch." I'm in full nighttime mask where I look like I'm totally uncomfortable and growing a beard. Actually I am in the most comfortable position in bed. The girls cuddle into their spots.

March 1, 2018

How Am I Doing?

Well, that's a loaded question that has a long overdue answer. Overdue because I don't like reflecting upon my poor health. For my commitment to educating, I will share with you what ALS is continuing to do to my body. After ALS turned me into a quadriplegic, it hasn't stopped there and continues wreaking havoc upon me.

Physically my lungs are slowing down, and we've had to decrease the air intake . . . three times. My lungs are not able to absorb all the air forced into me from my breathing machine. I don't feel short of breath, just that my lungs are slowing down. They're getting tired and weak.

I've been on a limited diet for the past six months, receiving most meals by formula in the tube. I still eat a little bit by mouth, depending on how strong my jaw is and how strong my epiglottis is. My tongue is weak, which is another reason I have a hard time eating—I can't move the food around in my mouth. My jaw is so weak I can't bite down even on a small piece of chocolate. Sometimes my esophagus is so weak, I can't even suck through a straw. It's okay; it's just that food is my love language, so I'll chalk it up with everything else ALS has stolen from me. With my jaw being so weak, I cannot keep it closed. It's hard to talk without closing your jaw, like the new game "Watch Ya Mouth!" I feel like we play every night when my mouth is tired. My family has to figure out what I'm saying word by word. I could use the Eyegaze; I'm just being lazy and making my family work for it.

Not that this really matters, but my hair is falling out. Doesn't seem to be a common symptom of ALS, so maybe it's a drug I'm on or wearing my straps 24/7 on my head. Either way, ALS can have my hair. I don't give a shit.

Emotionally, I'd say I'm struggling but doing as good as one could expect when I have to explain to my young child that I'm working really hard to not die before her school musical. The anxiety runs high for all of us, and when I say all, I mean my little family, my big family, my friends, my caregivers, and I'm sure many readers. It's a different kind of anxiety. Not if, but when.

These emotions are uncharted; they're obviously emotions I've never felt before, so I struggle with how to deal and often end up crying. There's no amount of medication, supplements, meditation, or essential oils that will ease the anxiety I'm feeling. I just have to feel it, process it, and move forward.

As I wrap up this blog, my mouth is currently strapped shut while my caregiver tries to interpret what I am saying. (Three cheers to Brittani Dodgeball!) Blogging is becoming harder. I feel like I need to devote my time and attention to my family, but I'm certainly not done educating. You will see this whole story of ALS play out to the bitter end. I may just need some helpers to do that.

March 2, 2018

My sweet Brittani Dodgeball! Brittani has been in our life since the very beginning of ALS. She is more than a caregiver and friend; she is like family. Thank you for sharing with such strong emotion, Brittani.

Photo by Weasie Gaines

Progression of a Caregiver

By Brittani "Dodgeball"

In August of 2014, I met Carrey. Her neighbor introduced us, as Carrey had been in search of a pair of hands to function as her hands since she had lost functioning of her arms to ALS. Immediately upon being greeted by Carrey, with her warm smile and tour of her home, I knew this was going to be a relationship to go down in history. Her little bits, Ian, Anne Marie, and Colleen shyly watched from the entryway as Carrey shuffled me around the first floor of her beautiful and welcoming home, discussing plans straight down to the times I would be making lunch and assisting with breakfast.

I came every morning to help her send her kids off to school. I helped craft her Rembrandt lunches for her little ones, complete with muffin liners and napkins corresponding to the time of year—even school-themed pieces. I helped style her girls with hair bows that matched their signature Matilda Jane outfits. I helped tidy the kitchen while she ran her errands, conducted PTA functions, and plan as well as execute perfect class parties for her children. Within the first year alone, I had a plethora of life lessons.

As we approached the second year, Carrey had begun to lose most of her upper body strength. I watched as her shoulders were taped up to prevent dislocation of her arms. Her breath began to become more labored, and my responsibilities started to change.

As Carrey progressed, so did her need for rest. I would come early in the morning, complete lunches and begin laundry as Carrey shifted her focus more on her relationships with her children than tasks needing to be done around the house. She and her sweet family began to fulfill her bucket list. Carrey planned a pirate-themed scavenger hunt that would lead her kids to the playhouse in her backyard to announce their Disney Cruise. She bravely skied in Colorado though her upper body strength was minimal. She kissed a dolphin with her family around her. She did it all with her family in mind.

She needed more help with tasks that were unexpected to me. Helping her on and off the potty. Helping pull her pants up and down. Support her up and down the staircase. She needed to rely on a new fancy machine called a Trilogy for an hour or so a day.

One day, she was particularly tired. She lay in bed resting while the day bustled, but still made sure to check her children's outfits, tell them she loves them, and wished them a great day as they headed out the door to catch the bus. I was in the laundry room when I thought I heard her calling for me, so I finished my task and headed up to her room. Carrey needed to use the restroom, had started to get up out of bed, lost her balance and fell. I found her lying on the ground, nose busted on her wedding ring. After maneuvering and problem-solving together, we were able to get her to the potty, onto a stool in the bathroom and, heartbroken, I carefully wiped the blood and tears off her face.

This was the first time I realized the depth of not only her progression, but mine as well.

Before I knew it, as we entered year three, gone were the days of working one on one with Carrey organizing her storage room, conducting PTA functions, going shopping in Hobby Lobby (thank God for FaceTime!), and preparing meals for her family. Before I knew it, Carrey was bound to her bed, with transfers becoming increasingly difficult as ALS robs her of her body, while her mind remains sharp. Suctioning saliva from her mouth became more and more necessary to prevent asphyxiation. Cough assist was terrifying, but a necessary evil. The first time I assisted Eric with the cough assist was a particularly rough episode as she had choked on something as simple as a McDonald's hash brown. I left boldly at the end of my shift as I didn't want Carrey to know it not only scared me but broke my heart. I watched Poppa Joe fearfully stand by as Dewey worked hard to help her cough up the hash brown. I cried to my parents when I was in the comfort of their home. This has been, without a doubt, an unexpectedly hard job.

As I write this post, I realize how much I've progressed alongside Carrey. I've become one of the few left comfortable feeding her. I don't bat an eye at using her feeding tube, cough assist, putting ointment on her sores, helping her potty in a new fashion, suctioning thick phlegm from her mouth and throat after she wakes up, and completing heartbreaking tasks as she prepares for her next phase of life. I squeeze Carrey's sweet nephews, and it's a bittersweet feeling because it's something she can no longer do. I stand over her bedside, translating for others as her jaw and tongue become more and more weak and her words begin to slur.

She's progressed so much, but as I stop and look at my fellow caregivers and assistants, Bossy Suzy, Karlee Fries, Becky Tiptoe, and more, so have we. As I stop and look at her family, Dewey, Ian, MeMe, Teeny-weeny, Poppa Joe, and Liz, I realize they too have progressed. We are all progressing alongside Carrey, but we get to come out standing on the other side.

Team Dewey is a part of my life that is so important, and as we continue to progress, I will hold even tighter to these new relationships as well as my sweet friend, Carrey.

March 9, 2018

Dancing with the Stars—Prospect Style!

When my dear friend Amy Nic told me Dancing with Prospect Stars invited her to be a participant this year instead of a judge, she shared with me she only accepted the challenge to raise awareness and funds for ALS in my honor. Amy Nic asked me to connect her with my charity of choice for ALS. Although I have several, I felt the ALS Association Kentucky Chapter would be the best fit for this fund-raiser. I put the date in the calendar as I often do for things to look forward to and whatnot.

"Amy Nic the Radio Chick" on Louisville's WAMZ used her celebrity platform on air, sharing my story with her sweet southern twang and genuine ginormous heart. Amy Nic's Facebook page was full of updates from my Team Dewey page, raising awareness, and posting nonstop efforts to fund-raise for the Kentucky Chapter of ALS Association. Amy Nic solicited friends, family, local businesses, her favorite little boutiques, and her listeners to help reach her financial goal of $4,000. She not only exceeded it but blew her goal out of the water again. There are so many organizations and charities to choose from, and for her to tap me and say, "I want to dance to honor you and raise funds for your disease" was truly a remarkable gift only Amy Nic could give, not just to me, but for all ALS patients. Genuine act of friendship!

I wanted to make sure I remembered the date so I could wish her good luck and follow along to what I was sure would be a cute southern boot scootin' boogie dance routine.

I didn't plan on attending; it's just too difficult to get out of the house with all of my equipment. I wanted to be there to support my dedicated and hardworking friend and sassy voice of WAMZ's *Corey & Amy* but honestly I had to be there for other ALS patients. I had to be there to show people what Amy Nic was really dancing for. What the disease really looks like. With the help of my sister, we were able to round up all my equipment and cheer Amy Nic on.

Amy did not win the disco ball, but the judges all agreed she looked like the dancer having the most fun, and anyone who knows Amy Nic is not surprised by that.

Thank you, Amy Nic, for riding cowboy for those of us who can't, and, finally, a special thanks to those who supported Amy Nic's fund-raising goal in my honor for the ALS Association Kentucky Chapter. Amy Nic trained with a professional dance instructor an hour a week for 12 weeks. And thank you to Amy Nic's posse who supported their mom and wife while she was busy fund-raising and dancing with her smokin' hot cowboy-trainer.

March 19, 2018

Big fat checkola—made it to Ian's performance not once, but twice this past weekend! Ian came out before the curtains opened and shared that the final performance would be dedicated to me. He later told me they said the Hail Mary for me prior to curtain call. Ian had a small part in the musical last year. It was a bit last-minute addition to the cast. His drama teacher wanted to make sure I saw Ian in one of the school musicals. After we left last year's final performance, Ian was overcome by emotion and I knew why. He put his head in my lap—he sobbed, and I sobbed too. We both knew that was likely the last performance I would see.

Truly a change in perspective Ian and I had going into this year's school musical. Not one of sadness, one of true gratitude that I am still here to receive this gift. It was an extremely proud moment and one of appreciation to see Ian in his second musical at Saint Patrick Catholic School, Louisville, Kentucky.

March 21, 2018

Once my cape is removed, you can see how I bear all the necessities to keep me secured in my chair. The black harness is attached to my chair, keeping my trunk upright. The cape also covers the long breathing tube and sometimes it covers my catheter bag (shown sitting in my lap in this photo). Additionally, I need to wear a neck brace to support my neck and chin from dropping down. The chin strap keeps my mouth together so I'm not drooling or slurring my words too much. Oh and one last important addition is the head support, also attached to the wheelchair. The strap keeps my head from getting whiplash for when we go around a corner or over a bump. Locked and loaded, ready to go.

March 22, 2018

A late post, which comes with deep appreciation to teachers and parents at Stopher Elementary. To make a long story short, the administration and the Stopher Elementary School PTA Board renamed the PTA office after me: "The Carrey Dewey Volunteer Center." I definitely felt undeserving because of the strong leaders who had come before me. Yes, I was involved in the PTA until my limbs gave out completely, but I did it by choice. I loved volunteering at Stopher. The staff and parents made it so easy to get involved. It really is an open door to those parents who want to participate.

I was humbled by the unexpected honor. It was be weird to go to Stopher in my wheelchair when I was no longer able to volunteer and see my name on the room in which I had met so many amazing people, organized events, and shared camaraderie while I served as a board member. Now, wheelchair-bound, I can't even fit in the room!

Thank you, Stopher, for allowing me to fulfill my goal of being involved in my children's school and of helping to cultivate the new and younger parents. My time spent in that room was, in hindsight, truly a gift.

April 6, 2018

Spring Break

Sorry I've been quiet. I am still here, and it is spring break. Half of Louisville has left town. My kids are healthy, the birds are busy visiting my second-story bird feeder, and my beautiful pink hydrangea plant is blooming in my room. I am enjoying various sentimental candles gifted to me by my friends and my twinning fireplace project turned out amazing. I've had a full week of watching and interacting with my children, and Eric took two days off work, so I get to see him breathe for the first time in a long time.

My only complaints are my shingle sores are still on my scalp and my tailbone hurts like a "mofo." We are still experimenting with my medication "recipe" to keep me comfortable and coherent. We're not there yet but getting close.

It has been a difficult month, physically and emotionally, which I guess is why I have been a little quiet. The reality of not being "done" vs. the reality of what ALS does to your body inside and out, whether you are ready or not, is my hardship. We're hangin' in, we're not done yet, and I'm waiting for my rose bush garden outside to bloom so I can smell them.

April 8, 2018

I know I've been quiet over the Lenten season. I had a wonderful service with Ian on Ash Wednesday. I felt very calm and reverent over the next 40 days. My brother died during Holy Week two years ago from chronic depression, and my priest shared with me there are more deaths during Holy Week than any other week of the year. He attributes that to the gates being swung wide open. How cool would that be? But, it wasn't my time. A lot of reverent prayer took place.

I didn't feel the need to go to Mass on Easter since I hadn't been any other Sunday in recent months. I certainly didn't want to be an "Easter lily." The few days before Easter I was yearning to join in the physical celebration of what makes me a Christian: believing Christ rose from the dead. So I called on my team to help me get ready and be at Easter Mass by nine o'clock. By looking at the picture, I'm not sure my hair got brushed or if Colleen's even wearing a dress that fits her, but either way I was happy to be able to join at the celebration at Mass.

Belated happy Easter!

April 12, 2018

The final chapter is by far the hardest. I don't know how long it will last or how it will happen—

Will I get pneumonia? Will I die of carbon monoxide poisoning? Will I go into respiratory failure? Will I suffocate on my own saliva or mucus? Will God tap me on the head and tell me calmly it's my turn? Will I say, "This is enough" and schedule hospice to remove my mask?

I pray I can make it to Colleen's musical where she will "star" as a golden napkin in *Beauty and the Beast, Junior* next week. It looks like God will keep me here until then, but you never know. I may roll out of the bed and hit my head. Oh, wait! I'm a quadriplegic and I can't roll. So that will be unlikely. Either way, I don't know how many pages I have to my final chapter.

I am a believer in Christ. I am a believer in Heaven where I will one day see my Maker, as well as my mom, my brother, my aunt, and my best friend, Debbie, who died when we were 16. I have lived through ALS almost four years, allowing me to get my affairs in order. So what does that really mean? Legal documents taken care of, my financial documents in order, school choices, bedrooms created, letters written, special gifts tucked away, and bucket list vacations traveled. But now that we have reached what I call the final chapter, I feel like I have so much work left undone! While I'm not scared, I am sad. I'd still like to live out my dream marriage we've had for so long. But there are some strong logistics coming into play. While I have handed over my parenting responsibilities to Eric, I have to watch my girls go to church in plaid and polka-dots, or accept "Yep" as a respectful reply to an adult, or seeing them go shoe shopping and coming home with four pair of shoes, or letting our older child stay home from school because he fell off a few steps of his bunk bed, additionally getting him out of cutting the grass not one day but two days and missing two days of swim team.

Eric reports to me I see only 10 percent of what is going on, I don't see the other 90 percent of good happening. He is right, I am critical of the 10 percent I see. Today, after questioning Eric on the logic behind Ian missing swimming for the second time this week, he was defensive. He gave his reasoning with harsh eyes and left with his head hanging down. I cried. He probably got in the Jeep and cried, too.

Is Eric a good dad? Is Eric a great dad? Does Eric know my priorities in parenting? Yes, he is all of those things. If I had to choose one person to raise our three kids I know nobody can do it better than Eric Dewey. I will absolutely use my energy I have left to have a kind and merciful heart for the 90 percent I don't see and the 10 percent I do.

I wish when I was diagnosed with ALS there would have been a book about raising children, parenting, and keeping your marriage strong while slowly dying of ALS. I guess that's why I'm here still, sharing my stories and hardships of what ALS looks like on the inside.

I'm okay. I'm not done yet.

April 13, 2018

Friday night means caregiver Melissa, a.k.a. MC Hammer, is on duty. Every Friday night. How cool is that?

April 17, 2018

Taping Tuesday Still in the Works

Here is an updated picture of me getting my arm sockets taped back in place; this used to provide tremendous relief. The taping still helps, especially during a transfer when my hand may fall. This taping used to be done with just me and my physical therapist friend, but now we need backup—literally. Friend one sits behind me to support my upper body since I no longer have core strength. Friend two is busy taping my arms back together with Kinesio tape. Friend three holds my chin up and my mask in place so my face doesn't drop and I'm still getting air supply.

April 21, 2018

As expected, Stopher Elementary, under the direction of Ms. Deanna Allen Williams, pulled off another over-the-top musical performance! Colleen did an amazing job starring as a beautiful napkin in *Beauty and the Beast, Junior*. But it was more than being a napkin. It was about me being there to share and celebrate Colleen's pride and excitement with her. Colleen and I both worked hard to share this bucket list moment. I loved seeing her big smile so much that I had to go back for more at the final performance. I couldn't miss out. I will have her smile locked inside me, and I know she will have the joy and flattery locked inside her as well.

So, now what? After I finish recuperating from two nights out, I will continue to live freely without a bucket list and feel very accomplished that I made it this far making all moments big and small count.

April 26, 2018

Trying to catch up. I am in my final chapter of this horrific disease that wipes you out completely; that causes suffocation; that disables your ability to suck from a straw; that completely paralyzes all limbs, upper body, and neck muscles; and, depending on my energy level, destroys my ability to articulate sounds that are supposed to be audible words, while making me unable to chew because my jaw muscles are weakened. If you ever see a strap on my head that's under my chin, it's a chin strap keeping my mouth shut, which helps with speaking and drooling. I know my friend Mel B would monogram it for me, but I'm so annoyed I'd rather nobody notice it. I have no idea how many pages this chapter will entail, but I have been told it will be the hardest chapter of them all. Oh great, it gets worse? That has proven to be true. No one had told me about the final chapter, so I'll do my best to share my version of the first couple of pages.

Please continue to pray for God to wrap his loving arms around me and all those I love, the same way he held my hand gently, while I'm surrounded by my family. This is what I've prayed for. I've heard it could be pretty scary if we're not prepared. Prepared? I'm the queen of prepared! Lists, delegating . . . I am the master of organization. I guess that's what has carried me through all the other chapters.

My neuropathy at night is unbearable and treated with high levels of medication to combat this internal fight. When properly medicated, I feel okay. My caregivers are up with me several times in the middle of the night massaging and administering medications for the neuropathy. It hurts like a b*tch, but it's more than nighttime pain. I have zero neck or upper body support. When we do our transfers now, I just close my eyes because I can't help in any way.

I'm so far behind on my blog intended to educate and advocate from a patient's point of view, a patient who is in the prime of their life, a patient who is still raising their young children, a patient who is happily married. The final chapters make it difficult to have waking hours to write and bring emotions I'd rather not revisit. I have about 10 blogs I've started but not finished and countless thank-you notes sitting on my dresser to write.

How do I know it's my final chapter? I am retaining higher CO2 levels, which give me headaches so bad that I often say goofy things. My caregiver BTD says she's keeping a log of all the crazy stuff I talk about, but if anyone is growing cranberries, don't worry: I've prayed for them. I'm short of breath. I sleep a lot. I don't have energy for visitors. It's always "call me before you come, and I'll tell you if it's a good time."

Marriage in the final chapter brings situations and scenarios that my heart mentally cannot process. I think it's excruciatingly painful for Eric to see me, his wife, in this condition, completely paralyzed, unable to eat, constantly drooling, and when I have to have a bowel movement, I must call on his services. It's horrific. I can't imagine *his* pain in this final chapter. I don't know what to say to him. Our fears are very different. I knew I would clock out of this ALS race when I no longer could support my family. I'm certainly not giving up; I'm just protecting those closest to me. Like I said, I have no idea how many pages this last chapter will be. I'm hopeful to complete my unpublished blogs. And I guarantee I am making every day count for my family, although Eric says the additional decor does not help prepare our party of five to transition to a party of four. Silly me, I thought it would! I think people don't say much about the final chapter because it's so difficult. I hope to finish those waiting blogs and updates on the final chapter.

May 8, 2018

I'm pretty proud of my highly educated caregiving staff! Three of my gals graduated with a nursing degree, a doctorate in physical therapy, and an early education degree—all in the last six months. Insert Karlee with a degree in health and physical education—that would make number four. You always need someone strong when you need your ass lifted all the time. And I know Suzy has a degree, I just can't remember in what. I also have MC Hammer, who has a bachelor's in exercise science and is in her first of four years of PT school. She hangs with me every Friday.

All of these educated, hard-working team members are hired privately. If I hired through an agency, the cost would be between $20 to 26 an hour, which means no medical assistance . . . they can't even suction. The ALS KY chapter offers a one-time annual grant of $500. Let me do the math here; if I went with the lowest rate, would be 25 hours of care and they still wouldn't be able to suction my mouth.

In the middle of this blog, my current caregiver, Becky "Tiptoe," had to stop and suction the mucus out of me and when that didn't work, she had to do cough assist to help me cough up the mucus. If I had hired her through the agency, such medical care would not be allowed. Thanks for the thought, but the grant for me is just a drop in the bucket. All private care is covered out of pocket. But, if you come to work with Team Dewey, I can guarantee you'll get a college degree or something like that.

My advice in this rambling blog post is hire someone in college or with a degree, and if someone offers to have a fund-raiser to support your outrageous medical expenses say "yes." Or in my case, if someone starts planning a medical fund-raiser without asking, like Mike and Dawn Ansert did, don't stop them! The sheer cost of living with ALS is astronomically outrageous.

May 10, 2018

Cooking with Colleen

One of the most difficult losses—because hell, it's all difficult—is cooking, or should I say *not* cooking, with Colleen. She has a real love for chopping, stirring, zesting, and spicing up different creative recipes she's found on Pinterest. I have a darling friend who comes in from Cincinnati once a month to cook with Colleen. A little collaboration is done over the phone between Colleen and Suzanne to discuss logistics and shopping lists based on inventory of who has what. Colleen loves to cook, much like her brother Ian, only Ian has learned the ropes of the kitchen; I had the honor of teaching him.

Cooking with Colleen is just an image for me. She's downstairs, proudly playing master chef, and I'm upstairs in my bed, unable to move, smell (because I have my breathing mask on) or taste her cuisine because I'm no longer able to eat food. Proud of her? Absolutely! Disappointed? Heck yeah! It's just one more loss that makes ALS so brutally and emotionally exhausting.

May 11, 2018

Since I am not able to eat, swallow, or suck through a straw, we've adopted a method we call "baby bird." I'm sure there is a proper technique for it, but it's much like a momma bird sharing through her beak. My caregiver sucks up water into the syringe and passes it on to me by squirting it in my mouth. Not the most pleasant, but nothing with ALS is pleasant.

May 13, 2018

Happy Mother's Day to all! My kiddos, with help, made me a photo board and thank-you letters with some of their favorite pictures. It's bittersweet I'm not celebrating on my mom's back porch, but I certainly do appreciate the times we did, and the memories my children chose for the photo board. A special happy Mother's Day to those newly diagnosed moms and moms who have lost their daughters to ALS. I deeply miss my mom, but I'm glad she didn't have to witness the continued attacks ALS has made on me.

May 14, 2018

ALS Walk, Louisville, Kentucky

I was humbled by the many walkers we had this year. I'll share more when I recover from the year's walk!

At Louisville's ALS Walk, a Memory for Mother's Day

Louisville, Ky. (WDRB)—A day before Mother's Day, Carrey Robinson Dewey could've done the easy thing and stayed home, could've checked out of the long process of preparing to leave the house, the travails of being wheeled into Louisville Slugger Field, the challenge of every little thing that comes with the end stages of amyotrophic lateral sclerosis.

Instead, Dewey and her family were front and center at Louisville's annual Walk to Defeat ALS, sponsored by the ALS Association of Kentucky.

They cut the ribbon to start the walk. Their large entourage, along with others from around the region, completed the short walk around the Louisville waterfront.

Appreciation for mothers will come in many forms today.

Few will teach a lesson as important as Carrey Dewey taught on Saturday—finish the course. Keep fighting.

She has done that with humor and honesty, tears and tenacity. Love isn't always a Hallmark-sounding thing. Her fight has spurred on many of those who walked with her Saturday, including her children, Ian, Anne Marie, and Colleen. Her husband Eric pushed her, continually leaning down to communicate.

In a blog on her Facebook page in which she has chronicled the experience of suffering from ALS in excruciating detail, and it is excruciating, Dewey wrote last week, "Yes, we'll be there again this year, but the cure will not come in my lifetime as I enter into the beginning stages of my body shutting down due to carbon dioxide retention."

She can't walk, swallow, or support her own weight. Her muscles have atrophied to the point where her joints easily dislocate.

But in her most recent writing, she has written about how hard all this must be on her husband and children.

And, of course, she notes her own frustrations. What you won't hear is regrets. She has made it to the plays, the cheerleading competitions, the church programs, and more. She spent Derby Day at home with her family, big hats included. She celebrated the degrees earned by several of her caregivers. She made it to the ALS Walk. She didn't let the disease stop her, nor did her support group around her.

"I'm so far behind on my blog intended to educate and advocate from a patient's point of view, a patient who is in the prime of their life, a patient who is still raising their young children, a patient who is happily married," she wrote in a recent Facebook post. "The final chapters make it difficult to have waking hours to write and bring emotions I'd rather not revisit. I have about 10 blogs I've started but not finished and countless thank-you notes sitting on my dresser to write. . . . I have no idea how many pages this last chapter will be. I'm hopeful to complete my unpublished blogs. And I guarantee I am making every day count for my family."

If there's a better Mother's Day message, I haven't heard it.

Her story is just one of many on display at the annual ALS event.

If you want to know more, or to do something to help, visit her Facebook page at Team Dewey: Kickin' ALS or the ALS Association.

May 16, 2018

Faithful prayer followers,

We are kindly asking for specific prayers for God to wrap His arms around Carrey so that she feels nothing but His peace and love as her respiratory system continues to significantly decline.

Thank you all,

Eric and Liz

*Carrey's sister,
Elizabeth Robinson
Sorg, with Carrey*

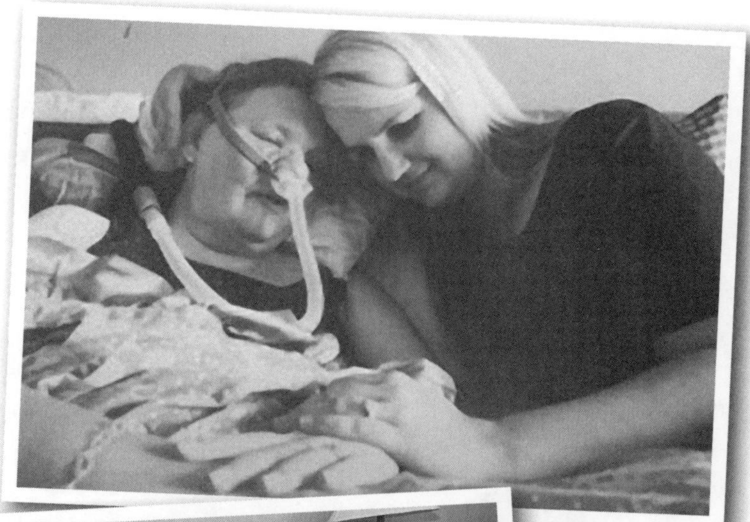

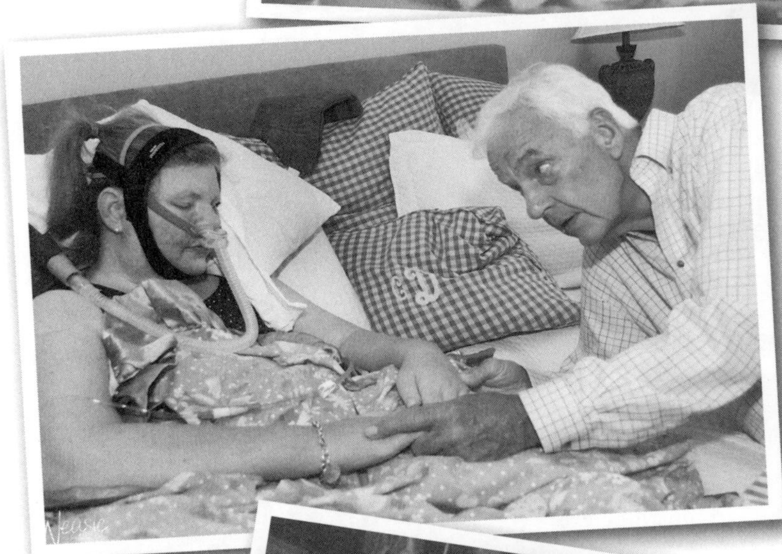

*Carrey's father,
Joseph Robinson,
with Carrey*

*Carrey's husband,
Eric Dewey,
with Carrey*

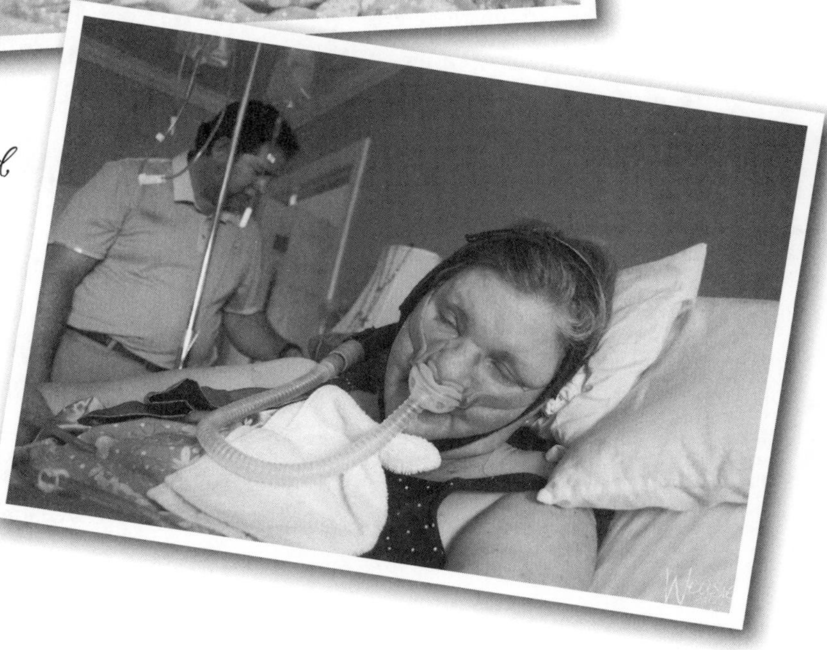

May 18, 2018

Our precious Carrey's four-year journey with ALS has come to an end. Yesterday, Carrey passed away peacefully in her home, surrounded by a bounty of peace and light with her family holding her tightly in endless love.

We are so thankful for your committed support and words of encouragement that cheered Carrey on through her brave journey.

Further details are forthcoming.

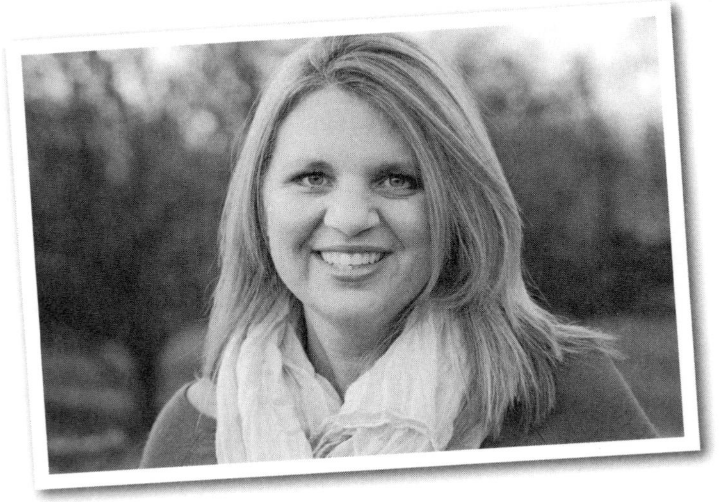

Carrey Robinson Dewey

Louisville—Carrey Robinson Dewey, 46, passed away of ALS on May 17, 2018, in Louisville. Born in Nashville, Tennessee, she was an alumni of Oldham County High School Class of 1989 (Buckner, Kentucky), a graduate of the University of Louisville where she received a BA in education in 1995 and later a MAT degree in 2001. She was a teacher for 10 years at Newburg Middle School before shifting careers to be a stay-at-home mom. She was a parishioner of both Epiphany Catholic Church and Saint Patrick Catholic Church.

She was preceded in death by her mother, Ellen McGuire Robinson, and brother Christopher Kerry Robinson.

She is survived by her husband, James Eric Dewey; children, Ian, Anne Marie, and Colleen Dewey; father, Joseph Patrick Robinson; brother, Ryan McGuire Robinson (Michelle); sister, Elizabeth Robinson Sorg (Michael); sister-in-law, Eva Robinson; and four nephews and one niece.

Carrey was a very active member of Stopher Elementary PTA. She loved to give and gift to others in any way she could. Organizing was a passion and she led Stopher to record Dare to Care donations for several years. Diagnosed in June of 2014 with ALS, she was an authentic and honest advocator and educator about ALS. She made it her mission through her Facebook page, Team Dewey Kickin' ALS, to convey to the world what ALS looked like from the inside. She was fearless in her openness and fought the disease with every ounce of physical, mental, emotional, and spiritual strength she had.

When diagnosed nearly four years ago, Carrey made a "bucket list" of places she wanted to visit and experiences she wanted to share with her family. Completing her list, she remained committed to showing her family her great love for them on a daily basis in ways large and small.

Carrey was a social butterfly and was affectionately known as "Care Bear" to many of her friends, and equally loved to designate nicknames to others. She was passionate about entertaining, and did so with meticulous attention to detail, creating a beautiful home with classic yet comfortable style—and relished shopping for a great bargain!

The Dewey family would like to graciously thank all of Team Dewey and Carrey Care for putting "faith into action" and their unfailing commitment and support through her brave and remarkable journey.

A Memorial Mass will be celebrated at 10 a.m. on Monday, May 21, 2018, at Epiphany Catholic Church, 914 Old Harrods Creek Road. Memorial visitation will be 11 a.m.–7 p.m. Sunday, May 20, 2018, at Ratterman Brothers Funeral Home East Louisville, 12900 Shelbyville Road.

Donations in lieu of flowers can be made to an education fund established for her children through PayPal at teamdeweykickinals@gmail.com, or at any Fifth Third Bank location in the name of "Team Dewey Fund." or PO Box 43365, Louisville, KY 40253. Or, if preferred, her favorite charity: Inheritance of Hope, PO Box 90, Pisgah Forest, NC 28768, www. inheritanceofhope.org.

May 19, 2018

Carrey wanted to post this earlier in the week, but as her health declined she did not get to it.

ALS has obviously altered my life plans. Obviously. But it has also altered the life plans of my children. Besides the obvious and horrible fact that they will finish growing up, becoming adults, and ultimately having their own children without me, ALS has taken away *my* ability to influence their life plans in many ways.

I've been thinking about this for a long time. Is it appropriate? Is it tacky? Is it rude? At this point in my life I really shouldn't care, but I do. I want to remain as proper in death as I have been in life. After thinking about it long and hard, I've decided I wanted to share in advance where my "In Memory" request will be directed. I would like you all—friends, family, and followers—to help contribute to one of my goals as a mother and wife to provide my children with a Christian education. The goal started in preschool when they were just starting to learn about Christianity and the beautiful world around us for all things living. This was all part of God's creations. We continued with sponsoring the Backside Mission, allowing my children to help teach Sunday preschool to the workers on the backside of Churchill Downs. We continued not just our weekly call to church on Sunday, but where the message led us throughout the weeks and months. A large call came when we started Ian in sixth grade on a path to a strong education with a Christian formation. Everything he did was woven into our family's beliefs, including his entire class starting the morning by saying a prayer for our family.

I have always planned to send my children to a Christian high school. It was one of my life goals. I was planning to go back to work to help fund this dream, but ALS has robbed me of my ability to make this contribution to the lives of my three kiddos. Eric is fully in support of this goal and would make every sacrifice to ensure my dream became reality, but not without worry and sacrifice. And damn it, hasn't he done enough of this?

In order to feel as though I am making a lasting contribution to my dream of sending my three kids to a Christian high school, I am establishing a fund. I will ask in my obituary "In lieu of flowers, which I will neither see nor smell at my funeral, please consider making a contribution to the Team Dewey Fund." Knowing that this fund exists gives me comfort as I am approaching the end of my wonderful life here with you all.

But at the same time, I want to be able to personally thank all those who contribute to this fund and to my dream. So I am humbly asking that if you would consider donating to this fund after I am gone, would you please consider donating to it now? I know there are many of you who have connected with me through my Facebook blog that have wanted to help me and my family but didn't know how. Here is your chance and it is *huge* and so important to me. And as an added bonus, I get to write you a thank-you note in first person from the bottom of my heart.

Here are the particulars:

PayPal payments can be sent to teamdeweykickinals@gmail.com. Make checks out to "Team Dewey Fund" and either take it to a Fifth Third Bank branch or mail it to Team Dewey Fund, PO Box 43365, Louisville, KY 40253.

I need to make sure you know that these contributions will not be tax deductible as the fund is not a 501(c)(3) organization, but rather it is a gift from your heart to mine.

May 24, 2018

Below is Carrey's final letter that was read at the memorial service on Monday. Wanted to post it for those who could not attend and those followers around the world:

Dear loved ones,

Writing a final letter makes me tearful for so many reasons. I am tearful because Eric and I knew we had a marriage that would last a lifetime—16 years is not nearly enough—but I am comforted to know that it isn't the end of our story because I know it will live on through our three beautiful children. I am tearful because I won't physically be here to comfort my children when life brings heartache like experiencing their first broken heart, losing a big meet, or arguing with a friend. I will also miss celebrating their big milestones and achievements such as making Eagle Scout, attending the prom, graduations, weddings, and the births of their own children, my grandchildren. I am also tearful when I think of leaving my dad and my siblings with yet another loss after the premature deaths of our mother and our brother. However, I also realize how blessed and fortunate I have been. Despite the sadness and loss this disease has brought, I feel immense appreciation for all the prayers, miracles, and blessings given to us, not just during ALS but before it as well. How can I feel anything but overwhelming gratitude?

My wonderful parents, Joe and Ellen, raised me in a home full of love, forgiveness, encouragement, and security. I grew up with my two brothers Chris and Ryan and my sister, Elizabeth (affectionately known as Lizzy). Lizzy walked my ALS journey step by step with me. She has been my biggest cheerleader and she never let me "go there." Showing true selflessness, Lizzy and her husband, Mickey, moved into a house next to ours, which allowed our families the chance to support each other through this journey. Their act of love and commitment lifted an enormous amount of anxiety and gave a priceless sense of peace to both Eric and me—peace knowing they will continue the journey with my family.

Throughout my life, I was never very good at picking the right guys, to say the least. Eventually I gave it up to God and became open to receiving whomever he sent. I'm so glad I listened because he blessed me with Eric: the most amazing husband, father, and friend. He is the kind of man I didn't know could even exist and one that I have loved with all my heart. I can see that Eric got so many of his great qualities from his own wonderful parents and family. They fostered the man he became. Not only did God bless us with a beautiful marriage, but he also gave us our greatest gifts of all, our three beautiful children: Ian, Anne Marie, and Colleen. I saw each of them grow and shine in ways that might not have developed in the same way without ALS in our lives. They have shown me great compassion and a willingness to help me no matter what. I saw how proud they were of Team Dewey, especially at public events. They have been amazing advocates.

At the beginning of my diagnosis we wondered, "How in the world are we going to manage?" But we trusted God to send us his people . . . and boy, did he come through! We couldn't possibly have imagined the outpouring of love, help, and support given by countless generous friends and strangers. He provided for all of our needs through all of you who are joining my family here today. All of you are our community. You are the people we live by, worship with, attend school with and work with. There are many of you with whom we have grown up our whole lives, and we are immensely blessed to have such valued lifelong friendships.

My family learned what the true meaning of faith in action looks like. It came from all of you coming together and providing us with everything from meals, housecleaning, and laundry to sewing, building, and scrapbooking. From creating schedules and running errands to carpools and problem-solving. The support we received from the medical fund benefit was crucial in lifting burdens and easing our fears. It helped provide medical and logistical needs and kept me comfortable with consistent care. The faithful prayers, thoughtful cards, flowers, texts, phone calls, and emails were wonderful; especially my treasured Carrey Care time. Watching so many groups of friends and family blend together and circle around our family has been a beautiful gift of that faith in action. It has given me strength to stay positive and has given me hopeful confidence for the future of my family. You have created a beautiful safety net that we could trust. Most importantly, I ask that you all continue keeping that safety net as strong as possible for my family in my absence.

Mother Teresa said, "I know God will not give me anything I can't handle. I just wish God wouldn't trust me so much!"

The cure for ALS may not have come in my lifetime but many answered prayers did. I have learned that at some point you just have to let go of what you thought should happen and live in what is happening. I accepted I could not do this alone and gave my fear to God and trusted Him. Philippians 4:13 says, "I can do everything through him who strengthens me." When you put your problems in God's hands, he puts peace in your heart. I believe if you listen, he will direct you. Find the quiet time to listen and be patient. If you trust in him, he will provide. I believe life is just a blink. I believe I will be able to watch from above as my children grow and that I will reunite with my mother and my brother.

Ian, Anne Marie, and Colleen . . . I want you to remember that God will never leave you as I have been physically forced to do. Continue growing in your faith, trusting that God will guide you and love you throughout your lives. I want you to be kind and loving to each other. Continue filling our home with love, enjoy our family traditions and share them with your own families someday. I have loved the three of you with everything I am, and that will never stop. Please remember I will always live inside of you because your first heartbeat started inside of me.

And Eric. I know I would not have lived as long without your care. You never said no to me. You were the perfect husband even before ALS. You displayed strength, compassion, and love beyond comprehension. Most couples will never need to go that deep. Our ALS years were just as good as the ones before it changed our lives. Thank you for loving me so completely.

Lastly, I want you all to know I adore you. God has blessed me through you beyond measure and I am eternally grateful for each of you.

May God bless you and keep you as you continue your journey, and if God allows, know I will be waiting to welcome you home.

COLOR RUN
THE COLOR RUN

Family Memories

By Eric Dewey

It's very hard to believe Carrey passed away in May of 2018. Time has flown by. Many days I ponder the question: "Did that just happen? Did we really have it all and then it was taken away over four years?" Carrey mentioned many times in her blog how we had the perfect plan, then something else happened. As I've struggled through the years to ask "Why?" it's become apparent that I may never know why. I do know that some amazing things happened from this and that helps answer why.

Carrey's positive attitude: When we received the second opinion that ALS is what we were dealing with and that Carrey's was progressing faster than average, that was followed with "A positive attitude will extend your life and make it much more enjoyable." Carrey couldn't have done that any better. She always had a positive attitude, smiling, joking, teasing people, and continually teaching and coaching those around her. For anyone facing the darkness of ALS or any other terminal illness, please take note of the power of a positive attitude and know that we lived it and it was extremely helpful. One motto was, "We are living with ALS, not dying by ALS." I am frequently stopped by people, most recently in Destin, Florida, while on spring break, with the following: "I don't know you, but I followed your wife's journey. She was an amazing person. We keep you in our prayers."

Team Dewey: Our community was the most amazing thing that came out of this darkness. The circles of all our contacts came together. People stepped up and planned things from day one. Fund-raisers, meal plans, shopping, carpools, Carrey Care, ramp building and home adjustments to name a few. We could not have made this journey four years without Team Dewey. The support that was given by Team Dewey to our family was unprecedented.

Caring for an ALS patient: Many times when people would see what we were doing, they couldn't believe all that we did and all that it takes to care for an ALS patient. My standard reply was, "We didn't go from zero to where we are today overnight. We've added new things to do every month, week, sometimes day. When there are already 10 things to do for the bedtime routine, what is one more?" When you are in the trenches, caring for someone daily, it is very hard to see and appreciate all that is going on around you. Anytime someone took a shift I was appreciative, especially when Carrey started getting so restless at night that I couldn't sleep. Now when I read through the blogs, I'm just amazed at all that we had to do and even more amazed at how Carrey handled it all.

Prepping me to be a single parent: Carrey wanted me to be as prepared as possible for single parenting. We had lots of discussions about schools, church, religion, piano lessons, not arguing with an eight-year-old. She would always say, "My hope is that when you are faced with decisions about the kids, you will hear my voice helping you to make a decision. And it better not have a nagging tone!"

Carrey on the Light: This concept, which was created by a team of caregivers, has amazing potential. Carrey shared her light with countless people before ALS. Through ALS, that number ballooned. What will you do to carry on the light?

The Light Within

This journey has been a shared blessing.
The path illuminated by God's light.
Shining brightly from the hearts of many.
No darkness or grief can diminish the light.
So keep your head up and smile
About the many good times.
Stay strong, so that the light within
Burns brightly for others
Carrey on the Light.

By Joe Robinson (a.k.a Papa Joe)

To know Carrey was to love her and she was *fun*.

I was with Carrey when she drew her first breath, as I helped Ellen in our first effort at natural childbirth. I was also with Carrey when she took her last breath. Elizabeth, Eric, and I held her hand and each other as she left this world. She had fought a tough battle and she was ready to meet Our Lord God, Our Creator. She was ready.

In between her first and last breaths, I had the pleasure of being close to Carrey and a big part of her life. While she brought joy to our family, she also brought a few challenges. Thank God for Outward Bound. That was a real turning point in her life. There were times when Ellen and I did not think she would make it out of high school. Yes, Carrey was definitely in the lower half of her class. I am proud to say she went on to earn her master's in education from University of Louisville. She became a teacher and was an inspiration to her students. Carrey had the ability to teach and motivate her students, especially the lower half of the class.

When she became a mother, she put all she had into raising her children. She and Eric were a great team. She was very involved in all their activities: room mother, PTA, and Epiphany Church activities, to name a few. Did I say Carrey was *fun*? She certainly was. Planning parties, sending gifts, writing notes of congratulations, sharing joy and excitement in all that she could. Then came ALS.

I want to thank all of you who are part of Team Dewey. So many of her high school friends, Facebook followers, caregivers, Carrey Care team members, nurses, church ladies, '89-ers, neighbors, Stopher moms and teachers, St. Patrick teachers and moms—all of you who helped Carrey and Eric's family. A thank-you to those who made donations to Team Dewey to help cushion the financial burden, as well. I am proud of my daughter Elizabeth and Carrey's husband, Eric. I am certain Carrey's life was extended by the constant care, knowledge, and comfort that they provided for her. Yes, we all love and miss Carrey. She certainly left her mark on anyone who really knew her. I truly do believe she left this world in a better place. God bless you, Carrey. I know you are at peace with your mother and brother.

By Ian Dewey, 14

My mom was many things. A wonderful mother, friend, sister, daughter, wife, and most importantly, a teacher. My mom taught me a lot about life. She taught others through her Facebook posts what it is like to be a mother, living and dying with ALS. One of the most important life lessons I learned from my mom was the importance of saying "good-bye." She taught me how to show thankfulness and appreciation for all that I have been given.

Every morning when I would leave for school, I was fully aware that my mom might not be there when I returned. So every morning before I left, I would say good-bye and accompany it with a hug and kiss on the cheek and an "I love you." And if the worst of the worst were to happen, I would know that the last encounter we had, I showed my care, love, thankfulness, and appreciation for her. So whenever I have regrets about choosing video games over spending time with someone, or getting in an argument about something unimportant, I know that we parted ways on a happy note. So the next time you are leaving someone, even for a few hours or a day or so, say good-bye, give a hug, do something that shows you care. It goes a long way. You may not realize it, but that can very easily be the last time you see them. Be sure you part ways in a fashion that you will not regret.

Thank you to everyone who showed support in the various ways throughout my family's journey. Because of the overwhelming care and love shown by others, we were able to get through the hard times. I cannot express how much I and my family greatly appreciate everything you have done. Thank you.

By Mimi Dewey, 12 (Anne Marie)

Carrey Dewey was my mom and my everything. She was my role model and my best friend (which I did not know at the time). My mom was an amazing wife, mother, sister, daughter, parent, friend, niece, cousin, and aunt. She would always come to my dance recitals, my cheer competitions, and my swim meets, even when it was difficult for her. And did you know my mom would always plan the best birthday parties for all of us?

I planned out my whole future with my mom. We talked about how my kids were going to come over all the time and visit with her and take care of her. We laughed about how funny it would be that she would be a grandma! I was excited to grow up and have her see all the amazing things I would do as an adult. I remember showing my mom my elementary school graduation cap. I told her that I was so excited for her to see me on my fifth-grade graduation, all dressed up with this cap that I had designed. She started tearing up and then just started crying. I grabbed her hand and she said, "I am sorry." I was confused. Then I realized she didn't think she was going to make it to my graduation. I knew she would not; there was no doubt in my mind that she would be gone by my graduation and she was.

I loved my mom much more than you can ever imagine. She would take care of me when I was sick. She would always know what to do for me. If a magical fairy asked me to change one thing, I would say to have spent more time with my mom. I always feel as if my mom is still here because I still cannot believe she is gone. When I was little, I could never imagine my life with my mom diagnosed with ALS. Now I cannot imagine my life without her. I always wonder, why her? What did she do wrong? I'm always confused because I know my mom was a great person, and she would never do anything bad to deserve to be diagnosed with ALS. My mom helped me understand that there is hope in everything, even when you do not notice it. ALS sucks! My mom was a perfect example of how to fight even when it is difficult. I think my mom really did kick ALS's butt! My mom could not have asked for a better group of supporters or a better Team Dewey. I would give anything to see her just one last time. Today I know she is watching over me and very proud of me. I just want to say thank you so much to all of the caregivers, supporters, friends, family, and Team Dewey for always having my mom's back and taking care of her. It's really hard knowing I will never see my mom again. I don't think life will ever be the same without her.

By Colleen Dewey, 10

I would like to tell you some things about my mom.

- I remember asking my mom what my kids could call her when I was a mother. She said call me "Gigi."
- I remember going to my mommy before school and telling her that I love her and good-bye. I was always afraid that it might be her last day.
- I would always get off the school bus and go straight to my mom's bedroom and get on her bed and tell her about my day.
- Mom made my bedroom really pretty.
- I was happy when my mom was a room parent at my school.
- I wish I would have kept my room cleaner 'cause that would have made my mom happy.
- My mom would dress me in Matilda Jane clothes.
- My mom would give me inspiration to be a better person.
- I really miss my mom.

A drawing by Colleen, at age 8

From Team Dewey, with Love

Karlee Puckett

Written before Carrey's death

Over the summer, I had the privilege to meet Carrey Robinson Dewey. Little did I know this woman would change my life. I came into her house expecting to clean, take care of her kids, and run errands for her, but that was not the case. Carrey was diagnosed with ALS two years ago. She is mostly in her bed, but that doesn't stop her from running a house full of craziness. This post is not about her disease but about how much she has changed my life.

Because of her I know what a buffet is; I know how to properly fold a bath towel; I know how to mail packages; I know how to make a bed; I know how to grocery shop in under an hour; I know how to return items without a receipt; I know how to use a coupon; I know how to cook (not anything amazing, mostly dips); I know what Cheddar Box and red pepper are; I know how to properly set a table for a special occasion; I know how to hide her children's items that she no longer wants them to have; I know how to change her space pants; I know how to help shuffle her feet during transport; I know how to push her farther up in her bed; I know how to feed her (making sure she talks less and adds extra sauce); I know her personal life and everyone who's involved; I know all about a sand dollar (we spent four hours on her post about them); I know the word "that" is an empty

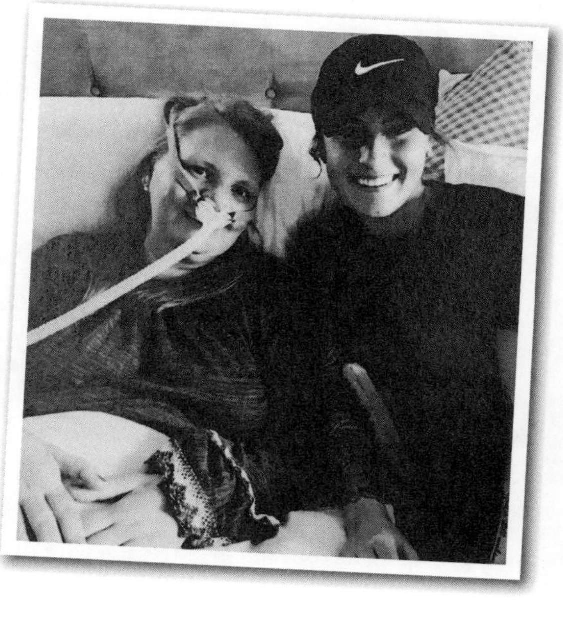

Carrey and Karlee Puckett

word which is not needed in a sentence. I know how to shop online using Dewey's credit card; I know how to write a thank-you, sympathy, and birthday card. And I know Carrey will always have a place in my heart.

I never thought I would have gained so many feelings and memories through this journey. Her kids are close to my heart, and Poppa Joe is like a father to me (always making sure I make good choices). Some days are hard, I'm tired and overwhelmed, but I would do anything for her, and for that, I have to push through it.

Because of her, I haven't gained just one new family but two. The Sorg family has rocked my world as well. Joey and Jameson have become like little brothers to me. They surprise me every day with their unconditional love and laughter. Elizabeth Robinson Sorg has become like an older sister, and I am blessed to be able to talk to her about anything and everything.

I know it's not her time right now, but eventually it will be, and, sadly, I'm not going to be prepared for that. I love walking into Carrey's room and hearing her call me "Karlee Fries," and telling me how late I am. I love how she looks out for me like a second mom, reminding me how I spend money on dumb stuff (coffee, tattoos, blah, blah, blah). I love how she kicks her feet at random moments. I love how she randomly yells, "What?" at something I say or do. I love when she texts someone, "Hot damn dog!" I love when she comments on how I always wear black. I love how she cares for me even though she has 100 other things going on. I love that she got me addicted to Twix. I love lying in bed next to her writing posts for her Team Dewey page. I love when she starts telling me what to type on her phone and goes too fast and expects my fingers to keep up. I love that she showed me a movie about a woman who was caregiving for a woman who had ALS and it reminded her of me. (Thanks, I cried like a baby!) I love that on my birthday she had a cake, and the whole Dewey and Sorg families were there to sing to me and give me presents. I love that her birthday party was absolutely perfect and how beautiful she looked. I love that during her birthday speech, she told everyone she got to meet my new boyfriend and to look for the girl with the tattoos. I love that she invited me to take a trip with her family to Great Wolf Lodge. I love that her kids are so beautiful inside and out.

Out of all the things I love about Carrey, her faith is my favorite. Her faith is like no other. Even though she has this horrible disease, she remains close to the Lord. She is the most caring and humbling woman I've ever met.

I know this post is long, but I wanted to let it all out before it was too late. She's nowhere close to leaving us, but life is crazy. Because of Carrey, I've gained two new families, and I've become so humbled and selfless. I would do anything for her, her family, and the Sorg family. I am forever grateful that God brought her into my life. I'm truly blessed and honored to have had this opportunity to be a part of [the life of] such an amazing woman.

Brittani "Dodgeball" Dodge

My time with Carrey was humbling. Standing beside her as she fought taught me compassion, zest for life, tenacity, and the talents I had hidden deep inside my soul. My short four years with Carrey brought me a new family, new friends, and, in the most bittersweet sense fathomable, a kick-ass guardian angel. She taught me what it is to "Carrey on." It's impossible to put into words the gratitude I have for Carrey Dewey, Team Dewey, and further rippling circles of friends.

Erin Rowland

I think about Carrey nearly every day. Carrey was my safe place to vent and swear and get feedback about things I thought were crazy or unfair. When I was assigned my own Trilogy machine to assist with my breathing last week, Carrey was the one I wished I could talk to. I am sad and scared and angry about the decline in my health, and she would know all about how that feels. She was a wise parental mentor and a sassy and gossiping sidekick for me. I loved to make her laugh and could talk to her for hours. I miss her a lot.

Janine Knoer

Carrey and I were an unlikely pair to become lifelong friends. She was young, single, and starting out on her life and career as a teacher, while I was older, married with children, and well on my way with both. But bond we did and what a gift that friendship turned out to be!

I treasure every second of the journey I took with Carrey Robinson Dewey. There are no words to describe what it felt to witness the joy and the tears, the strength and the courage, and most of all, the love of the Robinson and Dewey families. I do know that I am forever changed and eternally grateful.

Becky "Tiptoe" Tipton

The balance required of a caregiver is a delicate one. We must love with empathy and patience but maintain professional boundaries. When I entered the Dewey house, I was not given an option. I was welcomed into the family with a love that ran so strong and deep that my guards and walls stood no chance.

I didn't have the privilege of knowing Carrey for nearly as long as the multitude of friends and caregivers who surrounded her, yet I felt like I had known her all my life. We were kindred spirits communicating on a wavelength all its own. When she cried, it took everything I had in me to hold back a floodgate of mutual response. When she laughed, it dissipated the reality of her situation and infected all those around her. There wasn't even a single remnant of bitterness in her.

I spent many nights by Carrey's side, holding her hand, listening to her emotional struggles, and providing comfort to her unrelenting pains. I had immersed myself into Carrey's life, sensing her needs without even a word and tending to her holistically. I hugged Carrey often because it was one thing she desired so greatly to still be able to do. Amid the beautiful chaos that surrounded her, I wanted her to know she was loved and still seen beyond the destruction of her disease. I wanted her to know that I saw her. I saw the beauty amid the ashes. I had a glimpse of the whole picture and the beautiful image of her happily dancing with our Father in heaven. There are days when she is so heavily laid upon my heart that I feel like we are connecting once again on that private wavelength. I miss Carrey dearly but am also full of joy because I know she is.

Much love and many blessings.

Tammy Reid

It was an honor and a privilege to be one of Carrey's caregivers. What I wouldn't give to be able to spend one more afternoon crawled up with her in her bed laughing, crying, giving her advice and getting much better advice back, smiling at her "Carrey-isms." reminiscing and making jokes. I am a better person because of my time with her, but my heart has a missing piece without her.

Suzanne McHugh

It seems only fitting that I first met Carrey in baptism class for our sons at Epiphany Catholic Church, where we learned that the flame of the baptismal candle represents the Christ Light burning in all of us.

It was this Christ Light that brought Carrey and I together, fueled our friendship, and inspired me and so many others to be better people.

At first, after her diagnosis, Carrey questioned whether the programs in place at Epiphany would be enough to support her family on the long journey through her terminal illness. She quickly realized that instead, it would be the hundreds of people shining their Christ Light on her family that would illuminate the dark path of ALS. This was possible because Carrey and Eric opened their hearts and homes to receive the love and support that was offered despite how vulnerable it made them. Even though I was just one of many people who was drawn to share my Light with Carrey in her time of need, she always made me feel that what I had to offer was unique and appreciated.

At least once a month, I would drive from Cincinnati to Louisville to care for Carrey, cook with the girls, and share some faith-filled moments. Entering their home each month, I braced myself, knowing some aspect of Carrey's life would be different than the last time I was with her. Instead of being distraught by her failing muscle function, I was inspired by how Carrey handled life with ALS with faith, determination, and a wonderful sense of humor. I would leave my day with Carrey tired, but full of inspiration as to what is truly important in life and challenged to Carrey on the Light.

Kristin Kelley

I met Carrey only a few months before her diagnosis. My first impression was that she was someone who had that larger-than-life personality and who could fill a room with her positive energy. Our very first conversation was full of meaningful dialogue and lots of laughs. Her sincerity, strength, and authenticity were crystal clear. She learned all about me, my children, my husband, my job, etc. And on the day she died, she could still ask me specifically about things that I myself had already forgotten. She was a brilliant conversationalist.

We were joined together on a monthly basis throughout the next three years by a women's prayer group, called the Eucharist Sisters. We literally formed the group one month before we knew she had ALS, and it proved to be a great source of strength and sharing for us all, as we journeyed through the disease with her and her family.

At first, Carrey was concerned about the use of her hands and arms, so we assisted each month making sure she was comfortable. We would pick her up and take her home and put her seat belt on; we would bring wine to her lips (always making sure a straw was handy); we would put her in the chair easiest to get in and out of; we would pray with her as she gradually let go of each bodily freedom. Eventually, we spent our last year meeting in her bedroom with her comfortably tucked in bed, unable to move, completely exposed, completely in tune. We would encircle her with entertainment, gossip, and the faith of vulnerable relationship and prayer.

We all had no idea how much our faith and hope would be challenged throughout that time, but it seemed that each meeting, she would share one of her deepest fears and it would transport us to true compassion and empathy. I am so grateful for those real, vulnerable experiences we shared. And the greatest gift she gave us was the perspective to look at our own lives through a different lens. A lens that truly didn't want to take any little things (like hugging your child) for granted. We became more real, more connected, with ourselves. What a gift her vulnerability and honesty were.

The one sharing that stands out to me the most was our discussion one evening about her beliefs in the afterlife. After a few questions, she revealed that she didn't believe in Hell, she only believed in Heaven. I was impressed since we grew up in a religion that didn't teach us this. But intuitively, she said she just knew that the God who loved her unconditionally would care for her when the body was ready to transition. After this open dialogue about such a personal belief, she seemed to shift somehow. I observed a newfound peace, and today just thinking about it still brings me to tears. It was a powerful conversation that she needed to have. We all needed to have . . .

Carrey left an everlasting impression on me. I consider myself one of the very lucky ones to have cared for her in large and small ways. But to Carrey, *every* single act of caring and kindness were important, and she let you know it. In fact, she wouldn't let you forget it!

Beth Tinsley

Carrey changed my life and the lives of so many others in amazing ways. She had an unconditional belief in and love for God. She was always paying it forward in some way, shape, or form.

When the monster of all monsters, ALS, shoved its way into her life, Carrey took it apart piece by piece, dissecting it, and showing the world the reality and ugliness of what ALS does to a person and to a family. Carrey gave ALS a good swift kick in the *ass*! I would say she made more than a dent in promoting the awareness of the disease. She advocated tirelessly for ALS education and support.

I miss Carrey so much! A big part of my life is gone now, but Carrey left me with such a beautiful imprint of what it means to love life, no matter what.

Melinda Hileman

"He who plants kindness gathers love." —St. Basil

Carrey was *the* most kind and loving, courageous woman I have ever known! I *always* received so much love and joy assisting on my Carrey Care days. She changed my life and she will forever be in the fabric of my soul. Love Carrey and her party of five!

"Cincinnati's in the house," I can still hear her say.

Becky Brown

The day Carrey told my family of her potential diagnosis was a sad day, and the day her diagnosis was confirmed was sad, too—from pre-, during, and even post-ALS. We had so many laughs, cries, ups and downs throughout those short four years after she was diagnosed.

After our first time together, I left our play date saying we definitely need more time together; at our final farewell time soon before she died, I left again saying I still need more time with you.

I learned about how much fun it can be volunteering our time together at the backside of Churchill Downs, singing and playing together with our babes, organizing our lives, even getting a dead fish out of the aquarium if my husband wasn't home in time to get to it.

Through my time with Carrey during her ALS diagnosis, I learned that patience, hope, perspective, and perseverance are and will continue to be a deep part of this life for me. I didn't know I could feel so much honor, worthiness, and purity as I did as part of Team Dewey. Carrey brought out the best in me, from how I felt about personal issues, to how well I cared for her. I have been blessed with tons of awesome memories. I continue to and will hopefully forever remember our best memories from years before, during, and after.

"Sally-Wal" McMahon

I met Carrey in seventh grade, loved her immediately, and knew we would be forever friends. I miss talking to Carrey. Before she was diagnosed with ALS, we walked in the park each week and talked the entire time. We also talked on the phone in between. I called her for matters big and small. It didn't matter when, where, or what the reason, she picked up the phone.

Even though Carrey is gone from this earth, we are still friends. The relationship has changed, not ended. I think of Carrey often. I share stories about her with my husband and children. She visits me in my dreams. I still rely on her advice. I wear her red Churchill Weaver scarf and use her Vera Bradley lunch bag.

I'm inspired by how she lived her life, even to the very end. She was courageous, honest, and considerate. She could be so funny, even in the worst of situations. She drew close to her faith for strength. She accepted help from friends, neighbors, and strangers. She remained open. She welcomed people into her home, even when she didn't feel well. She thought the best of people. She made people feel special with nicknames.

I am also inspired by Carrey's loving family and all of the other caretakers—they responded with love and grace. These are traits I hope to "Carrey On" in my own life.

Mellissa Desmet

When I think of Carrey, so many amazing things come to mind. Not only was she one of the most thoughtful, honest, and giving people that I've ever had the pleasure to call my friend, but she was also very funny and downright raw. She could make you laugh and cry in the same breath with her openly honest vulnerability. I was honored to be a regular Tuesday caregiver, which were very busy days of bath time, physical therapy, nursing, and hospice visits, not to mention the pop-in visits and never ending "to do" list.

We rarely got quiet time together, but when we did, I savored her wisdom and guidance. She never failed to ask how my family was doing because she was always thinking of others, despite her own situation. Shortly after her diagnosis of ALS, she told me that she would make ALS her legacy, she would turn this diagnosis into good in some way, and ultimately thought of ALS as a gift. Carrey *lived* with ALS, she *taught* with ALS, she *advocated* for ALS research.

Carrey was a *gift*. Carrey still lives in each of us today because she taught us so much. She was always so very grateful for the love and support that everyone showed her, but truly we are the ones who received more than we gave. I miss you so much, dear friend, and promise to Carrey on your Light!

Debbie "Thursday" Robson

When Carrey was first diagnosed with ALS, my first thought was how could I help. I knew right away that I wanted to be there for Carrey and her family on this journey. When Carrey started having difficulties with the use of her arms, I offered to be Carrey's "hands" on a weekly basis. For the next four years, I spent one day a week with Carrey, earning the nickname "Debbie Thursday." Spending time with Carrey was such a blessing to my life. She taught me to live every day in the moment, to help others, and to be compassionate about what they were going through. Carrey had a special way of making you feel that whatever was going on in your life was just as important as her life journey. There isn't a day that goes by that I don't think of Carrey and all the caregivers. Through Carrey, a community was built, and I miss them all every day. We are so fortunate to have all Carrey's posts to look back on, and we remember the life lessons and awareness about ALS she taught us. I *miss* and *love* you, Carrey Dewey!

Crista Gilkey

I have procrastinated writing this for far too long, wondering how I could ever put into words this journey I have shared with you. So, I sit here, pen to paper, wrapped up in a blanket you gave me and eyes swelling with tears. I miss you! I miss spending my Friday afternoons with you. I miss your family. I miss your friendship.

When I signed up for your Carrey Care calendar four years ago, I never could have imagined the adventure ahead. I looked forward to seeing you every week, sometimes with a little bit of apprehension. Mostly the apprehension came from never knowing what a day with Carrey had in store. Running mad errands, hosting teacher luncheons, magazine shoots, picking out the perfect gifts, being driver and pit crew for your wheelchair van, and securing a must-have bathroom vanity that was not sold in stores. As your disease progressed, my apprehension turned to what ALS had stolen from you since our last visit. A breathing machine, suction machine, cough assist, feeding tube, catheter bag, and Hoyer lift became the norm. I often left your home overwhelmed and distraught, wondering how I could continue to witness the physical and emotional pain endured by you and your family, all the while knowing the final chapter.

Carrey, I am so thankful that you allowed me to share this journey with you. I am thankful for your friendship and the lessons learned from your battle with ALS. I am constantly reminded by your journey that life is a gift to be cherished every day. Your relentless faith in God even through all your struggles has strengthened my own faith. I have learned that living my faith in action—as you liked to call my days with you—has been given back to me tenfold.

Now that you are gone, life has strangely continued moving forward without you and I find myself feeling lost. Carrey, your illness, as ugly as it was, beautifully brought so many people together. I have made so many new friendships through this journey with you. I know we are all struggling with your passing, but you continue to be our angel when we need you most, still gifting us from heaven.

Carrey, it was a privilege to be a part of Carrey Care, an honor to call you friend, and a blessing to share your journey. I will do my best to Carrey on your light.

All my love,

Crista

"Crazy Lisa" Wilson

We don't choose the cards we are dealt. Through her actions, Carrey taught us the way you play your hand is what matters. She showed so much faith, strength, bravery, grace, and gratitude. She knew what was ahead for her, and she made every minute count for herself and for those around her.

Carrey taught me the most important life lesson I will ever learn: whatever our circumstances, we are only able to choose our attitude and how we respond to our circumstances. We all need to choose wisely.

Barbara Victoria

When I left the Deweys' home the first day I visited Carrey, I knew there was nothing I would not do for her or for the family. I was overtaken immediately by the immensity of the challenges she and her loved ones faced, and I longed to become worthy of the privilege of just being among her caregivers. Receiving a Team Dewey T-shirt was like buttercream icing slathered on devil's food cake—and I am all about icing! Carrey was, too. (And chocolate . . . and so many lovely, yummy, girly, motherly, human pleasures).

Carrey and Barbara Victoria

To a person, everyone whose life Carrey Dewey touched was drawn to her in a way that established a unique connection. She brought out the best in each of us. She made us want to be better people—for her, for her family, for ourselves, and for the Creator of us all. There was not a day I failed to leave the Dewey home with a lighter step, a clearer perspective, and determination to live in gratitude for having enough and more than enough.

From the moment she was diagnosed with ALS on June 5, 2014, Carrey was determined to show ALS from the inside. She did so with every word she wrote in her blog postings—and more. Far more. She showed the good and the bad and the ugly, the gritty, the poignant, the heartbreaking, and the particular, as the vagaries of ALS ravaged the dreams she was forced to relinquish day by day for her husband, her children, the life they had created, and the life and people they held dear. Her trust and unwavering faith—no matter how painful or humbling her disease became physically and emotionally—lit her path and illuminated all who were blessed to be drawn to her. As ALS claimed her body, her spirit and heart grew exponentially, lit from within by a resolve larger than a pernicious disease.

When Poppa Joe began discussing the publication of Carrey's writings, he was self-effacing. Maybe it would be a book just for family and friends, he surmised. He didn't think a broad spectrum of people would be interested in reading about ALS. But I was adamant: Carrey's story offers so much more! I shared with him William Faulkner's Nobel Prize acceptance speech delivered in December 1950.

Faulkner proclaimed that writers must put fear behind them forever and hold to the eternal truths of the human heart and soul. Carrey Dewey lived with courage, honor, hope, pride, compassion and sacrifice—the verities Faulkner lauded as worth the ardor and privilege of the written word. Every day she survived ALS she quelled fear and lived poetically the truths that Faulkner upheld. Moreover, she magnified those qualities in all whose lives she touched.

Carrey Dewey's story would make Faulkner weep, and it would make him proud for our shared humanity. May she be widely read.

Resources for ALS Patients and Their Families

ALS Association, Kentucky Chapter
webky.alsa.org

The Steve Gleason Initiative Foundation
www.teamgleason.org/gleason-initiative-foundation/

ALS Therapy Development Institute (IDT)
www.als.net

Hope Loves Company: Children of Patients with ALS
www.hopelovescompany.org

Inheritance of Hope
https://inheritanceofhope.org

Team Dewey on Facebook
www.facebook.com/TeamDeweyALS